George:

It has be[...]

to know you. I look forward to future conversations and collaborations.

Best wishes,

HEALTH-CARE
INVESTING

HEALTH-CARE INVESTING

Profiting from the New World of Pharma, Biotech, and Health-Care Services

Les Funtleyder

New York   Chicago   San Francisco
Lisbon   London   Madrid   Mexico City
Milan   New Delhi   San Juan   Seoul
Singapore   Sydney   Toronto

1 2 3 4 5 6 7 8 9 0   DOC/DOC   0 1 0 9 8

ISBN: 978-0-07-159748-7
MHID: 0-07-159748-4

This publication is designed to provide accurate and authoritative information in regard to the subject matter covered. It is sold with the understanding that the publisher is not engaged in rendering legal, accounting, or other professional service. If legal advice or other expert assistance is required, the services of a competent professional person should be sought.

—From a declaration of principles jointly adopted
by a committee of the American Bar Association
and a committee of publishers.

McGraw-Hill books are available at special quantity discounts to use as premiums and sales promotions, or for use in corporate training programs. To contact a representative, please visit the Contact Us pages at www.mhprofessional.com.

To Chloe and Gale, the loves of my life, who make it worth getting up each day.

CONTENTS

Chapter 8

ACKNOWLEDGMENTS

A lot of people participated in the making of this book. I would like to thank Tony Crescenzi for talking me into doing a book in the first place; if he hadn't made it sound easy (it wasn't), I probably wouldn't have done it. Larry Wine endured reading the early manuscript while being delayed at airports across America. A similar endurance award goes to John Schaetzl. In addition to encouragement, Steve Bright provided me with a great deal of information free of charge, which is unheard of on Wall Street. J. C. Davies was a big help with the med tech section and the reform section as well as providing last-minute inspiration. Ona Wu and Jonathon Swersey provided me with encouragement and a belief that what I had to say was worth saying. Fred and Catherine Golliard and Anastasia Mills Healy also did their part as a cheerleading section.

Kenneth Thorpe, Paul Ginsburg, and Sherry Glied all graciously shared their views on health-care reform issues. Lambert Van De Wald provided guidance on Medicare questions. David Nikodem and Jon Penshorn provided information on biotech and managed care, respectively. Phil Roth was extremely generous with his encyclopedic knowledge of investing. Given the vast wisdom of all these people, it should be clear that I am responsible for any errors made in the book.

I would like to thank the team at McGraw-Hill: Jeanne Glasser, Sophia Efthimiatou, and Pattie Amoroso for helping to shepherd this project through the shoals of publishing, and Alice Manning for copyediting the manuscript. Also thanks to the team at Miller Tabak, especially Jeff Miller and Jeff Tabak, for indulging me in my quest to be the author of a book with their encouragement and helpful comments. Interns Michael Serviansky and Todd Fernley tracked down information that I needed, in the nick of time.

Finally, I would like to thank Chloe and Gale, who endured my mental and physical absences with understanding.

INTRODUCTION

As goes GM, so goes the nation, as the adage goes. If that adage is still true today, the United States could be in for some trouble. General Motors, once the very pinnacle of the auto industry, has fallen on hard times over the last decade. The price of its shares has actually declined in nominal terms since 1997 while the S&P 500 has increased. One of the reasons GM has given for its poor performance is that it is at a significant cost disadvantage compared with other automobile manufacturers domiciled outside the United States. GM believes that disadvantage has equated to about $1500 a car. In 2007 the automaker took steps to remediate the problem by reaching a deal with its unions to offload some of its health-care expenses to its union members in the form of a VEBA (voluntary employee beneficiary association). It is unclear whether this new structure will allow GM to succeed, but it does eliminate some of the health-care price pressure the company was facing. For the workers it means they have more responsibility over their health care, including exposure to cost inflation. This is a change for the labor union members, who had fairly rich benefits packages by relative standards. It remains to be seen how workers adapt to the new paradigm.

In a global economy, a competitive disadvantage this large will be hard to overcome. GM felt that it simply couldn't compete effectively against companies whose local markets provided health-care benefits to employees. This story of competitive disadvantage is likely to be repeated across numerous companies as America's employee-based health-care system seems structurally designed to put U.S. companies at a disadvantage. As globalization continues to become a factor and U.S. companies are forced to compete more aggressively against non-U.S. companies, there will be more pressure on the government to take steps to help both employers and employees, leading to change in the health-care system.

The problems facing GM are not exclusive to GM or even to the auto industry; rather, globalization, unsustainable cost inflation, and changing demographics threaten to overwhelm the entire public health infrastructure. Either the government or market forces will respond to these challenges, eventually leading to significant changes in the way health care is paid for and delivered, and new treatments are discovered. This upheaval may not be all bad; there may be a way for the prescient person to benefit. If investors embrace these changes and seek out opportunities in the capital markets, there may be a way to see financial gain while contributing to improving the system. Understanding potential changes and their impacts on the health-care system ahead of their arrival will allow the investor to navigate the uncertainty that change creates in its wake and allow the investor to leverage analytical techniques to identify profitable stock opportunities and prosper. The goal of this book is to accomplish just that: to alert the reader to what may come to pass in health care, some important analytical approaches to use when approaching the health sector, and then finally, some industry-specific and subsector nuances to bear in mind when investing. Preparation cannot guarantee profitable results, but it couldn't hurt.

PART ONE

A MACRO VIEW ON HEALTH-CARE INVESTING

CHAPTER 1

The Investment Case for Health Care

Benjamin Graham and David Dodd famously defined an investment as an operation that, upon thorough analysis, promises safety of principal and adequate return.[1] Investors want above-average returns with no more than average and preferably below-average risk. While achieving above-average returns with average risk is no easy feat to accomplish on a routine basis, the possibility of doing so cannot be dismissed out of hand. Health care is an industry that has undergone significant change since its inception as therapies and delivery mechanisms have evolved. This industry is entering an era of reform, and with reform comes change and the opportunity for investment gain. According to Graham and Dodd, "Detecting change earlier than the rest of the market and acting promptly on the conviction of change are the critical steps to exploiting mis-priced securities."[2]

Some investors will be skeptical[3] about the broad macro thesis that health care is about to change radically and that the mispricing of risk and reward will result in significant opportunity. However, several other factors make this industry worthy of analysis. The health-care market is big and is growing rapidly. It is a complex market, something that often leads to share mispricings (a disconnection between value and price). There is also a social interest component, meaning that socially conscious investors can contribute to positive change by rewarding those companies that address health care in the most socially efficient way. Health care also represents a significant portion of the overall investable market, so that for an investor to be diversified, he must participate in health care.

Health-care demand is not as elastic as demand in most other industries, which makes it more predictable and less sensitive to shifts in the economic landscape. There are major inefficiencies in the system, leading to investment opportunities in companies providing products and services that can improve them. There are numerous significant health problems that have not been addressed; if these are solved, the result will be revolutionary changes in health care, which can lead to extraordinary stock returns. There are several factors that make health care a particularly attractive industry to invest in, even in the absence of large-scale reform.

SIZE AND COMPLEXITY

At $2 trillion annually in the United States, and double that globally,[4] there are few markets that are as large in absolute terms, and opportunity is in proportion to the size of the market. Health care as a sector is growing faster than the rate of general inflation in the United States (and even faster globally), which by definition suggests that investing in health care will deliver above-average returns (returns greater than the growth rate of GDP), assuming that investors do not overpay for the growth rate.

Health care is different from other industries, which makes traditional investors cautious when investing in a health-care service or product. There is a wide range of investments within the sector, from the smallest biotech or service company addressing a profitable niche to a mega-cap multiline pharmaceutical company, and the investor needs to weigh the advantages and disadvantages of each.

Health care is a highly regulated industry, with numerous bodies, all with differing agendas and requirements, overseeing its operations. A drug needs to be approved by the FDA, not run afoul of patents, be advertised appropriately, and be eligible for reimbursement by insurance companies. What is required for approval can change between the time a drug or therapy begins clinical trials and the time it reaches the market (typically as long as 7 to 10 years), depending on the development of other treatments and medical understanding. The delivery of services is similarly challenging, with insurance and antikickback laws dictating how and when services may be provided. There are numerous reimbursement systems. Health care has a bewildering number of payment systems, each with its own methodologies for paying for services and products. The almost mind-numbing complexity of reimbursement causes many investors to give up and decide that investments in this industry are not worth the time it takes to understand the risks.

Despite all its complexities, the health-care industry is unique in its opportunity for differentiation. There is no one definitive approach to most medical problems, and any drug or service available to the market is subject to direct competition. Different treatments and services can be provided for any one ailment, but there is often no consensus on optimal therapy—which means there is always room for improvement, and ultimately profit.

SOCIAL INTEREST

Public health has always been one of society's biggest challenges. There are societal pressures to ensure that adequate health care is provided for citizens. Besides access to food and housing, access to health care has remained one of the bright lines between the haves and have-nots. Religious groups, charitable organizations, and advocacy groups exist to promote health-care issues ranging from vaccinations to universal care to more research into particular diseases. If investors fund only those products or services that improve health, this is also a form of public advocacy. If the market rewards products that lead to good health, then companies whose products do not lead to better health will need to adapt by improving their product or service or will be made extinct by market forces alone. Health-care investors could create a virtuous health circle by rewarding good companies. There is a role for the capital markets to play in restructuring health care,[5] though that role is still to be defined.

DIVERSIFICATION

Diversification is a cornerstone of investment policy. The idea is to reduce the amount of risk by investing in different types of assets. When investing in stocks, it is prudent to invest across several different industries to reduce concentration risk. Over the last 10 years, health care has accounted for between 8 and 15 percent of the S&P

500, or about $2.5 trillion in market capitalization. Health care represents a similar proportion of the smaller-cap indexes (e.g., the Russell 2000), though the market capitalization is smaller ($280 billion). Although major pharmaceutical companies (the DRG index) are the largest component of the sector, with roughly $1.2 trillion in market capitalization, there are ample opportunities in other subsectors in health care, such as managed care and biotech.[6] If investors want to be diversified from an industry perspective, they simply cannot avoid being in health care, given the striking performance of some of the subsectors and companies and their respective stocks.

INELASTIC DEMAND

Investors do not like uncertainty because it can lead to more volatile business performance, which translates into more volatile share price performance. For most products, demand is elastic: the lower the price, the more of that product is demanded, and the higher the price, the less of that product is demanded. Demand for health care is relatively inelastic. If a patient has a heart attack or some other type of acute disease, the demand will be completely inelastic. With chronic diseases and elective procedures, there is a little more elasticity, with the level being dependent on the demographics of the sample.[7] This inelasticity makes health care more resistant to changes in the economic cycle. At the margins, elective and cosmetic procedures may be affected by changes in the overall economic picture, but overall, changes in the economy should not alter demand in a material way, unless the financial burden on patients is raised significantly. In general, the predictability of the demand for health-care products and services means that investors can have more confidence in the revenue projections of these companies. Reliability, being prized by investors, is often rewarded a premium valuation, which is a plus for health-care investors.

MARKET INEFFICIENCIES TO EXPLOIT AND REVOLUTIONARY POTENTIAL

Health care is an inefficient industry, with variations in care, costs, process, and outcomes that are greater than those in most other industries. Even if demand stays at its current level, innovations that can improve efficiencies and drive profits provide ample opportunity for investors. Health care has advanced significantly over the last 50 years. The rate of change has accelerated, and new discoveries that are being made at the molecular level are changing the way we view disease. There are still numerous conditions for which there is no completely effective treatment: strokes, Alzheimer's disease, cancer, and heart attacks, to name just a few killers. A company that can find a cure or even a more effective treatment for any of these maladies will benefit financially, and the opportunity that this provides is enormous. Health care remains one of the few areas where the possibility of a revolutionary change exists, and with it the potential for dramatic profit. Health care policy has not kept up with the innovation in the industry and thus investors can profit by trolling in the wake of policy failures over the last 50 years.

WHAT HEALTH-CARE INVESTING ISN'T

Health care is not contrarian investment most of the time. Being a "contrarian" investor is a prized distinction. It means that the investor does not run with the herd; instead, she goes out on her own and is able to find opportunity. Contrarian investing has been shown to outperform many other strategies.[8] However, the opportunity for contrarian investing will occasionally also present itself in health care. Changes in the political and regulatory climate happen with some regularity. When these changes occur, they create uncertainty for the health-care industry and the stocks of companies in that industry. One of the more famous examples is the reaction of the pharmaceutical group to the whirlwind of news flow surrounding the first Clinton health-care reform package in 1993. The shares sold off substantially, but they ultimately recovered and outperformed once the outcome of the program was known.

If earnings power and valuation are the key determinants of long-term share price, then changes in share prices that are unrelated to changes in the businesses' core operations and are the result of investor sentiment offer the chance of contrarian profits. Analysis and understanding of companies are much more important in times of stress for the industry's stocks. A plan for reforming health care could lead to further upheaval in stocks and open the door to contrarian profits.

Health Care Is Not a Monolith

Health-care investment opportunities can be found anywhere within the industry, from the execution of cutting-edge research into unmet medical needs to the disposal of medical waste. Given the diversity of the companies involved, it is often difficult to generalize about the industry, yet these companies do share some common traits: the more patients treated and the greater the reimbursement, the more opportunity there is to capture and generate returns for shareholders. Although there can be some competition between various parts of the health care industry (HMOs versus pharmaceutical companies, for example), ultimately the entire sector is competing with other parts of the economy for resources.

Change Drivers

Two trillion dollars is a lot of money. Health-care inflation has substantially outpaced the growth in gross domestic product (GDP) for at least 50 years.[9] Medicare forecasts that health-care spending will outpace inflation by at least 1 percent for the foreseeable future. While that might not seem like a very large percentage increase, the current growth rate is much higher than that both in the United States and globally, and the change amounts to multiple billions of dollars in absolute terms (see Figure 1-1).

When basic health statistics and costs for the United States are compared to those for the rest of the world, it appears that Americans are not getting their money's worth.[10] Making the public health metrics look worse is the fact that, while most other industrialized nations provide at least basic care for their populations, the United States does not provide basic care for roughly 45.7 million people (15 percent of its population).[11] There are also wide variations in the quality and cost of care in different geographical areas, for patients with different economic status, and for patients of different ethnicities that cannot be explained by chance alone. However, the health-care system is not a complete failure. The United States has been, and continues to be, on the cutting edge of most health-care breakthroughs, from polio vaccine to the present-day biotechnology wonder drugs and robotic surgery. Although many people view

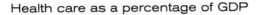

F I G U R E   1-1

Health care as a percentage of GDP

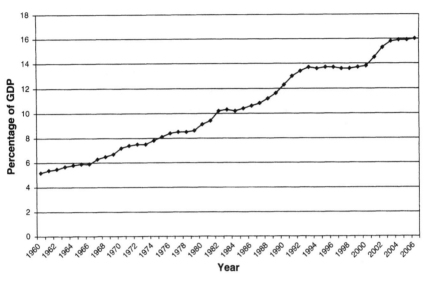

Source: National Center for Health Statistics, Health 2007.

the access to care as inadequate, emergency care is available to everyone.

In terms of perception, the negatives outweigh the positives in the mind of the public. There has been perpetual and arguably growing dissatisfaction with the way health care is delivered and accessed. Americans are more dissatisfied with their health-care system than people in most other industrialized nations.[12] Presidents have proposed universal health care or other health-care reform efforts since Theodore Roosevelt. However, vested interests, entrenched constituencies, and institutional inertia have made the progress toward increased access slow.

What does the public's dissatisfaction with health care have to do with investing? Reformers and investors have common goals. Both would like to see change. Change will improve the system and provide investment opportunities. With the growing problems of the uninsured and public dissatisfaction with its operations, the health-care system is on the cusp of major change. Determination of the true rewards and risks will be difficult for investors who are not prepared. In the confusion resulting from times of radical change, there will be ample opportunity for above-average investment returns.

Change need not even be radical; even moderate movement toward reform that stops well short of universal health care will be enough to generate outsized returns.

REFORM IS ON THE WAY

Polls consistently show that Americans favor some type of health-care reform.[13] But why should the movement suddenly be picking up speed after nearly 100 years of slow development? There are four interdependent reasons why this movement is inevitable: unsustainable cost inflation, demographics, globalization, and technology changes.

Globalization and Increasing Economic Insecurity

Markets are becoming more global. Both human and financial capital are freer to travel than ever before. This trend is going to accelerate as less-developed countries continue to gain economic clout. The United States is the only industrialized nation without a universal health-care system. The lack of universal health care puts American corporations at a significant cost disadvantage relative to their international peers, as companies and industries in other regions are not burdened by health-care costs or retiree benefits.[14]

The lack of universal health care has other less quantifiable but still important impacts on American economic life. Globalization has increased competition for reasons other than health-care costs, and this has fostered increased economic insecurity among Americans. Catastrophic health-care issues are a leading cause of bankruptcies.[15] Fear of financial ruin can lead to "job lock," or lack of workforce mobility. This concern probably also leads at least some potential entrepreneurs to defer any attempt to leave a corporate job in order to develop a new product or service. Since entrepreneurialism is a cornerstone of American economic life and a key contributor to its standing in the world, any diminution of this process will be harmful to the economy, and potentially to society as a whole. If people were less concerned about their health-care security, they would be more likely to take more financial risks, including investing in the stock market.[16] Increased investment in risky assets would be a positive for all markets, including equities.

Another economic consequence is that workers may defer their basic health-care needs as a result of cost concerns. Although the economic impact of deferred health maintenance has been difficult to quantify, certain screening procedures have been shown to be cost-effective compared to later treatments for acute disease episodes, so deferral of at least these tests could lead to higher costs downstream.[17] Deferred health care also hurts the economy in that workers' failure to deal with easily solvable health-care issues involving either themselves or their dependents leads to a loss of worker productivity; this is an insidious but tangible impact of the lack of a safety net.

Globalization and its associated economic insecurity will eventually lead the voting public to put pressure on elected officials to ameliorate the problem. One way politicians can do this is to establish a greater health-care safety net or face the possibility of being turned out of office. It will be in politicians' best interests as well as the country's to address the issue.

Demographics

As people age, their health-care utilization increases. In absolute terms, the older a population gets, the more expensive its health care will be for society.[18] The biggest generational cohort, the baby boomers (those born between 1945 and 1962), will soon be entering their prime medical utilization years (age 70 and above). People are living longer, ironically as a result of better health care. Potential patients will live longer in their high health-care utilization years. This demographic shift will put increased pressure on the government, which will need to respond in some way. The Medicare Trust has forecast that the system will be bankrupt by the year 2019.[19] The government has few options: it can reduce benefits in some way, increase revenues to pay for the program, let the program go bankrupt, or expand the program to broaden the risk pool.

None of these options is politically appealing. The path of least resistance (if history is a guide) is to respond to voters who want more care. This path almost always requires raising taxes, though there may be a quid pro quo involved: as the government expands the safety net (a move toward universal care) and reduces cost pressures on the uninsured and businesses alike, the employed and the employers are likely to face an increased tax burden.

Costs

Independent of the increasing utilization associated with the aging population, health-care costs per patient are rising. There are several reasons for this. The most obvious is that new technologies cost more than old technologies. New technologies have advanced health care to the point where previously fatal diseases like certain forms of cancer are now survivable.

While improving health outcomes has very positive benefits for society, it does mean that costs will increase substantially. As people age, they tend to have an increased number of comorbidities (multiple diseases). Medicine can now manage multiple diseases simultaneously, but we are the victims of our own success, as multiple diseases lead to multiples of cost.

The cost of technological advances comes on top of the normal wage and raw material inflation, and this is the reason why inflation in health care is growing faster than general cost inflation (see Figure 1-2). As a society, we have been able to accommodate above-GDP rates of health care inflation over the past few decades by asking patients to shoulder more of the payment burden, but since the cost pressures on business are rising faster than they can raise prices on their products, the pain threshold will eventually be hit (if it has not been hit already), and this will spur business leaders and the U.S. populace to demand change.

Technology

With the advent of the Internet, patients are now more aware of disease and potential treatments than ever before. This new awareness has been encouraged by both advocacy groups and the health-care industry and has spurred the demand for health care. Patients are also more aware of other health-care systems, and this not only has spawned heretofore unheard-of industries like medical tourism, but allows U.S. patients to access care

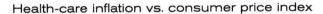

F I G U R E   1-2

Health-care inflation vs. consumer price index

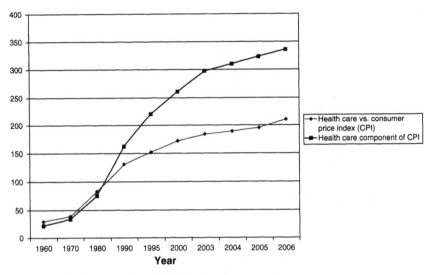

Source: Health 2006, CMS; National Center for Health Statistics, Health 2007.

from other places, such as obtaining prescription drugs from other countries.

As more data about procedures and outcomes become available, patients will be engaged as consumers, just as they are in other areas of the economy. Advances in technology have already started to hasten this process. Managed-care companies and Medicare are already posting outcomes data for certain treatments and conditions on their Web sites. The movement toward transparency in both price and outcomes is unlikely to abate. Patients seeking more control over their health status are likely to demand more data, and the providers will eventually have to respond.

Eventually there will be a portable electronic medical record (EMR), where patients and providers alike will be able to monitor their health status. The advantages of connectivity, such as reducing medical errors and ensuring continuity of treatment, are obvious, but costs and privacy issues have restrained the development of these systems. While connectivity may not in and of itself be a catalyst for change, government encouragement of EMRs will allow a reform scheme to be implemented more effectively, which would reduce opposition to such a plan.

NOTES

1. As cited in *The Intelligent Investor*, rev. ed. (New York: HarperCollins, 2003), p. 18.
2. Sidney Cottle, Roger F. Murray, and Frank E. Block, *Graham and Dodd's Security Analysis*, 5th ed. (New York: McGraw-Hill, 1988), p. 541.
3. An homage to John Burr Willams, *Theory of Investment Value* (Cambridge, Mass.: Harvard University Press, 1938), p. 186.
4. U.S. figures from Centers for Medicare and Medicaid; global figures from the World Health Organization, http://www.who.int/mediacentre/factsheets/fs319.pdf.
5. J. B. Silvers, "The Role of the Capital Markets in Restructuring Health Care," *Journal of Health Politics, Policy and Law* 26, no. 5 (2001): 1019–1030.
6. Bloomberg statistics.
7. Jeanne S. Ringel, Susan D. Hosek, Ben A. Vollaard, and Sergej Mahnovski, "The Elasticity of Demand for Health Care: A Review of the Literature and Its Application to the Military Health System," Rand Institute Monograph, 2002.
8. Josef Lakonishok, Robert Vishny, and Andrei Shleifer, "Contrarian Extrapolation, Investment and Risk," NBER Working Paper 4360, 1993.
9. Follette Glenn and Louise Sheiner, "The Sustainability of Health Spending Growth," Finance and Economics Discussion Series 2005-60, Board of Governors of the Federal Reserve System.
10. K. Davis, C. Schoen, S. C. Schoenbaum, M. M. Doty, A. L. Holmgren, J. L. Kriss, and K. K. Shea, "Mirror, Mirror on the Wall: An International Update on the Comparative Performance of American Health Care," The Commonwealth Fund, May 2007.
11. Carmen DeNavas-Walt, Bernadette D. Proctor, and Jessica C. Smith, U.S. Census Bureau, Current Population Reports, P60-235, "Income, Poverty, and Health Insurance Coverage in the United States, 2007," U.S. Government Printing Office, Washington, D.C., 2008.
12. C. Schoen, R. Osborn, M. M. Doty, M. Bishop, J. Peugh, and N. Murukutla, "Toward Higher-Performance Health Systems: Adults' Health Care Experiences in Seven Countries," *Health Affairs* Web Exclusive 26, no. 6 (2007): W717–W734.
13. The Henry J. Kaiser Foundation/ABC News Poll, "Health Care in America Survey, 2006," October 2006, http://www.kff.org/kaiserpolls/upload/7572.pdf.
14. Lee Hudson Teslik, "Health Care Costs and US Competitiveness," Backgrounder, Council on Foreign Relations, May 14, 2007, http://www.cfr.org/publication/13325/.
15. David U. Himmelstein, Elizabeth Warren, Deborah Thorne, and Steffie Woolhandler, "Illness and Injury as Contributors to Bankruptcy," *Health Affairs* Web Exclusive (2005): W63–W73.
16. Paul F. Smith and David Love, "Do Households Have Enough Wealth for Retirement?" Federal Reserve Board Finance and Economics Discussion Series 2007-17, 2007.
17. Michael Pignone et al., "Cost-Effectiveness Analyses of Colorectal Cancer Screening," *Annals of Internal Medicine* 137, no. 2 (2002).
18. National Center for Health Statistics, "Ambulatory Medical Care Estimates for 2004," http://www.cdc.gov/nchs/products/pubs/pubd/hestats/estimates2004/estimates04.htm.
19. 2007 Annual Report of the Boards of Trustees of the Federal Hospital Insurance and Federal Supplementary Medical Insurance, http://www.cms.hhs.gov/ReportsTrustFunds/downloads/tr2007.pdf.

CHAPTER 2

What Ails the Health-Care System

Coulda, woulda, shoulda is an old trader's lament about missed investment or trading opportunities. It refers to investors' wishes that they had done something that they had wanted to do but in fact had not done. This serves as a good metaphor for the problems the health-care system faces. Health care should cost less, it could be better in terms of quality, and it would be nice if everyone in the United States had access to health-care services. Fortunately for health-care investors (and unfortunately for public health), the glaring problems in health care and the drivers of reform offer ample opportunity for investment gain.

WHERE DOES THE MONEY GO?

Figure 2-1 breaks down by percentage the various cost components of health care in the United States. The United States spends about $480 billion more than it would cost in other countries to achieve the same outcomes.[1] Five disease states (cardiac, pulmonary, mental health, cancer, and hypertension) account for 31 percent of all spending; when the next 10 diseases are added, they account for 56 percent.[2] Furthermore, 1 percent of the population accounts for 22 percent of health-care spending, and 5 percent accounts for 49 percent.[3] The bottom 50 percent of the population (the well people)

F I G U R E   2-1

Health-care cost components

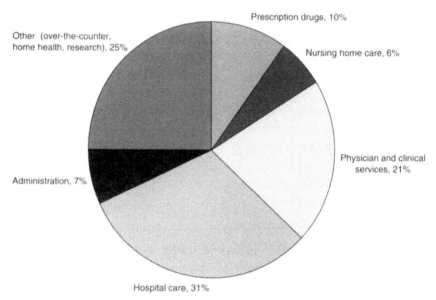

Source: Centers for Medicare and Medicaid Services; National Center for Health Statistics, Health 2007.

incurs about 3 percent of all health-care costs. About 30 percent of health-care spending involves patients in their last year of life. Medicare and Medicaid account for about one-third of all spending, private insurance accounts for about one-third, and out-of-pocket payments account for about 10 percent of spending. If all public funds are included, the government covers about 46 percent of health-care spending.[4]

The United States also spends a great deal of money on paperwork: about $1,059 per patient on the administration of health-care insurance in 2003.[5] This is roughly 3.5 times the per capita rate in Canada. Why is there such a disparity? Because of the way the payment system in the United States is constructed. There are about 2,000 commercial plans, as well as numerous government entities. Each of these systems has its own forms and processes. These processes require people, technology, and time, all of which add up to increased spending compared to that in countries where there is a single system with one set of forms and one set of processes.

Market Failure

Health care has some unique qualities that lead to market failure. Detailed explanations of all of these factors are beyond the scope of an investment book and have been the basis for several Nobel prizes. Investors should be aware of these market failures and related externalities because companies that develop products or services that can overcome them could see substantial investment returns.

Health-care providers are rational actors when it comes to delivering health care. As things stand today, the more service provided, the more revenue generated. On a purely economic basis, it is better for providers to give more care than to give less. One would think that more care would be better for patients, but in fact, there is limited evidence showing that performing additional procedures or tests actually improves outcomes. In fact, the opposite may be true. More care may in fact be hurting patients as well as leading to excess costs. In addition, because the system is fragmented, redundant procedures and tests are often performed because of a lack of communication between various sites or providers of care.[6] Economic incentives for providers may not always be aligned with patient needs (to receive optimal care at optimal cost). In theory, this incentive misalignment should be remedied by the market, but when providers benefit from the status quo, inertia appears to be the rule, not the exception.

Over 40 years ago, Kenneth Arrow wrote the seminal piece on health-care economics, in which he laid out the thesis that there were information asymmetries in health care, and that this was a cause of many of the problems in the industry.[7] Physicians and other health-care providers know more about the problem (the disease) than the patients do. This situation is not unusual; it is also found in areas like real estate and car sales, where one party has more information than the other. Since Arrow's work, there have been substantial changes in the health-care industry, and yet the problems persist, despite the fact that there are strategies for dealing with asymmetries of information: signaling and screening.[8] Signaling is a way in which one party transmits information about him- or herself to the other party. Screening is a way in which the underinformed party can draw out information from the better-informed party. However, no company has been able to apply these techniques to contend effectively with the problems of information asymmetries in health care. The Internet has given patients the ability to gather more information about their conditions, but it has yet to close the gap completely. Makers of health-care products have suggested that direct-to-consumer advertising also serves to close the information gap, but given the fact that they are not a disinterested party, this argument has been somewhat discounted.

Asymmetry of information leads to the principal-agent problem, which is well known to investors: the incentives of management are not always aligned with those of shareholders. In the health-care system, the principal-agent problem causes inefficiencies like those found in other industries where it exists.[9] Providers like physicians and hospitals can have motivations (such as profit) that may not align perfectly with the needs of the patients. Activist investors are occasionally able to force management to act in a more shareholder-friendly way. Though there are advocacy groups that could presumably do this for patients, their reach and economic power have yet to reach a critical mass that would enable them to change the health-care paradigm. Managed-care organizations suggest that they are capable of overcoming the principal-agent problem because they have the ability to pool resources and act as an educated purchaser. However, because they are not a disinterested party (they benefit from lower cost, not necessarily better care), both consumers and providers are often skeptical of their motives.

Wrong incentives and asymmetry of information can work both ways. Patients can have more knowledge about their health status than "the system" or physicians because of the fragmentation of the system. This knowledge can lead to adverse selection, with the healthiest patients recognizing that they do not need as much insurance and sick people recognizing they need increased insurance. The principle behind insurance is that risk is spread among all people, with the healthy functionally subsidizing the sick. Adverse selection results in the high utilizers of health care not being offset by low utilizers. For companies with a sick population, the financial results can be disastrous.

Moral hazard in health care is the term used to describe the utilization pattern of a patient who does not directly pay for care.[10] The underlying premise of moral hazard is that when patients are free of economic consequences (bills, for example), they will use unnecessary amounts of care. This is an example of a misincentive, but one directed at patients. Strategies that expose patients to more of the cost of health care include raising copays, deductibles, and coinsurance; these can place more of the financial burden on the patients and bring down utilization. These strategies for dealing with moral hazard have their limits; at a certain point, when costs get too high, patients use less than the optimal amount of care, and the longer-term costs are actually higher. Giving away free certain drugs for diseases like asthma, blood pressure, and diabetes actually lowers patient costs, so moral hazard can be a two-edged sword.[11] People tend to have a difficult time estimating low-probability events like disease, which makes their ability to understand their insurance and medical needs in an optimal way open to question, further complicating the moral hazard argument.[12]

There are inefficiencies on a collective basis, too. The Nash equilibrium in game theory explains why noncooperative actors make decisions.[13] But insurance companies and providers like hospitals can often seem to be at odds in determining which party should bear what risk. The same situation may be true if physicians are considered as a collective facing the government or other payers. Prevailing social and business norms can alter resource allocation from what would be obtained under an individual optimization (Nash equilibrium),[14] which leads to systemwide inefficiencies. As with resolving the individual market failures, companies that can alter the equilibrium on a large scale are likely to be able to create shareholder value, although there are significant roadblocks to be overcome.

QUALITY

What is high-quality health care? The Institute of Medicine defines the quality of health care as the degree to which health-care services for individuals and populations increase the likelihood that desired health outcomes occur and are consistent with professional knowledge.[15] For the layman, a better definition is that when a patient goes to a doctor, he gets better (or at least not worse). The problem is that there is often no definition of what *better* is, particularly for chronic diseases, which tend to be progressive over time. If there is no definitive cure—and that is the case for many, if not most, disease states—an objective successful outcome cannot be defined. For many diseases, there is no absolute consensus on what an optimal treatment is, even when a disease can be treated. In the gray area of no objective success, there is a lot of room for alternative outcomes.

VARIATIONS

There are wide and unexplained variations in the delivery, outcomes, and cost of health care. Care can vary widely by geography and site of care without having a significant positive impact on outcomes (living, dying, service intensity, and so on). Though the causes of these wide variations aren't agreed upon, barriers to reducing variations can include poor patient decision making, misaligned incentives, limited clinical knowledge, and a cultural bias that says that more is better and that physicians know best.[16] There may also be a misallocation of the number of specialists relative to generalists, which adds to the number of tests and coordination costs,[17] and to supply-induced demand. The cost of specialists can also be significantly higher than that of generalists, and yet the value they add may be out of proportion to the needs of society (i.e., the cost and value-added of a plastic surgeon versus those of a pediatrician). Variations may also be driven by the fact that there is no overarching body driving standardization, so that while in other industries the same processes or products will be used in similar situations, there is no guarantee of such an outcome in medicine.

The asymmetries of information persist in part because it appears that an asymmetrical information paradigm gives suppliers power over customers (in this case, patients). There is no incentive for providers to give up that power. In other industries, price discovery and quality discovery are relatively easy to obtain, as there are objective and transparent pricing and quality metrics. Not so in health care. One of the primary issues in health care is the lack of objective data. The health-care system is far behind other industries in its adoption of technology to obtain this data.

A patient is exposed to numerous treatments, so given the fragmented system, it is difficult to determine which treatment is actually driving a particular outcome. It is not in a provider's best interests to share pricing data. Sharing pricing data when others in a field do not also puts a provider at a competitive disadvantage. Given the lack of an information technology infrastructure, it is not clear that providers even understand the exact cost per patient when time and supplies are considered. Lack of ability to obtain price data means that price discovery for various treatments is impossible, and without price discovery, the basic laws of supply and demand do not function.

Measuring quality in health care has been and continues to be an inexact science. Survival data are easy to measure; however, quality of life, patient satisfaction, disease progression, and other health dimensions are not objective measures and are open to interpretation. Providers point to the lack of objective measures and to the wide variability in initial disease states (some patients are sicker than others) as reasons that outcome data cannot be interpreted and that sharing them would not be illustrative.

For therapeutics, head-to-head (comparative) trials, where one product or service used to treat a condition is compared to another, are rare. Though this information would be quite valuable, companies are reluctant to conduct such studies. The first reason is expense; the cost of clinical trials large enough to show a significant difference among several drugs would be prohibitive. Enrolling large numbers of patients in randomized trials is difficult when patients are already on an effective treatment. In the past, comparative trials have had negative financial outcomes for companies that engaged in them, as, after having invested significant resources in a study, they may find that their product is actually inferior to the alternative.

Medicine, like the children in Lake Wobegon, operates on the assumption that every treatment is above average—who wants to receive or provide below-average care? However, mathematically, this is not possible. Regardless of whether this is due to bad luck, bad skill, or unusually sick patients, the quality provided by half of all providers will be below average. If patients and payers had access to these quality data, their decisions on where and when to obtain care would be altered. This would be especially true if quality data were paired with price data. The potential longer-term problems of providing such transparency are that providers would start turning away sicker patients to improve their scores (gaming the system) and that there might not be equitable access to the higher-quality providers because of either economics or geography. Providers might also "study for the test" by providing care for only those things that are measured, to the exclusion of other high-quality actions.

MEDICAL ERRORS

In 2000, the Institute of Medicine released a report titled "To Err Is Human."[18] This was one of the first large-scale reports that looked at the impact of medical errors. The report suggested that between 44,000 and 98,000 people die in any given year because of preventable medical mistakes and another 1,000,000 people are injured nonfatally because of preventable mistakes. The report also calculated the direct economic costs beyond the personal toll to be in the billions of dollars. Though medical errors had been discussed for many years, the magnitude of the problem surprised many people, including politicians, clinicians, and the public. Since then, greater attention has been paid to the issue, but progress has been slow. Why all the errors? Health care as an industry has been slow to adopt many of the procedures used in other industries, such as quality control. Deming's work on quality control, developed in the middle of the twentieth century, has come into health care only slowly.[19] Other industries, where Six Sigma or some other quality approach is the norm, not the exception, are beyond what occurs in health care generally.

Malpractice

Malpractice is one of the more divisive issues in health care. The purpose of malpractice suits is to redress a wrong done to a patient by a provider. One side, the attorneys, suggests that the number of malpractice cases is low when compared to the number of medical errors. The providers counter that there are too many "frivolous" lawsuits filed, as sicker patients often become sicker irrespective of provider interventions. The states, having heard the complaints from both sides, are exploring ways of altering tort law to accommodate both sides. Such changes include caps on damage awards, limiting the percentage of awards paid to attorneys, expert witness standards, and greater accountability and transparency on the part of malpractice insurers.[20] Malpractice and other tort reform fixes are likely to be an area of reform, and although the devil will be in the details, it is important to watch this area because it could affect the cost structures of several parts of the health-care system. As patients will always need a way to redress wrongs (and the better technology gets, the more likely it is that these wrongs will be exposed) committed upon them by the health-care system or individual providers, malpractice protection will always be needed, but so is a more effective way of dealing with it.

THE UNINSURED

There are about 45.7 million people in the United States who do not have health insurance.[21] Roughly eight in ten of them come from working families. Usually the person is not insured because his employer does not offer insurance. There is roughly a 50/50 split of the uninsured between Caucasians and minorities, although as a percentage of their respective populations, minorities are far more likely to be uninsured. The uninsured tend to be sicker than the insured. Most importantly for investors, the number of uninsured has been growing until very recently.[22]

The economic cycle leads to changes in enrollment, but Medicaid offsets some of this change, as a weak economy makes more people eligible for government programs. One reason for the lack of coverage, irrespective of the economic cycle, is that fewer employers are offering health-care benefits. Some of the reasons that have been given for the decline in employer-sponsored coverage are double-digit health-care inflation, the change in the types of jobs (production to service) created in the United States, and the decline of unions. All of these trends continue to be in force today; therefore, barring a markedly improving economy, we can expect that the number of the uninsured will grow if the issues that created the uninsured are left unchecked.[23]

A QUICK HISTORY LESSON

Given the economic preeminence that America enjoyed during the twentieth century, one would intuitively assume that the country could have developed a superior health-care system. That assumption would be incorrect. Other countries developed national systems of health-care insurance far earlier than the United States. Germany is acknowledged to have developed the first social health insurance plan in 1883 under Bismarck.[24] Many other countries developed systems in the late nineteenth and early twentieth centuries, including Austria, Portugal, and the Netherlands.

So why was no such system developed in the United States? Unfortunately, there is no one definite answer. American exceptionalism cannot be explained by any one factor; rather, different sets of circumstances (political and economic) at different points in time have affected the success of health-care reform.[25] A considerable amount of scholarship has been dedicated to the history of social benefits in the United States. A common theme is that it has been tumultuous, with vested interests that benefit from maintaining the status quo usually facing off against politicians who were responding to their constituents. Over time, however, more and more people received coverage of some type, although the increases tended to be small and incremental, with occasional spikes (like Medicare). A quick snapshot of health-care reform will be instructive, as previous efforts provide a road map for the likely battle lines and ultimate outcomes of any proposed reform.

The first political candidate to propose a wide-scale health insurance plan was Theodore Roosevelt in 1912. The problem was that he lost the election to Woodrow Wilson. Even after Roosevelt's defeat, the progressive party that nominated him did its best to keep the program alive. Ultimately, however, the progressives lost out in a political fight with the American Medical Association (AMA) in 1917.[26] It wasn't just the AMA; labor unions at the time were also against universal plans. Samuel Gompers, the famous labor leader, felt that universal health care was too paternalistic, and that his members could do better on their own.[27]

Franklin Roosevelt put forth the next serious health reform proposal (universal coverage) in the aftermath of the Great Depression and the stock market crash of 1929. The economic situation of the United States dictated some extreme measures on the part of the government. As Roosevelt added proposals to what would eventually become social security, health-care insurance was included. However, the AMA intervened, as it had before, and helped to derail the plan by opposing it. In an act of political expediency, the Council of Economic Security (CES), which was driving the long-term changes that Roosevelt wanted implemented, dropped the health insurance mandate. Through the 1930s, ideas for universal plans were brought up by politicians, only to be defeated by the AMA, and when the United States entered World War II, national priorities changed, pushing health reform to the back burner. The intransigence of the

AMA's leadership was surprising given that polls showed 7 out of 10 members of the AMA actually supported universal care.[28] World War II did have a lasting impact on health care. To deal with inflation caused by the war, the government placed caps on wages; so to attract workers, companies began to offer health-care benefits. Combined with later tax advantages, employer-sponsored health care became quite beneficial to both employees and employers.[29] However, the employer-based system of insurance has created some of its own problems, and some reforms seek to do away with it altogether.

The next reform attempt came from President Truman in the late 1940s. His programs were very similar to some of the earlier proposals from the Roosevelt era. Again, the AMA was one of the key constituencies against the proposal. However, the AMA's tactics had changed somewhat, and now the movement toward health-care reform was labeled "socialized medicine," which, in a period when people were concerned about potential Russian infiltration, was quite effective in scaring American citizens.

The 1960s was a period in which the government was able to overcome contrary vested interests and expand social insurance to include health-care benefits. The election of Lyndon Johnson and the amount by which he won helped to increase the chances for a health-care expansion.[30] In 1965, Medicare and Medicaid were signed into law, ensuring that aged and poor people would have access to health care. This first large comprehensive government-sponsored health-care plan eventually had a profound impact on both the system and investment opportunities. The factors that led to Medicare should be instructive to investors as a template by which to measure the chances of meaningful reform.

President Nixon was the next to try to expand health-care coverage. In 1974, both health-care price inflation, which had jumped following the expiration of Nixon's price controls, and inflation related to the increased demand brought about by Medicare had made health-care costs a major political issue. There were several competing plans proposed, but all of them had the goal of expanding care to everyone. It looked to many observers as if something would eventually pass. However, organized labor believed that the 1974 elections would lead to a political environment that was more in tune with its positions and refused to go along with any of the proposals.[31] While the unions turned out to be correct in their political forecast that the fallout from the Watergate affair would change the political landscape, the weakening economy and other such factors did not allow the passage of a reform plan in the years that immediately followed. Nixon (along with Senator Ted Kennedy) was successful in passing the HMO act of 1973, which set the stage for the publicly traded managed-care industry.

President Clinton was the next president to attempt a wide-scale health-care reform effort. His wife, First Lady Hillary Clinton, spearheaded the endeavor. The driving force behind the proposal was the increasing costs of health care. As in 1974, the initial plan was complicated and led to a proliferation of other plans. Ultimately the plan did not become law. There is still disagreement as to why it failed. Explanations range from the complexity of the proposal, which included mandates and health alliances, to a lack of support from the insurance industry and large corporations.

While the definitive reason for the failure of the Clinton plan may never be agreed upon, its defeat in 1993 followed the same pattern as many other failed attempts at reform. It was a complex plan that did not have enough political momentum to overcome vested interests that opposed any change, including opponents from industry, the opposing political party, and even certain factions within the administration and different wings of the incumbent party.[32]

BARRIERS TO REFORM

Despite the logic and moral obligation of supporting expanded access to health care, as well as cost containment and quality improvement, there are many reasons, in addition to economic or employment-related vested interests, for reluctance to support health-care reform. Possibly the biggest roadblock is perceived or real equality and social justice concerns. Critics raise questions about how much responsibility citizens have for taking care of other citizens who have not taken care of themselves. The relative financial burden of a reform plan may not be evenly distributed among all income levels, and this also raises questions of fairness. People who are insured may not feel that they have a social obligation to pay for the less fortunate. People may also feel that their freedom to choose health-care coverage or health-care providers would be limited under a reform plan.

Budget constraints facing the government may not allow some types of reform. There may also be philosophical reasons why a plan doesn't get approved, including free-market versus a single-payer government approach to a program.

Is Wall Street to Blame?

There is a constituency in the health-care policy universe that believes that Wall Street is to blame for much of the mess. Headlines decrying pharmaceutical companies placing profits ahead of patients and managed-care executive salaries that are beyond ordinary workers' imaginations abound. Wall Street does have a history of boom and bust cycles, which can lead to overallocation of capital, and this can have negative consequences. However, investors have the ability to move more quickly than government or nonprofits, making them a more effective change agent than governmental reformers under the right circumstances. A key for reformers will be to align societal and capital market priorities, which appears to be the direction in which the country is headed, given the obvious stress that health care is putting on corporations. If the priorities are aligned, then Wall Street may be part of the solution to the health-care problem. Companies will respond when their shareholders make them act sensibly toward their workers in terms of health care. Moreover, politicians respond to both Wall Street and corporate America, and if corporate America is in favor of health-care reform, it adds significant weight to the argument. It also appears that one would have great difficulty in removing the profit motive from health care. Even if one could, this might not be in the best interests of patients or the system. Even in single-payer programs, profit is one of the driving forces for care and innovation. Without a profit motive, medicine could potentially stand still. The existing nonprofit system is no guarantee against system failure, as even in 1963, before much of medicine was corporatized, Arrow identified some of the problems that are still with us today, suggesting that a profit motive, while a potential cause of the issues, is at most only one of many.[33]

There are also executional challenges to a reform plan. If a reform plan is not articulated well enough for citizens to understand it or if the reform movement fails to generate enough momentum to overcome the political challenge of garnering support from lawmakers, a plan will fail. There may be legal questions that would preclude the development of a plan, such as constitutional objections. There are numerous ways in which critics could stall a plan legislatively, so objections from critics must be addressed in order for any reform plan to be successful. While health care is an important issue, it isn't the only issue faced by legislators. Government priorities can be dictated by current events, which may cause a shift in where health care is on the agenda. Given the magnitude of the health-care problem, it will continue to reemerge as other problems recede. Finally, given the size of health care, it is easy for inertia to set in and for change to be stifled by the weight of the system itself.

GLEEVEC

Prior to 2001, people diagnosed with chronic myelogenous leukemia (CML) or gastrointestinal stromal tumors (GIST) had poor prognoses. That changed following the approval of the drug Gleevec; suddenly two types of cancer could be cured. Not only could patients be cured, but they also could do so by taking a pill with limited side effects. Of course, this major change in treatment came at a significant cost. Novartis, the manufacturer, priced the product at about $32,000 a year.

Gleevec exemplifies the two fundamental and contradictory forces at play in health care—improving technology versus astronomical costs. The drug is the first member of a new class of drugs that inhibits tyrosine kinase enzymes. The drug was designed using molecular techniques tailored to a very specific target to minimize side effects. Gleevec was also designed to be orally available. The science worked and developed a cure for two heretofore not well-treated diseases. Is $32,000 a year worth the price? CML survivors would certainly say so. If Gleevec was the only one of its kind, the health-care system could easily absorb the costs. However, technology keeps improving and new life-saving compounds keep coming to the market at substantial costs. The tradeoff between cost and improving therapies will be one of the issues that drives change to the health care system.

NOTES

1. C. Schoen, R. Osborn, M. M. Doty, M. Bishop, J. Peugh, and N. Murukutla, "Toward Higher-Performance Health Systems: Adults' Health Care Experiences in Seven Countries," *Health Affairs* Web Exclusive 26, no. 6 (2007): W717–W734.
2. Kenneth E. Thorpe, Curtis S. Florence, and Peter Joski, "Trends: Which Medical Conditions Account for the Rise in Health Care Spending?" *Health Affairs* Web Exclusives, Aug. 25, 2004, 10, no. 4, pp. W437–W445.
3. Agency for Health Care Research and Quality, June 2006, http://www.ahrq.gov/research/ria19/expendria.pdf.
4. CMS statistics, http://www.cms.hhs.gov/NationalHealthExpendData/02_NationalHealthAccountsHistorical.asp#TopOfPage.
5. Steffie Woolhandler, Terry Campbell, and David Himmelstein, "Costs of Health Care Administration in the United States and Canada," *New England Journal of Medicine* 349 (2003): 768–775.
6. See Shannon Brownlee, *Overtreated: Why Too Much Medicine Is Making Us Sicker and Poorer* (New York: Bloomsbury USA, 2007) for a discussion of the topic in greater detail.
7. Kenneth J. Arrow, "Uncertainty and the Welfare Economics of Medical Care," *American Economic Review* 53, no. 3 (1963): 941–973.
8. For more information on asymmetry of information, see http://en.wikipedia.org/wiki/Information_asymmetry.
9. Maria Goddard, Russell Mannion, and Peter Smith, "Enhancing Performance in Health Care: A Theoretical Perspective on Agency and the Role of Information, *Health Economics* 9, no. 2 (2000): 95–107.
10. Willard Manning and Susan Marquis, "Health Insurance: The Tradeoff between Risk Pooling and Moral Hazard," Rand Institute Monograph, 1996.
11. Malcolm Gladwell, "The Moral Hazard Myth," *New Yorker*, Aug. 29, 2005.
12. Daniel Kahneman, Paul Slovic, and Amos Tversky (eds.), *Judgment under Uncertainty: Heuristics and Biases* (Cambridge and New York: Cambridge University Press, 1982).
13. John Nash, "Equilibrium Points in *n*-Person Games," *Proceedings of the National Academy of Sciences* 36, no. 1 (1950): 48–49.
14. Peter J. Hammer (ed.), *Uncertain Times: Kenneth Arrow and the Changing Economics of Health Care* (Durham, N.C.: Duke University Press, 2003), p. 234.
15. "Crossing the Quality Chasm: A New Health Care System for the 21st Century," Committee on Quality of Health Care in America, Institute of Medicine, 2001.
16. John Wennberg, "Practice Variations and Health Care Reform: Connecting the Dots," *Health Affairs*, Web Exclusive, October 2004, pp. W140–W144.
17. Shannon Brownlee, "Overdose," *Atlantic*, December 2007, http://www.theatlantic.com/doc/prem/200712/health-care.
18. Committee on Quality of Health Care in America, Institute of Medicine, "To Err Is Human: Building a Safer Health Care System," eds. Linda T. Kohn, Janet M. Corrigan, and Molla S. Donaldson (Washington, D.C.: National Academies Press, 2000).
19. W. Edwards Deming, Wikipedia citation, http://de.wikipedia.org/wiki/William_Edwards_Deming.
20. National Conference of State Legislatures, Feb. 8, 2007, http://www.ncsl.org/standcomm/sclaw/medmaloverview.htm.

21. Carmen De-Navas-Walt, Bernadette D. Proctor, Jessica C. Smith, U.S. Census Bureau, Current Population Reports, P 60–235, "Income, Poverty, and Health Insurance Coverage in the United States, 2007," U.S. Government Printing Office, Washington, D.C., 2008.
22. The Kaiser Commission on Medicaid and the Uninsured, "The Uninsured: A Primer," October 16, 2007. P1 http://www.kff.org/uninsured/7451.cfm.
23. Ibid.
24. Paul Starr, *The Social Transformation of American Medicine* (New York: Basic Books, 1982), p. 237.
25. Rick Mayes, *Universal Coverage, The Elusive Quest for National Health Insurance* (Ann Arbor: University of Michigan Press, 2005), p. 2.
26. See Ronald L. Numbers, *Almost Persuaded: American Physicians and Compulsory Health Insurance, 1912–1920* (Baltimore: Johns Hopkins University Press, 1978), for a greater discussion about this time period.
27. Starr, *Social Transformation of American Medicine,* p. 249.
28. Ibid., p. 273.
29. Victor Fuchs, "The Clinton Plan: A Researcher Examines Reform," *Health Affairs,* Spring 1994, 13(1), 102–114.
30. Numbers, *Almost Persuaded,* p. 68.
31. Numbers, *Almost Persuaded,* p. 93.
32. Paul Starr, "The Hillarycare Mythology," *American Prospect,* October 2007, http://www.prospect.org/cs/articles?article=the_hillarycare_mythology.
33. Kenneth J. Arrow, "Uncertainty and the Welfare Economics of Medical Care."

CHAPTER 3

Reform Proposals and Their Significance to Investors

Americans' interest in reforming health care has waxed and waned over the past few decades. The increased interest in the early twenty-first century has a lot to do with some of the factors discussed earlier. Either out of political expediency or out of a sense that they need to improve the system, politicians have put out a number of health reform proposals in response to what they see as the public's demands. However, a proposal is just that: a proposal. Even when a proposal becomes actual policy, real-world conditions and the complex details of execution can lead to unintended outcomes. Investors need to stay attuned to the actual proposals to get a sense of the direction of a policy, the potential for details to change, and the possible unintended consequences in order to gauge, in a macro sense, where opportunities may be found.

The government has surprisingly few levers to pull when it comes to its ability to reform health care, and these levers are blunt instruments. The government can alter laws, regulations, financing schemes, and tax regulations, and it can use its bully pulpit and moral suasion to jawbone participants to engage in better behavior. The government can also choose to intervene in either a direct or an indirect way. A reform plan sponsored by the government can order providers to take a certain action, such as mandating a minimum benefit level for patients, or it can offer such inducements as tax incentives to encourage providers indirectly. The interaction of these levers and the way the government executes them is what will ultimately drive health-care policy and lead to investment opportunities.

Another consideration that investors should not ignore is the speed with which any reform proposal could be implemented. It will not be just the plan itself but the speed of diffusion of information about the plan that will affect the reactions of the stocks and the time it takes for stocks to recover from mispricings. Since the market can be a discounting mechanism as information diffuses informally via opinions or projections, stock prices may move in advance of any formal announcement. The media and other information channels will be important factors in the speed of information diffusion. The accuracy of the information will also be important, as misinformation can slow down the momentum of any change.

There are long-cycle-time reforms and short-cycle-time reforms. In general, the larger reform packages (most recently Medicare Part D) have time frames on the order of years. Simple regulatory changes like Medicare National Coverage Decisions (NCDs) may take only a few months. The trade-off is that larger programs create larger opportunities because of their size, but do so slowly, whereas shorter-duration actions create smaller opportunities more quickly. The risk profile for the companies involved is the inverse—a longer lead time allows them to prepare better so that they can take advantage of the opportunities, whereas a quick regulatory change may be difficult to respond to in an optimal way. A major reform plan could take on the order of decades if it is a massive system overhaul. However, even the quickest government changes are not instantaneous, as there are usually comment periods and certain mandated points in the year in which they can be enacted.

Another consideration that investors must be attuned to is the level of controversy that a given reform provision generates. There are some subjects on which Americans simply cannot agree. These politically "taboo" subjects can slow the process down, or at worst derail the plan. When an item on which a substantial portion of the population does not agree is included in a package, this will reduce buy-in to the plan, and also reduce its chances of passage. Controversial subjects include, but are not limited to, abortion, stem cell research, animal testing, tax increases, and treatment of illegal immigrants. Although the major impact of these controversial subjects is likely to be on timetables for reform, there may also be investment opportunities in companies that can deal with these issues without inflaming the debate. Those companies that are not sensitive to the negative consequences of controversy are in danger of destroying shareholder value.

A final consideration is the level of complexity that any plan may have. The less complex the plan is (the fewer rules it requires), the easier it will be to forecast an outcome. Complexity benefits investors, as a more complex program will lead to increased uncertainty, and that will lead to greater mispricings. Most large programs that involve a significant portion of the population will not be able to manage a one-size-fits-all solution. A substantial level of exceptions (economic, geographic, disease- or condition-specific, and so on) and laws governing the provision of care will make for a very complicated program, in all likelihood.

Health-care reforms span a wide gamut. Generally speaking, they can be considered on a continuum of level of regulation (from none to full) and what type of entity enforces system discipline (market versus government). These are imperfect categorizations[1] but for investing purposes, they should be descriptive enough. In terms of a comprehensive system change, the extremes are represented by single-payer centered (predominantly the government taking responsibility for care), and free-market centered (predominantly individuals taking responsibility for their own care), with a private/public mix (a government/corporate/individual hybrid of responsibility for health-care insurance) representing a middle ground and more or less the system we have today.

Market-centric and government-centric approaches are diametrically opposed, and their proponents have often come into conflict. Unworkable as an ideologically pure system may be, that has not stopped proponents of each of the opposing views from trying. The adherents of one philosophy will inevitably point out the flaws in the other: a market-centric system does not self-correct due to uneven market discipline, is prone to misallocations of capital, exposes patients to imperfect markets, and won't necessarily cover the entire population;[2] a highly regulated system is impractical to develop due to imperfect regulations or regulators, will lead to interference in choice, won't impose cost discipline, and may not address malincentives.[3] Depending on the political climate, elements of each plan have become standards for the reimbursement and provision of health care. Health savings accounts (from the market-centric proponents) and coverage of end-stage renal disease (from the government-sponsored supporters) are now part of the health-care landscape.

Though there are an infinite number of potential reforms to the system, there are five categories into which a reform program may fit: cost control, process, financing, quality, and access.

COST CONTROL

Cost-containment provisions are fairly straightforward in that they are designed to reduce the growth rate of medical costs (or the absolute costs themselves). There are relatively few ways a reform can contain costs: It can cut prices or price growth, or it can reduce volume (of products and services) or volume growth. From an investment point of view, cost-control initiatives are a two-edged sword. If an investment leads to cost control, either through less expensive services or products or improved longer-term clinical outcomes, then that investment will benefit from cost-control efforts. If a company offers a service or product that is deemed too expensive or otherwise inefficient, that company is at risk of seeing its product's use curtailed, with negative consequences for the share price. Determining whether a product or service creates a cost-control benefit is not always easily done. Often a product or service may cost more on the front end, like screening, but provide longer-term cost benefits at a later date. Delaying a treatment will save money early on but will potentially cause significant cost issues later. Fraud and waste in the system should be easier to determine, but given the complexity of the system, even these issues may not always be clear. It is therefore important for the company to prove its value proposition to investors using very conservative assumptions.

There is an inherent conflict for many companies in that the more the health-care system spends, the better it will be for industry financial results. In an expanding market, the environment is not a zero-sum game, and organic growth is more important than market share shift. A rapidly expanding market is somewhat incompatible with the societal desire to reduce health-care spending. Companies that can show that they do, in fact, save the system money, either directly or indirectly, are the ones that are most worthy of investment consideration.

As with the rest of health-care reform, there is a wide variety of health-care cost-reduction ideas. They span the political spectrum and involve both direct and indirect modes of execution. It is inevitable that cost-control provisions will be a risk to companies in terms of either market growth or outright business, so watching the cost-control measures is of paramount importance for health-care investors.

Widely Considered Cost Reforms

Price Controls

Although they are not often specifically proposed in the United States, outright price controls, sometimes called reference pricing, have been a feature of cost-control schemes in other countries. With these arrangements, prices and price increases or decreases are determined by a central government authority. In general, companies' experience with price controls has been negative. There is a political component to these pricing schemes, so companies with better political connections can sometimes buffer some of the issues, but that is the exception, not the rule. The United States has its own subtle form of price controls in the form of payments from Medicare and Medicaid, which functionally set the prices for products and services. Commercial insurers then use Medicare and Medicaid pricing as a starting point for determining their own pricing schemes. Outright price controls seem unlikely in the United States, given the unpopularity of price controls in other segments of the economy throughout the history of the country. Nevertheless, if they should emerge, price controls would be interpreted as a negative by the vast majority of health-care investors.

As draconian as direct price controls may seem, there are more stringent restrictions that governments can place on health-care utilization. The government can institute utilization caps, which dictate that patients are allowed only a certain amount of health care per year, per lifetime, or for some other period. This is a form of rationing, and it is not an attractive option to propose from a politician's standpoint. A more likely rationing approach is means testing, which uses a predetermined level of income to determine whether a patient can obtain government payment for services. Medicaid and SCHIP (State Children's Health Insurance Program) have eligibility requirements for health care based on household income, so this concept is not unknown in the United States. The idea is that above a certain level of income, a person should be able to shoulder some or all of the costs associated with health care rather than relying on society. The levels can vary based upon geographic location, although the question of what income level defines "poor" has been the subject of debate for some time. From an investment perspective, less stringent rules on income levels are preferred because government and health plans are more reliable (less economically sensitive) payers of health-care costs than individuals are.

Market Incentives

Market-centric approaches to cost control tend to involve the use of financial incentives to encourage prospective patients to choose low-cost options. Often these financial incentives take the form of a tax refund or subsidy to patients. With a tax-based scheme, the patient has a financial incentive to seek out the lowest-cost health-care option. For a market-centric approach to be successful, outcomes data must be available so that the patient can make an informed choice, the lowest-cost options must be available to the patient, and the incentives must be large enough to actually change behavior. The most prominent example of free-market incentive-based thinking is the development of the health savings account (HSA). This product takes money tax-free and puts it into a savings account that can be used for medical expenses; it is often paired with a high-deductible catastrophic-care plan. The premise is that patients can save money if they remain healthy and make prudent health choices. For such a plan to be successful, the underlying assumptions that the moral hazard level is high enough and that care is unnecessary must be correct, so that when an individual is spending her own money, she will choose the optimum level of resources without underutilizing. This proposal may be a mixed blessing for investors, as providers of free-market-type products like HSAs are likely to benefit, while providers of services or products that would benefit if the money were payer-directed rather than individual-directed will be hurt by losing the incremental patients who may choose not to utilize, if given a choice.

The market approach also implies that providers' behavior can be changed through incentives as well. Under the free-market approach, providers who deliver optimal care from a cost and quality perspective should benefit financially. Incentives include bonuses for optimal care as well as information dissemination about providers' quality standards, which could drive patient traffic.

Screening and Prevention

Preventing a disease or treating it early in its progression may lead to long-term savings to the overall health-care system. There are screening tests for a number of illnesses that are underutilized, like a colonoscopy. However, the data on whether prevention works depend very much on the intervention and the addressable population. Not all interventions are created equal;[4] some are highly successful, and some are not.

Cost-effectiveness analysis of prevention initiatives, like valuation analyses of stocks, can often be an art rather than a science. Because of its intuitive appeal and easily explainable nature, almost all reform plans contain a preventive medicine element. It is almost a given that some increase in prevention will be part of a reform package, but how broad this is depends on the details of the program. From an investment point of view, diagnostic companies stand out as the most likely to benefit. As diagnostic tests become more advanced, we may be able to screen at the molecular level in ways that were unachievable before. While this opens up bioethical questions like privacy and discrimination, more sensitive predictions may allow medicine to narrowly define at-risk patients and address their problems before they become a large expense item.

Risk Pooling

One of the basic mechanisms of insurance is to pool risk. In any population, there will be a certain number of negative events requiring insurance coverage. The cost of these events will be borne by a broad population, most of whom will not have an event, and this makes insurance affordable for the entire population. The larger the pool of people to spread the risk among, the more predictable the risk profile and the lower the individual cost should be. Many reform proposals contain an element of allowing individuals and small groups of people to band together in larger pools to reduce their individual costs. The risk is that people who are currently healthy will all band together in a way that allows them to achieve the lowest possible cost, excluding the sick people and forcing them to band together into high-cost plans. This is referred to as adverse selection. Most insurance companies would rather insure healthy people than sick people, as the costs and risks of doing so are lower. If an insurance plan or the government is forced to take care of the sick patients exclusively, it is unlikely to be of any help to the system. Any risk-pooling programs will have to take into account the potential for adverse selection, and the possibility that individuals will be excluded from private insurance on the basis of preexisting conditions.

Mandating minimum expenditure ratios for care and maximum expenditure ratios for administration is another cost-control proposal that has been floated by reformers. The ratio used to define how much of medical cost is spent on patient care is known as the medical care ratio (MCR), and the amount spent on administration (paperwork, salaries, advertising) is known as the administrative ratio. Some proposals define minimum and maximum ratios. There is no one-size-fits-all definition for a given population, so a proposal with a hard-and-fast level is likely to represent a risk for companies that may have to comply with the defined ratios, as they limit the flexibility of operations.

Reimportation

Health-care products and services are less expensive outside the United States, although the magnitude of the price difference and availability is a function of which country and what the currency exchange rate is. The reasons that products are less expensive outside the United States often have to do with local price controls or local labor costs. There are indications that much of the world is "free riding" on U.S. innovation, and that local innovative industries have suffered as a result, but there is nevertheless a near-term cost advantage for an individual (though perhaps not for society) from procuring items in other countries. The reimportation proposals generally revolve around lowering barriers to cross-border procurement of products or services. Proper safety protocols will have to be enacted to ensure that all products entering the U.S. supply chain are of typical high quality under reimportation. There will have to be safeguards against innovation destruction as a result of reduced R&D caused by lower profit margins, or else entire industry segments are at risk of value destruction. It is not clear exactly how much longer-term benefit reimportation will have. The laws of supply and demand may result in higher prices in the countries outside the United States rather than lowering costs in the United States. The United States dwarfs all other health-care markets, so there is really no practical way for any other country in the world to supply the U.S. market without seeing material disruption of its own prices and availability of goods.

DTC Fixes

The government changed the laws governing direct-to-consumer advertising for pharmaceuticals (DTC) in 1997. This allowed pharmaceutical companies to start marketing directly to consumers in ways that they had been unable to before. The result was a major increase in pharmaceutical company advertising spending and an uptick in drug usage. Pharmaceutical companies were not the first to advertise to the public; hospitals and even individual physicians had been advertising to consumers for some time before that. The consequence, the potential reformers believe, has been that DTC leads to increased utilization, much of which is unnecessary. Regardless of whether this sequence of events is correct (and opinions vary), if DTC curbs are put into place, it will hurt companies that rely on DTC as a marketing tool.

Pricing Information

Lack of pricing information is one of the key problems in health care. Patients and payers generally do not know how much a service or product actually costs, nor do they know the relative health outcome (benefit) of a service or product. Many reform proposals have some mechanism for identifying both cost and quality metrics and releasing those data to the public. The details on how to accomplish this goal are varied. Possibilities include creating an agency to determine cost-effectiveness, similar to the United Kingdom's National Institute for Health and Clinical Excellence (NICE), which decides the relative value of a product or service. Many companies have had negative interactions with NICE in the past, and there is reason to believe that companies with products that are expensive or of questionable effectiveness would have trouble with a similar agency in the United States. There is no consensus on how to obtain good data beyond running comparative clinical trials, and these tend to require a great deal of time, expense, and logistical difficulty. It is unclear how such an agency would make decisions in the absence of good data. Investors in "good" companies with superior products should welcome such an agency, as it will allow those companies, their products, and their share prices to rise commensurate with their cost-effectiveness. Dissemination of pricing information will allow patients and payers alike to comparison-shop to get the best deals on their health care.

PROCESS REFORMS

Process issues are a bit more complex to implement from a policy level. They can also be difficult for reformers to explain to the public at large, making it hard to achieve broad support. Vested interests that look at regulation narrowly can get in the way of changes in statutes. As part of a larger reform package, process fixes can be codified, making resistance to individual items potentially less likely. The U.S. health-care industry is behind its peers when it comes to many outcome measures and efficiency. Process reforms, while not addressing care directly, address some of the tangential issues that get in the way of quality care.

Reduction in Medical Errors

Many medical errors are preventable,[5] but preventing them will be a challenge. The most common proposal is to increase reporting of errors, because the level of information about which procedures, drugs, and patients are most likely to be at risk of suboptimal outcomes is currently limited. As it stands, however, the culture of "naming, blaming, and shaming"[6] keeps most errors unknown. Manufacturers of medical products are required to report malfunctions and adverse events associated with their products, and providers should be required to do so as well. There is no standard set of reporting criteria for when a product on the market shows signs of negative outcomes.

Financial or other bonuses to providers who show that they are giving patients optimal care may be another way to reduce medical errors. In general, proposals to reduce medical errors should be a boon for companies that manufacture systems to track outcomes, provide better systems, and possibly help payers identify suboptimal care. There are relatively few proposals aimed at addressing the human failure component of medicine, beyond capping the number of hours worked.

Malpractice

If a provider or product maker acknowledges a preventable medical error, it opens itself up to the possibility of a medical malpractice suit. As with other parts of medicine, recommended methods of malpractice reform depend upon the ideology and vested interest of the proposer. Proposals for malpractice reform tend to focus on one of the three parties involved in the process: lawyers, courts, and insurance companies. For attorneys, proposals involve capping the amount of awards, penalizing attorneys for filing "frivolous" suits, and lowering the percentage of awards that lawyers are entitled to. For the courts, the proposals include reorganizing the way in which malpractice cases are heard in an attempt to hasten what is usually a multiyear process. For insurance companies, the proposals range from transparency on how much the insurers pay out to transparency on how they develop their malpractice rates. Some of the same dynamics hold true for other parts of the tort system, including lawsuits against product manufacturers. A system that makes the malpractice or tort system more efficient while still maintaining legal and economic justice will reduce financial friction in the system and be a positive for all involved parties and a positive for shareholder value.

Innovation

The United States has historically been one of the most innovative countries in the world when it comes to medicine. Other countries have seen their innovative industries decline, and some have suggested that this may be related to cost controls, but making the case with certainty is difficult because so many factors come into play in the success or failure of innovative industries.

Many health-care reforms acknowledge the danger that crimping costs could hurt innovative industries (pharmaceuticals, biotech, and medical technology) and take some steps to ameliorate any loss of productivity. These steps can include tax credits, direct investment, and intellectual property protections. Refinements to the patent process are of particular importance to investors, and changes may make gaining a patent either easier or more difficult and may make the ease of patent infringement and the penalties that go with it more or less onerous. For investors, these proposals are important to watch, as price controls and intellectual property (IP) protections are related to a reduction in innovation.[7] The lower the potential return, the less likely it is that investors will want to participate in the company at a given share price.

Approval Process

The regulatory process has also been a focus of health-care reform. The main regulatory agency in this area in the United States is the Food and Drug Administration (FDA). According to its charter, the FDA is the federal agency responsible for ensuring that foods are safe, wholesome, and sanitary; human and veterinary drugs, biological products, and medical devices are safe and effective; cosmetics are safe; and electronic products that emit radiation are safe.[8]

In 1992, the government passed the PDUFA (Prescription Drug User Fee Act) as a response to claims that the agency was not approving therapeutics in a timely way. The act calls for innovators to pay a fee; in return, the agency will respond within a predetermined time frame. This act attempts to balance the agency's responsibility for safety with the innovators' (and patients') need for speed to market. These two mandates can come into conflict, particularly because a clinical trial cannot be designed to determine how a product will be used in an infinite number of real-world situations.

Several widely sold drugs and devices have been recalled once they were on the market because of safety issues that were not anticipated by the clinical trials. Reforms could include increasing spending on the FDA to boost the number of regulators before and during the approval process, to monitor safety issues, and to be responsive to public health concerns once the product is on the market. The FDA does not have a mandate to determine the cost-benefit of any given device, but there have been calls to add this responsibility to its mandate. The FDA does not yet have a mechanism for approving lower-cost versions of advanced products like biogenerics (generic versions of biotech drugs). As more advanced therapies enter the market, it is inevitable that regulation will follow.

As medicine becomes more complex, the FDA's responsibilities will increase. The faster a product can get on the market, the more successful the company will be. However, if a devastating safety consequence arises after a product is on the market, there is the potential for a complete elimination of capital. If the FDA develops the capability to approve low-cost competitive products, investors must be aware that such a potential exists. It is incumbent on investors to watch the FDA and ensure that it is successfully balancing innovation and safety.

Allocation of Resources

Misallocation of resources is an issue that plagues the health-care system; the supply of resources is mismatched with the demand for resources. Such mismatches include geographic issues (physicians won't practice in certain locations, for example), too high a ratio of specialists to general practitioners in some locations, and too much capital equipment (MRI equipment, for example) for the number of patients who require it. These mismatches have led to increased costs.[9] In some regions, certificate of need programs are in place to curtail spending on unnecessary projects, but they are not nationwide, and criteria vary widely. Economic solutions have been proposed to rectify the imbalances in physician ratios, mainly by compensating physicians and hospitals for working in certain geographic areas and practicing certain types of medicine. Such proposals include altering the medical education process to either expand the field or make practicing medicine in underserved areas more lucrative. These efforts have not been successful in large measure, as shown by the current gaps in access. The same types of inducements could also be used to improve scientific education to develop new types of therapeutics, but the success of these efforts has also been limited.

As long as medical reimbursement is based upon procedure intensity, which favors procedure-based medical specialties, it is unlikely that these imbalances will be fixed. Capitation, which involves making a gatekeeper responsible for all care and reimbursing the provider based upon the care provided, was once considered a popular antidote for the procedure intensity issue. This system in its most common forms proved to be too restrictive to be adopted broadly by the market. If the government does become more involved in the allocation of resources, it will merit watching, as the products that the government favors and the companies that provide them will outperform those that the government decides are inefficient.

A Health-Care Federal Reserve or SEC

The United States does not have a health-care system per se, but rather a collection of programs and corporate entities, each of which provides care for a sector of the population. There is no one agency that oversees the proper functioning of the industry. In contrast, the financial markets have numerous regulatory bodies that oversee the functioning of the industry. In financial services, the Securities and Exchange Commission (SEC) is the government agency that makes sure that the industry functions correctly. The mission of the SEC is to protect investors; maintain fair, orderly, and efficient markets; and facilitate capital formation. Given the size of the U.S. health-care industry and its importance to the economy, it is surprising that there is no centralized agency that is responsible for the overall functioning of the market. There have been proposals for such an agency, but its design and responsibilities remain open to debate.[10] Creating such an agency may take time, so responsibilities such as making sure the market performs efficiently are likely to fall on the Centers for Medicare & Medicaid Services (CMS) and the FDA as an expansion of their mandates. From an investing point of view, increased regulation does impose a higher level of uncertainty on investments, but it does allow those companies that are able to fulfill all regulatory requirements a competitive edge.

FINANCING REFORMS

Any proposal, no matter how good its intentions or how positive its outcome, will need to be financed. Financing health care is an area where the government already plays a substantial role and at which many health-care reform proposals are directed. The financing approaches mirror the ideological approaches to health reform: private, mixed public and private, and entirely public financing. The overall goals of all the financing schemes are the same: to make sure that coverage is provided to a wide population, that the financial reasonability is fairly distributed among the people who pay for it, and that it will accomplish other reform goals (process, quality).

Market-centric proponents believe that health care can be reformed through the proper use of tax and other incentives. As it stands now, employers can deduct health insurance costs, whereas individuals cannot. Thus, there is an incentive for companies to supply insurance, and there is an incentive for individuals to not be insured. Employers receive the benefit of being able to pool risk over a larger group, whereas individuals, especially if they have preexisting conditions, are subject to market rates, which may not be financially palatable. The tax and financial incentives approach believes that if individuals can be turned into consumers, they will seek out the optimal care for their situation. The availability of multiple plans optimizes choice for the individual, which is a highly prized right. However, there are still significant disparities in the level of information in health care, and the market-centric approach does not explicitly counteract this problem. To be successful, market advocates will have to pair tax reforms with additional transparency requirements.

Even with an attractive tax profile or the availability of low-cost coverage through a pooled-risk program, employees and employers may still not wish to participate in the health-care system, and this can lead to adverse selection. Making health-care insurance compulsory is the solution that all three approaches can take. The rationale is that having more participants expands the risk pool and also makes purchasing less expensive. Although it is not a particularly libertarian approach by any means, in that it forces participants to do something, making health insurance, like auto insurance, compulsory does have some appeal from a logistical point of view. A purely free-market approach may not be palatable to citizens who do not trust strictly corporate-controlled health care and is rendered relatively unlikely by the fact that the government already pays for about one-third of health care directly and another 12 percent indirectly,[11] and that undoing this payment system would lead to substantial executional issues.

A mix of public and private mechanisms is the most commonly proposed reform. These reform programs can take a play-or-pay approach, which means that employers and individuals either join the system or pay into a fund that will pay for care. The system builds on the existing health-care infrastructure while expanding government programs. The risk is pooled over a larger group, so that the program will be actuarially sound. It also preserves plan choice, as employees and employers who are satisfied with their insurance will not be forced to make major changes. Paying for these plans may require a mix of increased taxes, employee and employer contributions, and payments from individuals who want to opt out of the program.

At the other end of the spectrum from a completely free-market approach is a purely public payment approach. Under this policy, known as a single-payer system, a single entity, most likely the government, will pay for all of health care. Since Medicare and Medicaid already pay for a substantial portion of health-care services, this proposal requires an expansion of those programs to pay for everyone. The program will be paid for by increased taxes on individuals and corporations. This approach does have some potential advantages, as the administrative burden should be lower. The efficiency of the administrative burden depends on the ultimate plan design in this system. The system will be less efficient if the government chooses to implement a health stamp type of system similar to food stamps rather than a direct-payment model similar to Medicare. A single-payer system does potentially reduce choice and forces the 85 percent of Americans who are enrolled in a program to change plans, so a health stamp-type of reimbursement program may overcome some of the choice issues, although it does carry a certain stigma of being enrolled in a public program. A government-centric approach need not be completely single-payer, as government may regulate the system more without necessarily becoming directly involved in the provision or reimbursement of care.

Another drawback of government programs, as they stand today, is that many providers are unable to earn a profit on government programs alone, making up the difference from private plans (cost shifting). Under a government-pay program, an inability to shift costs might create financial distress for some providers if they had been relying too heavily on commercial subsidies. A government-centric plan may also not be palatable to a certain part of the population that fears government control or does not wish to pay for others' poor health choices. In addition, of course, regardless of regulation, a government-centric plan cannot force an unwilling patient to make lifestyle choices (no matter how sound those choices may be).

The most likely outcome, if history is a guide, will be a mix of public and private financing. From an investing standpoint, this is the optimal outcome. More patients will be enrolled in a variety of health plans, growing the market. A growing market leads to investment opportunities. A public and private mix is not likely to require the draconian cuts in prices that would have to occur under a market–based plan or a government-based plan in order to make those programs financially feasible. Public/private plans are likely to contain elements from both the free-market approach and the single-payer approach. The ultimate mix will be important to investors, as it will determine which types of companies will benefit and to what degree.

QUALITY REFORMS

Government does not directly take care of patients; people take care of patients. There is relatively little direct impact that reform can have on health-care quality. However, government could use indirect methods to encourage the development of better outcomes. The government has three tools at its disposal: carrots (rewards), sticks (penalties), and information dissemination.

In most industries, high-performance products and services receive a premium price, not so in health care. Particularly where the government is concerned, all similar procedures and services are treated equally, regardless of outcomes or patient satisfaction. One of the few distinctions the government makes is to vary some of the payments by geographic areas and sites of care, noting that some geographies and sites are more expensive to operate in than others, and sometimes it needs to make adjustments for severity. Many proposals seek to reward best practices and best care while penalizing those who perform suboptimally. This change in payment methodology could be beneficial to those products and services (and the shares of companies that provide them) that lead to optimal care, and it has the appeal of making health care more like other industries, with payment being based on performance.

Because there is often little consensus about what constitutes high-quality care, many proposals call for an agency or an organization to collect the available data on given procedures and services and determine which is most efficacious. An unbiased organization would then disseminate the information to providers and patients so that there was informed decision making on both sides. Then the payer could accurately assess whether optimal care had been delivered. This information may require public expenditures in the form of state-run cost-effectiveness trials, as companies may not see an economic benefit from doing these trials themselves. A half measure may be for the government to collect outcomes data (if privacy concerns can be addressed) for procedures and services that it already pays for. Developing best practices across a broad cross section of health care is likely to be a multiyear process.

In recent years, the government has conducted some pilot programs on disseminating outcomes data for hospitals on certain procedures where there has been agreement on care standards. The pilot programs have found that publicizing both the good and the bad outcomes has raised the standards at underperforming facilities. These programs have not been done on the national scale that politicians envision in their proposals.

For investors, the details and execution will matter. If comparative trials of products and services are required, the costs of developing new therapies will be much higher, and that would be a negative. To the extent that companies can prove that their therapies are superior to others on the market, this represents an advantage. Gathering and disseminating comparative clinical data and outcomes results is a nascent industry, so if these proposals were to succeed, there would be an investment opportunity.

ACCESS REFORM

For health-care reform to work, patients must be able to access the system. One of the areas that will make or break a plan is access. Efficient access to products and services will allow companies to take advantage of increased opportunities and patients to receive necessary services.

There are some investment considerations to keep in mind with regard to access. From a corporate perspective, the more enrollees there are in a program, the better, as the size of the market increases. It may never be feasible to cover every single person, but roughly 15 percent of the market is uninsured, and a certain number are underinsured (people who have insurance but whose expenses are too high to allow them to utilize services), and therefore there is a substantial market expansion potential available. The simpler the enrollment process, the more likely it is that the plan will be a success, because the easier it is for patients to enroll, the more likely it is that they will participate. Along with the simplicity will come portability. In a mobile society, the ability to move among geographic regions easily will also be a positive reform.

Out-of-pocket expenses should be kept to a minimum because, all else being equal, high out-of-pocket costs will discourage necessary utilization, contradicting the goal of the plan. Some type of premium assistance program could be put into place to cap the maximum percentage of a person's income that could be spent on health care. Although the mechanics of such a proposal would have to be worked out via the tax code, it is a potential approach to keeping out-of-pocket expenses down.

In order to be successful, any plan will probably have to offer at least some options in terms of individual choice, although having insurance in any form, even without optimal choice, is most likely preferred to having no insurance at all. Plan choice probably will lead to increased costs to the service providers and may hinder visibility of earnings, but it seems unlikely that plans will offer infinite choice, so the confusion should be manageable.

Coverage in and of itself may be important, but if the plan does not cover needed services and products, it will not be helpful to patients or to companies' bottom lines. At present, there is no consensus on the optimal benefit design structure of a basic plan. Preventive and screening services are likely to be covered, as are catastrophic and emergency care. Treatments in the middle of the cost and value spectrum are likely to be the most contentious in terms of deciding whether they should be covered or not. These middle-ground treatments may also be where companies can capture value, assuming that they are included in a plan. For example, the way a plan deals with experimental treatments and "off-label" usage will have implications for more of the early-stage companies. The adjudication of judgment calls (where the evidence on optimal treatment is unknown) will also have an impact on how utilization evolves. A positive development would be if a plan designates an unproven product or service as being in a trial and receives a collection of data in return.

In order to make a plan successful for the public and for companies, providers must also participate in the program; their needs mirror those of patients. Providers need a simple plan that compensates them at a level consistent with profitable operations. They need some level of autonomy, or they will not want to be involved in the system. A program that encompasses a wide range of providers will be more successful because it will mean that access to the plan is available. A plan with few willing providers runs the risk of having care that is compensated but not available.

Reform Goals

Universal coverage is one of the goals often cited for health-care reform. One of the more common definitions of universal health care is the situation in which all the residents of a geographic or political region have access to most types of health care, regardless of their ability to pay. Of course, this definition is quite broad. It does not define a boundary between mandatory and elective care or how to choose that boundary. It does not define who should provide the care or how it should be paid for. The desire for universal health care also presumes that basic health care is a human right. Many members of the public use the terms *universal health care*, *single-payer*, and *socialized medicine* interchangeably, but they are not synonymous. As long as most of the population is covered, the participants should be indifferent as to how they are covered. Ideological and philosophical issues will play a role in determining the mechanics of a plan—who pays for and who delivers care—or how a system will work. Though people from most ideological viewpoints on the health-care debate ultimately appear to believe that there is a social contract to provide a health-care safety net, there are extreme, and often acrimonious, differences about how such a net should be enacted.

A plan need not be completely universal in order for investors to benefit. Most health reform programs have insurance coverage for at least most of the citizens as their primary goal. A move toward greater access will most likely be an evolutionary process that will have long-term consequences for investors. The goal will probably be full coverage of the entire population in a way that controls costs. If history is any guide, reality is likely to fall short of this goal in the short term.

Assuming that the future of health-care reform will not vary much from the past history of health care, incrementalism will prevail, and a mixed public/private-payer plan that increases the insured population, but not universally, and has only a modest impact on costs will ultimately be the result. Bolstering this view, a radical shift to a $2 trillion plan to fit an ideological mold simply does not seem feasible.

HOW OTHER PLACES DO IT

Though many health-care problems are not unique to the United States, health-care delivery systems are different. Universal health-care plans represent the predominant way health care is delivered outside the United States in the developed world. Examples of universal systems include the National Health Service of Britain, Health Canada, Medicare of Australia, the German system (GKV), and the Japanese system (Social Insurance or National Health Insurance).

These systems provide routine and preventive care at a modest fee to the patient, with services being heavily subsidized by the government. Elective procedures and nonessential and more advanced procedures or treatments are generally treated somewhat differently, with access determinations being made by government agencies like the British NICE.

Countries that do offer systems that provide health care for all are facing many of the same challenges that the United States is facing, including health-care cost inflation that is increasing faster than GDP. In other mature markets, countries that in the past had robust medical innovation industries have seen those industries wither, and though it is hard to pinpoint the cause of the loss of innovation, reduced spending on health care as a result of cost-control schemes is a possibility.

Although the less-developed nations have yet to fully grapple with their own public health issues, it appears that they will expand their universal health programs to accommodate upwardly mobile populations. Access to health care is one of the many hurdles developing economies must overcome if they want to be on a par with the developed world.

The health-care system in the United States is not a universal system in that many people without economic means cannot access the health-care system for their basic health-care needs. The United States has a mix of private and public payers for health-care services that manage to insure about 85 percent of the population. On the private side, employers generally pay for their employees' health-care benefits and receive some tax benefits for doing so. The government (state or federal) pays for citizens over 65 though Medicare, and economically challenged or otherwise disabled citizens are covered through Medicaid. The government also makes provisions for children of parents who either have jobs that do not offer health benefits or cannot afford insurance premiums through the SCHIP program.

The goals of reform will ultimately drive a reform program, and that will drive investment returns. The underlying philosophical approaches of the program will drive the goals, and it is paramount that investors understand the philosophical framework of any reform initiative. Either the authors of the program believe that government is more effective at running the health-care industry or they believe that the private sector is. Either the authors of the reform program believe that incentives (financial or otherwise) can bring about behavior change in terms of cost and clinical outcomes or they do not. Either the public is willing to accept the inevitable trade-offs required to expand access or control costs or it is not. Finally (and perhaps most importantly for investors), the authors of the reform plan either believe that profit should be a major component of health care or believe that it should not be. The basic facts underlying whatever reform philosophy emerges victorious may eventually prove incorrect, but for investors, the money will flow to where the program is heading, and that is where the upside will be garnered.

BBA 97: WHEN GOVERNMENT GOES TOO FAR IN CONTROLLING COSTS

In 1997 politicians were able to reach an agreement on measures that would help control costs of Medicare and Medicaid. The provisions were in a bill known as the Balanced Budget Act of 1997 (BBA 97). The bill provided for some radical changes in the way Medicare was paid for, and made substantial reductions in payments to home health agencies, managed care plans, skilled nursing facilities, and physicians. The results were not positive for many health-care companies and industry segments. The cost cuts resulted in severe financial stress placed on many providers across numerous industries. The HMO index of stocks dropped from $311 to $220 by the end of the year. Many nursing homes either went into bankruptcy or came very close.[12] In terms of quality, access was reduced substantially. Ultimately, even though it saved money initially, the program reduced competition, which eventually forced cost inflation back up, counter to the intent of the bill. On seeing the level of pain caused to organizations and patients alike, portions of the law eventually were modified via the Balanced Budget Refinement Act (BBRA) of 1999 and the Medicare, Medicaid Benefits Improvement, and Protection Act (BIPA) of 2000. From this experience, government came away with an understanding of how much could go wrong when a bill is aimed purely at the cost side of the equation. It also may be true that having been through this experience, the government may be less penal toward providers in future reforms.

NOTES

1. Joseph White, "Markets and Medical Care: The United States, 1993–2005," *Milbank Quarterly* 85, no. 3 (2007): 395–448.
2. Thomas Buchmueller, Sherry A. Glied, Anne Royalty, and Katherine Swartz, "Cost and Coverage Implications of the McCain Plan to Restructure Health Insurance," *Health Affairs* 27, no. 6 (2008): w472–w481 (published online September 16, 2008).
3. Joseph Antos, Gail Wilensky, and Hanns Kuttner, "The Obama Plan: More Regulation, Unsustainable Spending," *Health Affairs* 27, no. 6 (2008): w462–w471 (published online September 16, 2008).
4. Afschin Gandjour and Karl Wilhelm Lauterbach, "Does Prevention Save Costs? Considering Deferral of the Expensive Last Year of Life," *Journal of Health Economics* 24, no. 4 (2005): 715–724.
5. Committee on Quality of Health Care in America, Institute of Medicine, "To Err Is Human: Building a Safer Health System," ed. Linda T. Kohn, Janet M. Corrigan, and Molla S. Donaldson (Washington, D.C.: National Academies Press, 2000).
6. Ibid.
7. Joseph H. Golec and John A. Vernon, "European Pharmaceutical Price Regulation, Firm Profitability and R&D Spending," NBER Working Paper No. 12676, November 2006.
8. FDA mission statement, http://www.fda.gov/opacom/morechoices/mission.html.
9. W. P. Welch, M. E. Miller, H. G. Welch, et al., "Geographic Variation in Expenditures for Physicians' Services in the United States," *New England Journal of Medicine* 328 (1993): 21–27.
10. Lynn Etheredge, "Perspective: Promarket Regulation: An SEC-FASB Model," *Health Affairs* 16, no. 6 (1997): 22–25.
11. From CMS data set 2006, http://www.cms.hhs.gov/NationalHealthExpendData/02_NationalHealthAccountsHistorical.asp#TopOfPage.
12. Judy Y. Yip, Ph.D., Kathleen H. Wilber, Ph.D. and Robert C. Myrtle, DPA, "The Impact of the 1997 Balanced Budget Amendment's Prospective Payment System on Patient Case Mix and Rehabilitation Utilization in Skilled Nursing," *The Gerontologist* 42 (2002): 653–660.

CHAPTER 4

Anatomy of the Health-Care System

One of the maxims of investors is "invest in what you know." If all investors approached health-care investment in this way, very few of them would ever put their capital to work in the sector, because on the surface, the industry looks very complicated. There are many moving parts to the system, so many that it seems impossible that the system can work—it's very similar to a Rube Goldberg device. This seeming complexity conceals a plethora of investment opportunities for those who do their homework to understand the basic framework of the industry. An investing advantage derived from this perceived complexity is that it scares away many investors who would otherwise push up valuations and create competition for returns. The lower the valuation paid for a company, the more likely the investment is to be successful.

The health-care system has five constituencies, each with its own set of interests: patients, payers, politicians (government), product makers, and providers. Investment value is created by what can be described as a dance among the various groups. It does not necessarily need to be a zero-sum game, although shareholder value can be created that way. The market power of the various participants is often unequal and can change depending on the circumstances. Market power also can be divided into a hard component (the number of competitors) and a soft component (expectations, bargaining, and wherewithal), both of which can be altered by either external intervention or internal market forces.[1] Long-term shareholder value will be driven by the market power garnered by the product or service that aligns best with the greatest number of constituents. Those products and services (and representative stocks) that benefit from power shifts exclusively, rather than from providing actual value to multiple constituencies, may see a short-term upside, but they will be unlikely to maintain their momentum given the inevitability of future power shifts.

In order to determine where the value creation will occur, investors have to understand the motivations of the different groups. It is important to realize that changes in one part of the system can have a knock-on effect and lead to changes in other parts of the system. Constituent group preference curves vary in accordance with the interests of their members and can change over time. In some cases, the interests of the groups are aligned; in other cases, they are opposed. In some cases, there can even be opposing factions within a single group. Conflict between groups can lead to volatility in investment results because conflict reduces certainty, but the changes that come in the aftermath of conflict lead to investment opportunity—curing system balkanization can be profitable.

The amount of influence a given group has matters, as it can sway the outcome of a health reform process. The history of health-care reform has shown that various constituencies' power to influence health care has waxed and waned over time. Part of this power is derived from economic considerations—economic influence can lead to increasing power—but the ability to influence the political landscape and a sense of moral authority can also add to or diminish a group's power. Since nothing feeds success like success, the simplest way to determine where the power is heading is to look and see which group prevails in reimbursement, regulatory, or political battles. While power inflection points will be hard to determine, most of the time is spent in a trend, not at turning points.

In times of change, it is important to determine how a constituent group interacts with the upheaval. Though constituent groups may not be able to determine definitively whether a change is good or bad for them until some time after the fact, the best approach is probably to see if a plurality of the group reacts positively or negatively to a reform proposal. For example, if an individual group's members believe that they will somehow be harmed by a change, they will probably be vociferous in opposing that change. A group may either be vociferous in support of or quiet (but not oppositional) about a proposal or change that they believe benefits them (particularly financially).

When there is a major change, it takes time for industries to completely respond to the new operating environment. In some cases, stock prices may actually respond faster than industries, as investors are more aware of pending changes than the managements of companies or government officials because of their broader perspective. This is not always the case, however, and any time lag between environment changes, corporate changes, and share price changes represents an opportunity that investors can capitalize on. In order to do this, investors must determine what the new "normal" is, how long it will take for companies to sort it out, and how companies will respond. A method of anticipating outcomes is to run a sensitivity analysis of the most likely outcomes of a change and the most likely corporate responses. The better the anticipatory models an investor employs, the better the chances of a successful investment outcome. If an investor feels that he cannot reasonably anticipate the outcome, he probably should not be aggressive in his investment program.

The inputs into the sensitivity model are the five major constituencies. It is at the intersection of all these groups that a plan will be fashioned. No one group will completely dominate the process, but some will be able to influence the development of a reform plan more than others. Investors must watch the proposals and monitor the reforms to see which constituency is influencing the process most, then invest accordingly. It is also the level of "give" that each constituency has that will dictate the amount of flex the system has in response to change before a reform program will see pushback.

PATIENTS

Patients are the market. Without patients and potential patients, the health-care industry would not exist. Patients act differently from customers in other industries. They often have little choice as to whether to obtain the product or service, have relatively little information about providers and potential outcomes, and often are not responsible for the majority of the payment. They work collaboratively (or should) with providers to obtain an optimal outcome, which is different from the supplier or purchaser relationships found in many other industries. These factors can make the supply-demand equation difficult to calculate.

A common factor among all patients and potential patients is that they want to stay healthy, and if they become ill, they want to recover and not suffer undue financial hardship in the process. Since there is a trend toward greater financial responsibility and greater access to information, patients are demanding greater amounts of control over their health-care treatments. Informed patients are able to make better decisions. Patients also benefit when they aggregate through either collective insurance plans or advocacy groups. This is especially true given that the tax advantages for health-care coverage that are extended to companies are not available to individuals. It is possible that a health reform plan may mandate that individuals take action. Joining a collective organization is one way for an individual to offset some of the financial and administrative burden that this will entail. A collective organization can also address other issues that are important to patients, such as increasing access to insurance (limiting exclusions for preexisting illness or making sign-up convenient), allowing portability of plans, supplying information about providers, and providing protection from financial catastrophe. To the extent that patients can aggregate, they will gain power under a reform plan.

Patient advocacy groups grew in power and influence in the aftermath of the AIDS crisis and have been growing ever since. These groups now have a seat at the table in regulatory and product distribution discussions. They allow patients to act collectively and give individuals more power. The move toward patient collectivism shows no signs of abating, given the success that these groups have had in terms of funding for projects, awareness of diseases, and reimbursement for services. Advocacy groups are likely to be a feature of most major health reform discussions.

Given their greater financial burden, patients are acutely aware of cost issues. Patients, like consumers in any other industry, are starting to demand more information about cost and effectiveness. This information is not readily available today, and this represents an investment opportunity as well as a challenge for product makers and providers to spell out their value proposition. The ability of providers and manufacturers to communicate with patients effectively will be a value driver as information becomes more readily available. Given the increased level of information, patients are also more aware of alternative treatments like nutritional supplements, and therefore they will want access to a wider variety of therapies. Like successful consumer companies, successful health-care companies will be the ones that can deliver the types of care that patients require in a way that will create value.

Patients are not always well equipped to judge the potential for low-probability events like illness. The challenge for companies will be to help patients anticipate their current and future medical-care needs. The better patients can align their future health-care demand and costs, the more accurately they can plan for their financial future. Patients want to maintain their privacy and not have their current or future medical needs used against them when it comes to obtaining future care. Medicine has gotten better at anticipating future medical demand and looks as if it will get even more accurate over time. As a result, patients, companies, and the government face a bioethical dilemma of using predictive medicine to improve health, but not abusing it for the sake of controlling costs.

The demographics of patients are changing, particularly in the developed world, where the population is getting older. This "graying" of the population will have substantial influence on the way services and products are delivered and paid for. Medical utilization rises as a patient gets older, so as a population ages, it will demand new types of delivery as well as new types of therapies to deal with ailments that are more commonly found in older patients.

Given the change in demographics, a premium will be given to products and services that can prevent or reduce the occurrence of secondary illnesses. The health-care system has a much easier time dealing with problems that have already emerged than preventing problems that may emerge. The aging of the society will also have an impact on the way in which the society views aging and the diseases that come with it, as a broader swath of the population will have direct experience with both diseases and the system designed to treat them. This will include an ever-growing number of patient caregivers as well as the patients themselves.

Since political power tends to be driven by numbers of people, the older and sicker a large cohort of society gets, the greater the relative power of that voting bloc becomes. Since older people generally have more wealth than the younger cohort, this growing political bloc also has the financial wherewithal, through both political donations and buying power, to demand changes from the other constituents.

Although there is no voting bloc of the uninsured, there are advocacy groups. As the number of uninsured grows, the power of this demographic could begin to drive policy. A recognition that the uninsured are a powerful bloc means that even if there is no actual reform plan, more policy will be geared toward dealing with uninsured patients. Any company that can "fix" the uninsured for the government will see substantial returns.

Investors should watch what demands and requirements the patients have. It is important to watch how quickly companies adapt to the demands of this constituency. Reformers need to sell any plan to the population and make it part of the Zeitgeist to improve the chances of a successful reform outcome. How patients interface with the health-care system will be a test of the program's success.

The media (both old and new) can also play an important role in increasing patient power. They can alert the public to the ramifications of broad-scale changes to the health-care system and can engage the public in a debate over the direction of any potential program. The media can also be harnessed by the other health-care constituencies through advertising to make sure that their interests are heard. New treatments and services that may be available for conditions yet unrecognized by patients can be uncovered, moving market share. Exposés can also identify and uncover negative cost or quality situations and and thus help to reduce variations in care. If the media misinterpret information or promulgate incorrect information, the opposite will be true, and widespread attention will confuse patients rather than help them. Investors should not underestimate the power of the media to motivate patients in any health-care debate or on general health-care matters and the influence the media may have on sentiment regarding stocks.

Even if patients as a group fail to accumulate power for change, the market demand will be there for companies that accommodate patients. Investors should watch for companies that are patient-focused in practice. It is incumbent upon investors to sort out those companies from the companies that say they are patient-focused, but in reality are not. The power of information exchange will allow patients and advocacy groups to share experiences about companies and will give the genuinely patient-focused companies a competitive edge in the longer term.

PAYERS

Payers can be defined as entities that are responsible for paying for the cost of care. The range of payers is quite varied and can include employers, managed-care organizations, governments, and individuals. In terms of power dynamics, managed-care organizations and employers who self-insure tend to have more commonality than other payers, such as governments and individuals.

As health-care inflation has rapidly outpaced the costs of other items, it has put considerable pressure on payers to take action to preserve their profitability, and in some cases to preserve the viability of the corporations. Like government initiatives, corporate health-cost-control programs have gone through several iterations. Still, there is as yet no magic bullet in terms of a delivery model that successfully addresses cost control. Payers have tried several business models, including staff model HMOs, network model HMOs, and PPOs. While these models do work in certain instances, there is no one model that has been able to control costs on a large scale without incurring costs elsewhere, such as loss of membership or member satisfaction.

Although the payer models may vary, they have three tools to control costs: they can limit treatment options or quantity of services, pay providers less, or pass along a greater portion of the costs to patients. Payers that represent companies must use these tools judiciously, as they must balance cost control against other demands, which include attracting and retaining employees and keeping those employees productive. The power to offset costs by being restrictive with benefits can be a function of the economy. When labor is in short supply, employers have to be more generous with benefits, whereas in less robust times, the power is more in the payers' favor.

Payers are also looking for value for their payments. Not unlike the purchasers in any other purchaser-supplier arrangement, payers want to make sure they are getting value in return for their expenditures. In the past, determining whether a product or service provider was delivering care in line with the payment was difficult, if not impossible. Information technology has made data gathering and dissemination of this information more common. Industry coalitions have been created to advocate for more transparency and to help payers understand the value proposition of health-care payments.

In order to manage a business effectively, an employer needs to be able to understand what future costs will be, even if it cannot quite control them. The same holds true for companies that manage health-care benefits. In order to price their product effectively, managed-care organizations need to be able to anticipate future medical utilization. Actuarial predictability is a cornerstone of running a health plan, so a reform plan that aids a managed-care plan's forecasting will create value for that group. Companies that can better forecast their future medical costs will have a strategic advantage over those that cannot. In addition to using advanced forecasting tools, another way to anticipate future medical costs is through transparency in pricing and utilization of services. The more information the company has to put into its forecasting models, the more accurate the cost forecast will be.

Many of the same dynamics that apply to corporations also apply to unions and other third-party payers. They need to control costs, and they need predictability, particularly in the longer term, in order to make sure that the intake of revenue is consistent with fully funding the promised benefits. Unions have the additional responsibility of making sure that their members have viable employment. Since health-care costs threaten the ability of many companies to remain successful going concerns, unions need to be mindful of the balance between the benefits packages that their members require and the ability of a given company to maintain the maximum employment of their members. Unions have the same levers that other payers have, but they also have the ability to alter benefit packages on a large scale if it becomes necessary.

The regulated environment is one of the reasons for the high administrative burden placed upon insurers and employers when it comes to delivering services. Among the necessary administrative considerations are privacy, eligibility for services, financial responsibility, and adequacy of payments. Compounding the complexity is that each of the 50 states has its own set of insurance regulations, which can vary in scope and requirements. These regulations must be adhered to in the context of managing benefits to minimize disruption to and maintaining the satisfaction for patients.

In order to be successful, a reform plan must offer payers a clear line of sight concerning what is required. It is also important that there be some standardization in order to reduce complexity, which should lower costs and reduce the chances of error. A reform plan with guidelines like mandatory levels of revenue spent on care and minimum levels of access can diminish the power of the payers to control costs and earn a profit if the rules are too onerous.

Determining whether payers have power in a health reform initiative will be a function of how demanding the financial rules are. The more control regulators leave in the hands of the payers, the easier it will be for the publicly traded ones to deliver value to shareholders. Though they may be enacted under names such as the patient's bill of rights, patient-centered regulations will move power away from payers and toward patients and government, which would be a negative for the companies in this sector.

POLITICIANS (GOVERNMENT)

When it comes to health care, the government's basic functions are to execute on entitlement plans, provide a safety net for the less fortunate, and ensure that medical products are safe and effective. To manage these functions, the government has a dual role as both a regulator and a payer. This dual role can put the government into conflict with itself, as government can approve products that will ultimately put pressure on the payer function. A veritable alphabet soup of acronyms identifies the agencies responsible for the government's involvement in health care, including CMS (Centers for Medicare & Medicaid Services), FDA (Food and Drug Administration), and NIH (National Institutes of Health), among others. Since the government touches almost all of health care, it is incumbent on investors to be cognizant of the machinations of the government agencies. The government's health-care goals are generally the same as its other goals: to maintain social stability while balancing health care in the context of other social priorities.

The government has two main levers it can use to reach its goals. On the payer side, Medicare (for seniors) and Medicaid (for those with low income), along with other direct-pay parts of the government, decide what items they will pay for and how much they will pay for them. Because the government (through its collective programs) pays for such a large part of the market, the government is a price maker; it dictates the prices that most participants must take (price takers). The government has to balance its power to create prices with the fact that providers are citizens, too, and if prices are too low, providers may choose not to accept patients on government programs—hurting the goal of offering access to care for plan participants. The government can also use the payer function to provide incentives for behaviors it deems important by paying a premium for those procedures or services that it views as helpful to its goals.

The government has the final say on whether products can be available on the market. The FDA is the most important organization in this regard; it has established criteria for determining whether a product is safe and effective and what types of claims a product developer can make about the product. The agency must also maintain supply chain integrity so that products can reach patients safely. As a result, the FDA can have significant influence on the ultimate success of a product. In a later chapter, there will be more details about the FDA and how it relates to value creation/destruction for product makers. There are regulatory standards on both the state and federal levels that dictate minimum safety and service levels. The Federal Trade Commission regulates the competitive aspects of health care; the role of this agency is to make certain that no party disadvantages consumers by trying to control an overly large share of the market.

The regulatory and payer functions have generally been separate, but have a working relationship. In other nations, there are agencies that combine the two functions and look at the efficacy of products and services in the context of their cost. In the past, there have been proposals to establish a formal cost-effectiveness agency in either the FDA or the CMS, but they have not yet come to fruition.

Centers for Medicare & Medicaid Services

The Centers for Medicare & Medicaid (CMS), part of the U.S. Department of Health and Human Services, oversee Medicare, Medicaid, and the State Children's Health Insurance Program (SCHIP), and also regulates human laboratory testing through the Clinical Laboratory Improvement Amendment (CLIA) and administers portions of the Health Insurance Portability and Accountability Act (HIPAA). By virtue of its enormousness, and the fact that many CMS coverage and pricing decisions are duplicated by commercial insurers, CMS is an important agency for health-care investors to consider. CMS is likely to be the agency charged with overseeing many parts of whatever reform efforts the government may undertake.

Medicare currently is available for any U.S. citizen 65 years or older, severely disabled persons, and persons on dialysis. It is split into four financial and operational segments: Part A (hospital and nursing home insurance), Part B (health insurance—physicians, nursing, and certain drugs and medical equipment), Part C (managed-care plans, an alternative to Parts A and B), and Part D (the prescription drug benefit). Medicare is financed by payroll and income taxes and beneficiary premiums and coinsurance. Since there can be holes in coverage like copays and deductibles, there are "Medigap" insurance plans that are standardized by the government but sold by private organizations. Payment is made through Medicare contractors who interpret CMS coverage policy in determining what to pay for. Payment rates are set centrally by CMS, which decides what to cover and how much to pay. These policies are enforced by the regional contractors as they process billing claims.

Medicaid is a joint federal and state program that is run by the individual states, whose programs must conform to federal regulations in order to receive matching federal funds and grants. The program is intended to insure the less fortunate, and enrollees may qualify by income level, status as a child, residing in a nursing home, or disability level. SCHIP, like Medicaid, is a state-run program that receives guidance and matching funds from the federal government. The purpose of this program is to cover children in families whose incomes are too high to be eligible for Medicaid. The level of income eligibility varies by state.

To a large degree, CMS sets rates for most of the products and services offered by health-care companies. CMS's decisions can have significant influence on demand curves, given the financial incentives to choose one course of treatment over another. In recent years, the agency has also placed other demands on its payees, including withholding payment for medical errors, promoting higher quality through data gathering and dissemination, and paying bonuses for performance within predetermined quality guidelines. Beyond its direct impact on the fortunes of publicly traded companies, since CMS can be seen as "an honest broker" without a profit motive, there is a spillover effect from its decisions to commercial insurers, who can use CMS's policies as a starting point for their own strategies. In an era of health-care reform, CMS's power will only grow. If CMS becomes more assertive in its use of power, it could reshape the way health-care analysts value their companies.

Machinations Are a Risk

The government, as represented by politicians and civil servants, is beholden both to patients as citizens and to corporations (which pay lobbyists as well as taxes). The government must balance the needs of both groups while promoting its own social goals of safety and financial responsibility. This is not an easy task when many groups are placing pressure on it. From an investment perspective, companies that can navigate both the reimbursement and the regulatory areas of the government successfully will have a competitive advantage. Though the system that the government has created may seem byzantine, companies that have experience or are able to hire experienced personnel can overcome potential roadblocks that can vex less experienced companies.

For investors, government is a major source of risk, as the best case is that government acts the way it is expected to. Most of the actions that government can take outside of its normal operations will have negative consequences for companies. The government does not often surprise on the upside because there is no incentive for it to do so and because institutional inertia often prevents it.

A key determinant of how expansive a role a government takes in health care is the collective philosophical direction of the legislators. In general, the more conservative the leadership of the government is, the smaller the role that government will play in health care. The converse is also true; a more liberal-minded leadership may take a more activist role. Though some investors may believe that a hands-off approach is best for companies and corresponding share prices, this may not always be the case. A program like universal health care that substantially expands a market could be a positive for companies under the right set of circumstances. Programs that are more than just incremental changes do require more of an activist bent. The investment implication is that governmental actions can be mercurial and subject to the whims and changes in political fortunes, which adds uncertainty to the process.

The government always has a process, which can be complex and takes time to work through. When a change is potentially coming, investors have time to adjust their strategies depending on the probability of an outcome. Time to adjust one's investment strategy is a rare commodity on Wall Street, where change often happens before investors have time to react judiciously. Investors benefit from monitoring the philosophy of the major players in the government.

PRODUCT MAKERS

Investors in medical product makers (pharmaceuticals, medical devices, biotechnology) reflexively get concerned whenever the subject of health-care reform is raised. The concern is that reduced reimbursement, combined with increased regulations, will hurt profitability. The reality is somewhat more complex. To understand how a plan interacts with product makers, it is important to understand the companies' institutional priorities. They want to sell products without restriction at the maximum price. They also want to develop products and get them to market as quickly as possible, with limited interference.

Most reform plans seek to increase the number of people who have access to health care. By definition, this should expand the market for most products, as patients who previously did not use these products will now have access to them. Utilization of medical products differs between the insured and the uninsured,[2] with the insured using more. Increased access would be a net positive for most product makers, particularly those whose products are geared toward chronic and common diseases. Given its price-dictating role, government has the capability to decimate companies, as was the case with BBA 97 discussed previously, even if it does so unintentionally.

If regulations concerning the distribution or development of products are unclear or are subject to a wide range of interpretations, this is a problem in terms of both quantification of timelines and probabilities of success. Once a product is approved, severe restrictions on its distribution would be considered a negative. Controversy surrounding sales practices and direct-to-consumer (DTC) advertising has been a feature of health reform proposals.[3] Investors dislike uncertainty, so if the rules are vague, this could lead to discounted valuations. Some product makers would like unfettered access to patients and other buyers, but a reform plan is likely to put some restrictions on sales channels. This need not be an outright negative, however, as regulation may prevent overly aggressive tactics and ensure a level playing field for all product makers.

Cost-control efforts are another area of concern for product makers. While product makers would like to charge as much as the market will bear, they face a pushback from payers, both commercial and governmental, whose goal is to control costs. Product makers also face a pushback from consumers. Products, particularly pharmaceuticals, are one of the areas in health care where consumers are most directly exposed to price. If a reform plan takes steps to neutralize free-riding, it could remove some of the consumer pressure. If a reform plan fails to make a distinction in terms of value for services, this could hurt the industry, as price controls could reduce the level of innovation.[4]

One of the ways in which a reform plan may try to address the cost issue is through encouraging the use of generic (commodity) products and other less expensive treatments. The goal would be to make such products more available, and one way to do that is to loosen intellectual property regulations, an approach used by countries outside the United States. Some countries have been aggressive in limiting intellectual property rights when they felt that there was a public health need.[5] Although the chances of major changes in intellectual property regulations appear remote given all of the other nonhealth-care industries that would be negatively affected, the potential does exist and should be monitored by investors and companies alike.

The product makers have significant financial resources and employ a substantial number of workers. Their size and influence give them a seat at the table in any reform plan. The product makers spent $182 million in 2006 on lobbying efforts to reach policy makers at both the state and federal levels.[6] Substantial sums of lobbying money can move reform in favor of product makers.

It is doubtful that lobbying alone will be able to forestall all potentially negative (for the industry) consequences of reform, but it is a force that reformers must reckon with. Another lever that the product makers can pull is that of innovation. In the past, the product makers have developed many life-saving therapies. It is relatively easy for the industry to appeal to the future—creating treatments for disease states that have not existed before to assuage concerns raised by consumers and government about the prices of therapies. It is a compelling argument, but the industry must balance it with a way to keep its prices in line with the value delivered.

Because product makers encompass a diverse group of subsectors, it is difficult for investors to generalize. Despite the different risk and reward profiles in the industry, there are a few areas that investors need to monitor to determine whether a plan will be beneficial for the industry or not. The bigger the market, the better for all concerned. The degree of control a plan has in terms of centralizing the setting of prices will be important in determining how much flexibility the product makers will have in running their business. The more flexibility they have, the more likely it is that the companies will be able to deliver positive returns. Investors favor certainty, so the greater the visibility in regulatory and reimbursement policies, the more value the companies can create. To the extent that a plan can encourage innovation, speed to market and protections for intellectual property will be a positive. Although the industry is likely to have to alter its business model, this is probably better done organically rather than imposed from the outside.

PROVIDERS

Traditionally the bottleneck for reform efforts, providers (physicians and facilities) have become more enthusiastic about reform in recent years.[7] This change in sentiment has accompanied the changes that providers have seen in their businesses and business models. Reimbursement has become more restrictive and regulations have become more complex, leading to increased costs. As the practice of delivering care has gotten more difficult, provider dissatisfaction has grown to a level where the majority of providers are now in favor of reform.[8]

There are 900,000 physicians, about 5,700 hospitals, and numerous alternative site providers (nursing homes, ambulatory surgery centers, radiology centers, and so on).[9] Given the size of this cohort and its economic power, it is a formidable player in the development of a reform plan. While this group is not uniform in its preferences, investors can generalize that its members want to maximize their income and increase their autonomy.

A reform plan, by its nature, will tend to act in a top-down "command" way, which at times may be at odds with the autonomy of providers. Evidence-based medicine is one of the paradigm shifts happening in health care that a reform plan may use to dictate how care is delivered. Evidence-based medicine is sometimes referred to as "cookbook medicine" in a pejorative way. This term resonates with providers who do not want to be told how to deliver care, especially when questions of clinical judgment are involved. Providers want to be able to deliver care in the way they see fit, but guidelines that influence reimbursement will influence practice patterns and open up providers to malpractice suits if the care they offer deviates from the norm. Providers often practice "defensive medicine," overutilizing services and products to prevent negative legal ramifications. Neither cookbook medicine nor defensive medicine appears to be an optimal use of resources, so some middle ground must be found if a reform plan is to be truly successful. Providers will almost certainly want some say in how guidelines are developed, and investors need to be cognizant of the development and outcome of such discussions.

There have also been changes in the demographics and behavior of providers. Changes in provider behavior have been driven by the development of more specialized types of care, the movement away from center-based medicine to more outpatient services, and the delivery of care being directed by a different type of provider from those who directed it in the past; there has also been a change in the demographics of those entering the medical profession. These changes have not been without consequences. Among the unintended outcomes of these changes is the increasing number of turf battles in medicine.[10] A reform plan and corresponding reimbursement scheme will inevitably make top-down decisions on which specialty or site service is most appropriate for a particular type of treatment. This may lead to some internecine battles between various providers.

It is through the reimbursement mechanism that many of the behavior modification incentives will be driven. Defining what value is placed on what treatment has always been a challenge for the health-care industry, given its procedure-based structure. There is conflict here, as it is not always clear that a patient needs high-intensity levels of care. Ironically, lower-cost solutions for the system, like preventive services, are not given premium reimbursement; therefore, they are often not prescribed. Evidence does not equal certainty, which often puts providers in the position of not advocating certain preventive procedures.[11]

In addition to disagreeing with treatment directives from a reform plan, providers will no doubt be concerned about the potential for mandates that they have to pay for. Such unfunded mandates can include requirements like certain staffing levels or the use of information technology. Providers will probably want to make sure that they are compensated for any capabilities that a program requires them to have. This includes any of the potential cultural shifts that a broad-scale program may force upon a provider, although these are difficult to quantify.

First, providers tend to have more information about the patient and her treatment than either payers or patients. Providers also have a direct relationship with the patient and can themselves advocate for the patient when necessary. This doctor/patient relationship is important to the patient, as it is easier to trust someone you know than to trust a large, presumably faceless entity like the government or a payer.

Beyond directly investing in providers, investors should watch the provider cohort because it is the ultimate deciding factor for demand for products and services. Despite any mandates a program may muster that may move demand curves at the margin, the providers will have the final say in treatment. Watching their preference curves will be paramount when it comes to gauging actual demand and future changes in demand. Products that are tailored to helping providers meet any guidelines mandated by a reform initiative will be successful. In addition, products that help providers gain more efficiency through lower costs or time burdens will create value, as any plan will put additional cost pressure on providers. For investors, a key to interpreting how much leverage the providers will ultimately have will be to watch how restrictive the guidelines are, as well as how willing providers are to participate in a program. Follow the incentives to see where the value will be created.

NOTES

1. Joseph White, "Markets and Medical Care: The United States, 1993–2005," *Milbank Quarterly* 85, no. 3 (2007): 395–448.
2. Harvard Medical School, "Uninsured Adults Increase Medicare Costs, Harvard Study Finds," Science Daily.com, July 13, 2007; retrieved December 24, 2007, from http://www.sciencedaily.com/releases/2007/07/070712144615.htm.
3. Robert W. Dubois, "Pharmaceutical Promotion: Don't Throw the Baby Out with the Bathwater," *Health Affairs* Web Exclusive (2003): W93–W106.
4. "Pharmaceutical Price Controls in OECD Countries: Implications for U.S. Consumers, Pricing, Research and Development, and Innovation," U.S. Department of Commerce International Trade Administration Report, December 2004.
5. "Thailand Backs Patent Drug Copies," BBC News, Jan. 29, 2007, http://news.bbc.co.uk/2/hi/asia-pacific/6310515.stm.
6. "Pushing Prescriptions," a study done by the Center for Public Integrity, April 1, 2007, http://www.publicintegrity.org/rx/report.aspx?aid=823.
7. "Arizona Physicians: Attitudes toward Health System Reform," St Luke's Health Initiative, 2007, http://www.slhi.org/publications/studies_research/pdfs/PhysSurveyPub.pdf.
8. Bruce Landon, James D. Reschovsky, Hoangmai H. Pham, and David Blumenthal, "Leaving Medicine: The Consequences of Physician Dissatisfaction," *Medical Care* 44, no. 3 (2006).
9. Figures obtained from trade associations.
10. David Levin and Vijay Rao, "Turf Wars in Radiology: Emergency Department Ultrasound and Radiography," *Journal of the American College of Radiology* 2, no. 3 (2005): 271–273.
11. Eileen Salinsky, "Clinical Preventive Services: When Is the Juice Worth the Squeeze?" National Health Policy Forum Issue Brief 806, Aug. 24, 2005, http://www.nhpf.org/pdfs_ib/IB806_ClinicalPrevServices_08-24-05.pdf.

CHAPTER 5

Evaluating a Reform Plan

Successfully analyzing a reform plan from an investment perspective is a function of asking the right set of questions to assess which companies will create shareholder value. This process is made challenging by the fact that reform can be complex and can evolve over time. There will also be unintended consequences, and small details can lead to outsized gains. Since there is no major plan currently under way, much of the analysis of any reform must be anticipatory.

Given that there are no absolutes and that any program is likely to shift underneath the feet of investors, the best one can hope for, a priori, is to get a sense of the direction in which reform is moving and invest accordingly. With this in mind, there is a checklist of factors to evaluate that should allow the investor to develop a feel for where the program is heading and what magnitude of impact it may have on the companies in the industry.

THE PHILOSOPHY UNDERLYING THE SYSTEM

A reform program can fall anywhere on the continuum of completely regulated (government-centric) or unregulated (market-centric) sides of the range. Both systems have their strengths and weaknesses. A market arrangement allows greater flexibility among program designs and permits quicker innovation as capital is directed to profit-making ideas. The key weakness of this approach is that it exposes

73

participants to the mercurial nature of the market, which includes boom and bust cycles; probably limits recourse in the event of negative outcomes; and makes oversight more difficult. The strength of a government-directed plan is that it is likely to be simpler to administer, and government oversight should be relatively simple. Negatives are that it could be bureaucratic, limit choice, and be difficult to alter once it is in place.

Given that the orientation of the population is not fixed to one point on the regulation spectrum, one should expect that any reform plan will need to balance both ends in order to be achievable in terms of acceptance. Public opinion varies over time, so when a program is implemented it will influence the relative contribution of government and private-market solutions to the program.

From an investment perspective, the mix of market-based and government-based elements does matter. A market-based approach is likely to yield a greater number of investable opportunities, as private and therefore investable entities will be responsible for carrying out any reform plan. Since one cannot invest in government directly, the greater the proportion of the program that government provides, the fewer investment opportunities the program will have.

The character of the investments will also vary depending on the philosophy of the reform. For a company to be successful in a market-based program, it must deal with market issues, including competition, as well as creating an indisputable value proposition for payers and consumers. Investors may believe that a government-directed plan would be devoid of investment opportunities. This is not the case unless the government learns to develop products and services on its own, without the input of private industry.

A fully government-run health-care system is an unlikely scenario, so as long as either a profit motive or an altruistic motive exists, individuals will have the opportunity to build a better mousetrap. A government-dominated system does pose some specific issues for investments, however. Government programs tend to have a bureaucratic set of rules designed to protect the taxpayer from misuse of funds. While the intention of these rules is positive, they can make interaction with the government slow and often complex. Thus, in addition to successfully addressing market factors and being better than the competition, a company will need to be able to navigate a bureaucracy in order to be successful.

GOVERNMENT INVOLVEMENT

Investors must assume that there will be some government involvement in any reform plan. Government involvement can be channeled
in two ways, either directly or indirectly. In the direct way, the
government receives claims, pays bills, and is responsible for
determining what rates are paid and under what circumstances.
In the indirect method, government outsources these functions to
other entities like managed-care companies. The advantage of the
direct method is that it offers the government direct control over
the process; the disadvantage is that, depending on the agency, the
government may not be the optimal mechanism (since it is not
specialized) to direct such a plan. The advantage of outsourcing
to private entities is that it will allow more specialized companies
to run a program, the premise being that a focused company
should be able to deliver higher performance. The disadvantage is
that the increased performance may not be sufficient to offset the
increased costs to the system coming from the outside company's
profit margin. Given the stringent rules that may be associated with
such an arrangement, the risk that the outside company will run
afoul of policy is ever-present. With a direct government operation,
system rules, as cumbersome as they may be, are less likely to
change rapidly, leading to more consistent revenue visibility. For
investors, the indirect model is likely to yield more investable
opportunities.

GOVERNMENT INVOLVEMENT AT THE STATE
VERSUS THE FEDERAL LEVEL

Which level of the government will lead a health-care reform will
have an impact on investments. Government is a multilayered entity.
Government intervention at the federal level will lead to more
consistency across the entire system. Involvement at the state level
will provide a more nuanced approach that takes regional and local
issues into account in a way that an overarching federal program
could not. It is the ability to deal with nuances and work out
problems more quickly than could be done at the federal level that
has allowed states to often act as a laboratory for federal programs.[1]
The downside to states running a program is that they will need

incentives to conduct experiments, they will also need additional resources, and they are often not able to accommodate larger-scale programs.

An advantage of local or regional control over a plan is that it is easier to work out kinks in a reform plan on a smaller scale than it is at the national level. Starting at the state level may also allow for quicker innovation, as the populations involved are smaller, allowing greater attention to detail than in a large, monolithic federal program. The negatives are that multiple state programs increase the level of complexity and that the larger number of rules to follow means more systems, which leads to additional compliance costs. Added complexity also increases the chances of a regulatory failure, which increases the risk of penalties.

For investors, a state-level program will give companies the chance to experiment and develop new solutions. The process of interacting with smaller state agencies is much less cumbersome than that of working with a larger federal bureaucracy, which means that the initial capital expenditures would be smaller, lowering the risk and increasing the chances of positive return for company projects. Smaller projects can also allow investors to fund innovation, which may have a positive societal benefit.

A federal program would represent a larger potential return in absolute dollars. However, since there are fewer large-scale federal programs, it would mean that the risk-reward spectrum would be skewed, with a couple of larger winners and many losers. There would be a more varied investment spectrum with positive results if the states took the lead in health-care reform. Giving the states at least some control over the process also has the added advantage of involving one more constituency that is essential to the success of any program in the dialogue and removing one more barrier to implementation.

FINANCING THE REFORM PLAN

Any reform plan is going to require an initial outlay of funds and very likely an ongoing stream of revenue. How a reform is financed is important not just to the scale of any reform but also to its long-term viability. There are three financing mechanisms: government, private, and mixed government/private financing.

The initial outlay of capital will need to come from somewhere. The capital markets are probably too small to fund a major reform program, and in any event, it is unclear exactly how a direct capital market investment in reform would lead to a financial return. If financial conditions nationally warranted it, government could reallocate capital from other programs (e.g., defense) to fund at least part of the reform plan. This method of financing would entail difficult choices and seems unlikely given the recent history of government finances and public discourse. Increased tax revenue seems to be the most likely source of funds for any new program.

The ability of the reformers to present the value proposition to those who will be paying for it will be a key to understanding the viability of a reform initiative and how broad in scope it will be. Since the payees are likely to derive some value from expanded health care, they may see some value in participation. People get a safety net to protect them from economic harm in the event of job loss or serious illness, and corporations can get some relief from onerous health-care costs and retiree health benefits.

Investors need to observe how large such a program can become in order to quantify the size of the additional market for various goods and services created by a reform plan. Conversely, if the financing stream does not look viable or durable, it is likely that the plan will have to be scaled down or abandoned. Private payers tend to pay providers more per medical encounter than the government does, so investors should prefer a plan that favors corporate payers. If the plan involves placing more of the financial responsibility for health care on individuals, that increases the risk of nonpayment for the companies.

AN EMPLOYER-BASED SYSTEM

An employer-based system is the predominant way in which working-age people today interface with the health-care system.[2] This approach is an artifact of tax code changes made in the middle of the twentieth century to support labor negotiations. A combination of public indifference and institutional inertia on the part of other system stakeholders is the reason for the lack of alteration of this structure.

Given the greenfield opportunities associated with a completely new structure, many of the initial investments are likely to do well, although, as with other greenfield opportunities like the Internet in the late twentieth century, overinvestment and misallocation of resources are potential risk factors. A completely government-based solution appears somewhat unlikely because a substantial proportion of Americans fear government control over health care.[3] As long as at least a substantial minority is either against government-run health care or satisfied with their current health-care arrangement, the chances of a sea change in the government-sponsored direction are small. History suggests that investors should assume that the status quo will prevail over radical change in the reform arena.

COMPULSORY INSURANCE AND MANDATES

Health insurance, unlike many other forms of insurance, such as auto insurance, is not compulsory. People are not obligated to have it, nor are companies required to provide it to their employees. It is the lack of such mandatory actions that has contributed to the problem of the uninsured.[4] Among the barriers to such mandates are the perceived lack of fairness involved in requiring a low-income individual to pay for health insurance that he cannot afford or forcing a small employer who does not have the ability to spread health-care risk across a larger number of workers to purchase such insurance. Mandating that an insurance company take all patients, including high utilizers, without additional compensation would also be considered unfair.

The positives surrounding compulsory insurance are that it would mean that many of the uninsured would be covered and that the larger pool of people who are covered would help to reduce the risk of adverse selection. Compulsory insurance rather than a government-run single-payer plan is the most likely way that universal coverage will be provided. For investors, concerns include the management of actuarial risk, the potentially draconian cost-control measures associated with mandates, and the willingness of providers to offer expensive treatments. Should a compulsory plan be able to overcome these challenges (i.e., adverse selection and limited choice) and assuage the concerns of libertarians about government intrusion into their lives, it should expand the market for goods and services and be a positive for investors.

CENTRALIZING RESPONSIBILITY FOR HEALTH CARE

Depending on the extent of the reform, a new agency, either government or private, may be required to oversee the workings of the health-care industry. Since new agencies are difficult to create from scratch, the reform plan may require other agencies to come together to form a new entity. Some of the key factors for any centralized authority will include what tools it has to provide incentives for optimal behavior. The way the hierarchy of responsibilities is broken down within the agency and the way the leadership of the agency is chosen will be important. If there is a new agency and regulation to go along with it, companies and investors will have to adapt to the new framework. This will require companies to be able to accommodate the new agency and its standards in their business model.

WHAT WILL BE COVERED

In all likelihood, a comprehensive reform plan will mandate a minimum set of benefits in order to simplify the implementation. In addition to a delineation of what will be covered, simplicity of use, transportability across state lines, level of services, access to high-cost therapies, an appeals process for denial of services, reasonable out-of-pocket expenses, and patient choice of providers will be important factors. The key to making any reform plan work will be to managing the trade-offs between plan designs, thus making the plan palatable enough to be accepted by a majority of the patients while still being able to control costs.

From a patient's point of view, while the ability to obtain care and avoidance of financial ruin caused by a health-care crisis are probably highest on the hierarchy of demand, convenience, choice, and limited out-of-pocket costs should not be underrated. Given the diversity of patients, a narrow plan will be unlikely to succeed. Americans have grown accustomed to choice, whether it is holistic medicine or the very highest-tech treatment for the same malady. In the absence of definitive evidence of treatment efficacy for a given malady, it will be difficult for a plan to exclude treatments. If patients are not satisfied with the system, they will not participate in it.

Some patients may not wish to participate in a program, seeking instead to go outside of the minimum plan. A plan design is likely to have an opt-out mechanism to deal with these patients, although under a compulsory system there would have to be a guarantee that these patients were in fact obtaining insurance and were not free-riding on others within the system.

Making a plan palatable to providers will also be a key to its acceptance. The risk is that the program will either reimburse them at too low a rate or make it too difficult in terms of rules or benefit designs for providers to successfully accommodate patients. A plan design must incorporate input from providers before it is implemented so as to eliminate some potential hurdles.

The investment considerations involving plan design depend on the type of investment. For product makers, the issue will be what is included in the plan. If a product is not covered, it will have a very limited market. If the plan offers a wide range of therapies or has a relatively straightforward process for obtaining an excluded treatment, it would be a positive for the program and for companies. The wider the menu of options, the better for investors, but given the cost-control efforts associated with any reform plan, the program will probably favor lower-dollar prevention and generic treatments, saving more focused expensive treatments for later in the course of the disease. It will be incumbent on companies that produce expensive treatments to show a positive cost/benefit ratio for using these treatments either earlier in the course of a disease or in a wider population.

If a reform initiative mandates that providers offer only a very narrow band of services or prices, this will limit their ability to differentiate services and make actuarial predictability more difficult. Mandates on out-of-pocket expenses may introduce an element of moral hazard (raising costs) if the limits are too low, while if they are too high, they will effectively eliminate the market, reducing revenue potential. Portability and other issues may introduce increased costs, and if they are not able to generate the revenue required to cover the costs of implementation and maintenance, this will have a negative impact on the earnings power of the entity. Reform provisions that lower either the earnings stream from an investment or the visibility of that earnings stream will lower the value of that investment.

WHO WILL BE COVERED

Who will be covered is another important feature of a health-care reform plan that will have implications for investors. Previously uninsured patients have higher utilization rates upon becoming insured.[5] In the long run, insuring more people should reduce costs, but in the short run, there may be a large bolus of utilization resulting from previously unmet needs.

A reform plan is likely to have some elements directed at populations that have generally been neglected by the health-care system. These include patients with prior medical conditions and illegal immigrants. Insurers have generally avoided people with prior medical conditions, although this same group is often courted by product makers because chronic conditions are the source of a substantial part of health-care utilization. Insurers fear that these presumably high utilizers will raise costs beyond the risk pool's ability to spread those costs, leading to losses. Reform plans will need to put a mechanism in place to deal with patients with prior medical conditions, either through government insurance for these patients or meaningful reinsurance for companies that take on the risk of patients with preexisting conditions.

With respect to other "difficult" populations like illegal immigrants and the homeless, the reform plan becomes more complicated because dealing with these populations raises questions of how far into ancillary and not directly health-care-related issues (nutrition, poverty, and homelessness, for example) a program should go. Even if a reform plan does not address these populations directly, they will still interact with the health-care system, so providers will, as they have always done, deal with complex populations in an informal way. The more equitable the constituents of the reform plan view it and the more flexibility providers have in dealing with "difficult" populations, the more likely it is that the program will succeed.

The comprehensiveness of the safety net that a reform program implements needs to be monitored, as it relates directly to both market size and market risks. For product makers, the addition of high-utilizing patients who previously did not utilize at an optimal level represents a significant positive market shift. The benefit is likely to be seen most acutely in the area of treatment for chronic diseases.

Service providers could also see a significant uptick in demand under a plan that expands access. The challenge will be dealing with people who have limited experience with a health-care system and who lack a current provider. If there is a spike in utilization as heretofore uninsured people suddenly do have insurance, forecasting cost initially will be an actuarial challenge. Locating services may also be a challenge, as the locations of the newly insured may be mismatched with the locations of current providers. There is an opportunity for providers who can develop solutions to these challenges.

BENCHMARKS

Most programs will have a method or metrics to determine whether the initiative is succeeding. These metrics or benchmarks also serve as a target goal toward which program participants will direct their efforts, particularly if there are financial rewards associated with succeeding. There are difficulties with the development of benchmarks. Guidelines concerning which benchmarks to use need to be developed. In general, there should be quality, access, and cost benchmarks. Defining exactly which measures are most important and most indicative of the function of a health reform plan is necessary.

Once a benchmark is determined, measurement becomes a challenge. Many aspects of health care are not objective and are difficult to quantify. Diseases can progress regardless of treatment paradigms, so measurement of clinical outcomes can have a subjective element to it. Waiting times and satisfaction can be measured, but whether they are indicative of the success of a reform plan may be the subject of debate. Irrespective of reform, health-care benchmarks are a growing phenomenon, and investors should look at companies that either develop benchmarks or help providers and product makers achieve benchmarks as potential value creators.

CONTROLLING COSTS

If costs were manageable, it is arguable that access and quality issues would be much less severe. There are relatively few tools that can tackle the problem of spiraling costs successfully. To control costs, a system has to address either the supply side (prices and availability) or the demand side (utilization and product mix), or both. The few devices that have been developed to contend with higher prices have had only modest success and have either met with resistance or had unintended consequences.

On the supply side of the equation, a reform plan can deal with either price or availability. The most draconian way to control costs is with outright price caps. Reference pricing, a more modest form of price controls, has had limited success in controlling costs in areas where it has been tried. The danger of outright price controls is that they may damage an industry that is important to the economic future of the country. A less draconian method of controlling costs would be to acquire pricing power by becoming a bulk buyer and negotiating discounts from product makers and providers. This tactic has been used with some success by agencies like the Veterans Administration (VA). Buying products in bulk to drive discounts generally assumes that a plan can direct the majority of its members' utilization patterns so that the product maker receives a previously agreed-upon level of demand that justifies the initial discount. This approach is difficult and limits choice on the part of providers and patients.

Specifying the use of a low-cost network to deliver services and providing a guaranteed number of patients in return for discounts is another method that has been used to lower system cost. As with bulk purchasing of products, this removes choice and creates the possibility that only the lower-quality providers (those who could not win on quality alone) will join the network. Quality provisions could be enacted to prevent this from occurring, but the notion of a two-tier system would be anathema to many patients.

An initiative could also act on prices through caps on profitability levels, rather than by dictating a price. A mandatory maximum profit level could result in lower prices. This reform has been proposed in the past, particularly with regard to delivery of health-care services, with a dictated amount of revenue being dedicated to the provision of care. Such a reform has yet to be put into practice, but it could reduce companies' level of profitability and potential flexibility with no guarantee that it would stem spiraling costs.

A program could also influence the supply side by making products and services less available, thus decreasing utilization.

In its most draconian form, this is referred to as rationing. In this approach, a maximum number of products or services are budgeted per year, and people who require them are not able to obtain them if the quota has been met. With regard to medical services, such a harsh system seems inhumane and is not very practical, especially for urgent medical needs. Less severe restrictions on supply have been tried, including stringent rules about the point in a treatment course when certain therapies could be applied (i.e., step therapy) and tight preauthorization review prior to expensive procedures.

Cost-control plans have also paid attention to the demand side, eliminating the moral hazard phenomenon by exposing patients more directly to costs to make them more sensitive to the optimal level of utilization of products and services. Financial barriers like copays, deductibles, and coinsurance have been put in place and adjusted (usually upward) in an attempt to align patients' utilization with their needs. Higher financial outlays are presumed to discourage "unnecessary" utilization of health-care services and products.

Beyond moral hazard reduction, there are also positive financial incentives to steer patients and providers to lower-cost alternatives. Such mechanisms can include making generic drugs a more financially attractive option to patients and providers. There have also been schemes in which some of these savings have been returned to patients (health savings accounts) and providers (capitation). A problem with using financial rewards alone as a motivator of optimal behavior is that monetary proceeds are a relatively blunt instrument and may not contribute to positive outcomes, which are often related to nuances in the disease process.

The health-care industry is often less efficient than other industries because of its continued reliance on paper rather than digital communication and its significant level of fragmentation. Reform plans have promoted such tools as mandates to use electronic medical records, universal forms, and larger penalties for fraud as a way to address the efficiency gaps and reduce costs. There has been limited buy-in, as these programs usually require providers and product makers to make capital outlays without any corresponding revenue to compensate for the increased expenditure. While the programs put in place may make the system more efficient, it remains to be seen whether any savings from increased efficiency would be given back to the system.

For most companies, any reduction in either prices or utilization is a negative. Therefore, cost-control provisions will almost always have negative consequences for some industry participants. Services and products that are able to demonstrate that they add true value to public health, particularly with regard to the ability to control costs by either reducing prices, lowering utilization, or making the system more efficient, will be prized by any reform plan and add value to shareholders.

DETERMINING THE VALUE OF PRODUCTS AND REIMBURSEMENT

In order to grow, companies must have a continued flow of new products and services. Health-care innovation can come in many forms. New products that can improve clinical outcomes, cost, or efficiency will always be in demand. Given the cost and quality pressures evident in the system, there is a headwind facing innovative companies in that there is an incentive for payers not to reimburse for premium products without substantial evidence that they do deliver value. There is a chicken-and-egg problem in that innovators will not innovate without a reasonable expectation of return through reimbursement, while payers will not pay unless the innovator can prove that the new product is superior to existing methods.

How a reform plan balances the needs of the system with companies' ability to innovate will have a direct impact on the return potential for investments in the innovative industries. The system has a mishmash of approaches for determining the value of goods and services. In the future, health care will see a streamlining of these approaches, if for no other reason than that information technology has allowed payers and regulators to gather more information on utilization and outcome patterns in a shorter time frame. If a reform plan has explicit rules covering reimbursement, it will be incumbent on investors to understand the valuation methodology of the system in order to determine reimbursement rates.

To offset potential cost pressures that may come with increased cost/benefit scrutiny, a reform plan could institute steps to help lower the risk profile for innovators. Such steps include tax credits for innovation, greater collaboration with government-sponsored agencies like the National Institutes of Health (NIH), a less restrictive regulatory path, and greater intellectual property and competitive protections. Investors need to be cognizant of the quantification of trade-offs between cost pressures on the system and the ability to innovate. The extent to which one end of the scale (cost or innovation) holds sway will determine the risk profile of the product.

THE EFFECT OF THE PLAN ON MEDICAL PRACTICES

A reform initiative is likely to favor certain medical practices over others, with the goal of improving access, cost, or quality. This may or may not be a positive development, depending on the point of view of practitioners and patients. The potential for a slippery slope in which a plan, government, or other entity demands more command of health care is something that investors should be aware of.

Considerations include privacy issues, the relationship between patients and providers, and the possibility of one-size-fits-all treatments. The specter of privacy concerns will hang over any corporate or government intrusion into the health-care system. Patients hold their confidentiality sacrosanct, and any weakening of privacy protections will lead to pushback on a reform plan. The intrusion of a reform plan into medical practices is more of a risk than a potential opportunity, as it will limit the number of investable ideas, since the breadth of treatments, in all likelihood, would be narrowed. This process will take time, however, so investors will be able to make adjustments if the paradigm shifts in this direction.

CONTROLLING QUALITY

Quality is becoming a more important feature of the health-care landscape. This process has been evolving over time, but in the early twenty-first century, the pace of interest in quality improvement has accelerated. Information gathering and analysis have become more sophisticated, enabling better monitoring of quality. In 2003, a national clearinghouse of quality data sponsored by the Agency for Healthcare Research and Quality (AHRQ), the government agency designated to lead health-care quality, made its debut to publicize quality metrics to a broader audience. There are drawbacks to this, as the AHRQ suggests that not all guidelines are created equal, nor are all measures equally able to assess the varied aspects of quality care.[6]

Any explicit quality metrics set forth by a reform program will be an important investment consideration, in that they open an opportunity to fulfill a market need. Investments that encourage the promotion of price and quality discovery will be able to add to shareholder value. Any products or services that can aid in the improvement of a product or service's quality metrics will also be able to add to shareholder value.

INCENTIVES AND INITIATIVES

Incentives, both financial and otherwise, will drive the health-care reform process. Incentives are not always aligned with the efficient and effective functioning of an industry. A successful reform initiative should take aim at these malincentives (like paying for unnecessary procedures) and replace them with inducements for a more optimal delivery of care. There are both implicit and explicit incentives used in health care, including trust, payment, and regulatory incentives.[7] Since financial incentives can translate into practice patterns,[8] these are likely to be among the most commonly used methods of altering behavior.

What incentives a program uses will ultimately be a function of the philosophy of the program as well as the intended goals. Investors should track the incentives to get a sense of the direction in which a program is headed in order to anticipate where the value may be created. Incentives may not always have the anticipated effect; therefore, it is incumbent on investors to watch for the risk of unanticipated outcomes when it comes to quantifying the impact of an incentive-based program.

THE DIRECT MARKET IMPACT OF THE PLAN

Unless a reform plan is heavily tilted toward a free-market approach to the delivery of health care, there are likely to be provisions designed to ensure proper market functioning. Reforms of this nature can vary widely, from limiting anticompetitive actions by market participants to making sure that companies have enough capital to avoid a catastrophic failure of critical services. It is clear that health care has had difficulty allocating capital efficiently, and regulations have been put in place on a local level in the form of certificate of need (CON) programs in an attempt to assure efficient use of resources. States with CON programs do seem to have lower costs and better outcome measures in certain clinical areas.[9] And although the data showing that capital restrictions can work are far from conclusive, there is enough enthusiasm for programs of this type that a reform plan may have some capital-control provisions. Some of the mechanisms for allocating capital include limits on new facilities and the expansion of existing facilities or services, prohibitions on merger and acquisition activity, and caps on maximum market share. Flexibility is important to companies in their quest to generate returns, and market limitations could get in the way of growth potential. However, as long as all market participants have a level playing field and the process of ensuring superior products and/or services can be delivered, capital constraints may not pose as big a hurdle to positive returns as investors may intuitively believe.

Managing and monitoring financial risk levels are key concerns for health-care reformers and investors alike. Knowing which party bears the financial risk and having the ability to quantify that risk are important in understanding where a system may fail. Provisions regarding the prevention of financial risk include capital adequacy minimums, regulatory filing requirements, and availability of risk-mitigating factors like reinsurance and other hedges. Although there are already some provisions directed at risk mitigation, there is relatively little in terms of centralized ability to understand these issues at a national level. For investors, the greater the emphasis that a reform plan places on restraining excessive financial risk and the greater its ability to quantify existing risk, the easier it will be to price the risk of investments and understand the return potential.

Transparency is a hallmark of a successful system, as it lets all market participants know how the market is functioning, where issues may be arising, and where adjustments that will improve the system can be made. A reform plan may contain specific transparency minimums in order to ensure that the market participants are on a level playing field and to provide a greater understanding of the cost and quality of the services that the system is paying for.

Some proposals could include mandatory disclosure of financial data and the timeliness with which these data must be disclosed. The benefit from greater transparency is that it allows investments to be made in a more informed manner. A risk for investors is that what is uncovered in the transparency process may turn out to be a major impediment to the performance of companies.

Given the high level of fragmentation in health care, a reform plan, if it is to be successful, must have connectivity provisions in order to unite the highly disparate parts of the system. As in other industries, communication and information technology platform standards are imperative if the different parts of the system are to communicate effectively. The benefit of communication standards is that they will lower costs and potentially reduce negative clinical and financial outcomes by having systems that are designed to detect such unwanted occurrences. The impediment is that there is a lack of standardization in forms, platforms, software, and hardware. The current level of disorganization and the complexity of the existing infrastructure make this connectivity challenge even greater.[10] A reform plan will have to overcome this hurdle by reaching an agreement on what types of systems are best suited for an optimal health-care system. Connectivity has the potential to be a source of investment opportunity, as those companies that can overcome the substantial connectivity challenges and optimize the functioning of the health-care system will create shareholder value.

ADJUDICATION OF DISAGREEMENTS AMONG PARTICIPANTS

In any plan, there will be disagreements among program partici-pants. These disagreements can be financial (between payers and providers), breadth of services (between patients and providers), responsibility for payment (between patients and payers), or reg-ulatory (between providers and government). Disagreements can cause disruption in the system, and there are several very well known examples of payers and providers who could not agree to terms of payments, leading large populations to change either their providers or their payers, or both.[11] As market participants grow in influence, it is likely that more conflicts will arise. A reform plan must lay out a clear method of adjudication of these disputes if the parties cannot find a resolution on their own. The adjudication must be timely and allow for minimal disruption of health-care delivery, while still allowing market participants to achieve the necessary value for their services and products. The existence of a process may be enough of an inducement to reach a resolution without major disruption to the system. There is limited investment opportunity in adjudication processes, but in terms of risk mitigation, investors would view a clear process as a positive, as it allows for greater quantification of risk.

FEASIBILITY OF REFORM

Any reform can be proposed, and many have been. The announcement of reform can have a deleterious effect on the prices of health-care shares. Whether the impact is permanent or temporary (which would be an opportunity) will depend on whether the reform is enacted. History has shown (notably the Clinton program) that not all reforms are politically feasible. It is up to the investor to determine whether the political climate is amenable to passing reform. Investors must be cognizant of whether the reform is "sellable" to the public. The more popular the public response, the more likely it is to pass. A sellable reform will be one that the public does not tune out. It should rather be one that picks up and maintains political momentum. There is a certain political calculus that goes on between the public, the government, and special interests that needs to be monitored. Also, even if a reform (legislative or administrative) is implemented, the way it is implemented (i.e., speed, with caveats) will influence its impact on health-care companies.

NOTES

1. Guy Boulton, "Health Reform Looks to the States," *Milwaukee Journal Sentinel*, Nov. 26, 2006.
2. Center for Economic Development, "Affordable Health Care for All: Beyond the Employer-Based Health Care System," October 2007, http://www.ced.org/docs/report/report_healthcare200710.
3. John Goodman, "Health Care in a Free Society: Rebutting the Myths of National Health Insurance," Policy Analysis no. 532, Cato Institute, Jan. 27, 2005, http://www.cato.org/pub_display.php?pub_id=3627.
4. William C. Symonds, "In Massachusetts, Health Care for All?" *BusinessWeek*, Apr. 4, 2006, http://www.businessweek.com/investor/content/apr2006/pi20060404_152510.htm.
5. Harvard Medical School, "Uninsured Adults Increase Medicare Costs, Harvard Study Finds," Science Daily.com, July 13, 2007; retrieved December 24, 2007, from http://www.sciencedaily.com/releases/2007/07/070712144615.htm.
6. Information from AHRQ Web site, http://www.qualitymeasures.ahrq.gov/resources/commentary.aspx?file=season_for_change.inc.
7. Carl-Ardy Dubois, Martin McKee, and Ellen Nolte (eds.), *Human Resources for Health in Europe* (New York: Open University Press, 2006), European Observatory on Health Systems and Policies p. 144, http://www.phac-aspc.gc.ca/php-psp/pdf/human_resources_for_health_in_europe.pdf.
8. J. Hadley, J. S. Mandelblatt, J. M. Mitchell, J. C. Weeks, E. Guadagnoli, and Y. T. Hwang, "Medicare Breast Surgery Fees and Treatment Received by Older Women with Localized Breast Cancer," *Health Services Research* 38, no. 2 (2003): 553–573.
9. Thomas Piper, Director of Missouri Certificate of Need Program in FTC Hearings, June 10, 2003, http://www.ftc.gov/ogc/healthcarehearings/docs/030610piper.pdf.
10. *Achieving Electronic Connectivity in Healthcare*, Connecting for Health, Markel Foundation, July 2004.
11. Will Shanley, "Health-Plan Impasse May Delay Service, *Denver Post*, Aug. 31, 2006.

CHAPTER 6

Nonreform Trends

Some trends in health care will persist regardless of whether or not reform happens. Reformers should not ignore health-care trends that reform cannot influence directly; instead, they should acknowledge that these trends exist and either explicitly or implicitly prepare the health-care environment to accommodate them. For investors, understanding long-term trends is a key to driving above-average returns. One may believe that investors need clairvoyance if they are to model decades-long trends, but it is more a question of good observation that enables them to invest in a trend in its early stages.

Given the lack of a perfect vision of the future, it is important to bear in mind that there are trends that have yet to emerge, so it is incumbent on investors to watch for trends that have relevance to altering the health-care system. There are some trends that in the early twenty-first century appear as though they may be important to the health-care system and persist over a long period of time. Some of these trends are easier to quantify than others, but they are all worthy of observation, as they potentially may lead to value-creating investments.

PAY FOR PERFORMANCE AND EVIDENCE-BASED MEDICINE

Pay for performance, often referred to as P4P, is an emerging movement in health care that attempts to use financial incentives and disincentives to reward providers who achieve predetermined health-care benchmarks. Such benchmarks can include percentages of patients receiving certain tests and clinical or cost outcomes. The benchmarks are derived from another growing field: evidence-based medicine (EBM). This is an attempt to apply the standards of evidence gained through the scientific method more uniformly to certain aspects of medical practice. "Evidence-based medicine is the conscientious, explicit and judicious use of current best evidence in making decisions about the care of individual patients."[1] Variations from good medical practice, which include medical errors, can lead to negative clinical outcomes.

People from other industry groups may look at P4P initiatives and wonder why health care needs to mandate such activity. Other industries already incorporate such factors into their operations because the market has dictated it. Part of the reason that health-care practices have veered so far from those in other industries has to do with the special market failures found in the industry. Among these are lack of data, poor processes, lack of transparency, and the principal-agent problem.[2] The government has recognized that given the size of its health-care expenditures, it should incorporate P4P/EBM tools into some of its programs, including Medicare, and it looks as if those efforts are accelerating.[3] Government, because of its size, often tends to lead health-care innovation; if the government becomes more active in P4P, so will other parts of the system. How effective P4P programs have been in reducing costs and improving quality is inconclusive, given the paucity of data,[4] but P4P would appear to be an improvement over the approach we are using now.

There are several hurdles that a reform initiative must overcome in order to implement a P4P program. The first is deciding what constitutes evidence that a procedure works. Evidence-based medicine rests on two premises: that for any given diagnosis, there is a narrow range of optimal treatment outcomes, and that this information can be communicated to the patient and/or the caregiver.[5] There are many disease states for which some level of consensus has been reached; however, there is enough debate over many others that it may take time for clinical research to achieve consensus.

The second hurdle is what to measure. P4P programs have generally measured either process (did the patient get the optimal course of treatment?) or outcome (did the patient recover?). Whether process or outcome should be measured depends a great deal on the type of disease and the type of patient. How exactly to measure qualitative issues like compliance with the regimen or to define an optimal recovery is open to debate.

A third issue is how to provide incentives for optimal behavior. A plan or program has relatively few tools, some hard (defined by statute) and some soft (indirect), to cajole potentially reluctant providers into delivering care. The hard goals are financial—paying bonuses or withholding payment based upon predetermined process or outcome measures. Pricing such a bonus and determining at what level (system, group, or physician) to pay it can be difficult.[6] A program can also include regulatory provisions defining optimal care, making it illegal or financially impractical to provide certain types of care either entirely (e.g., off-label prescribing) or in certain settings. Indirect incentives would involve making quality and cost data more transparent to patients and other payers. These incentives would work through soft motivations like prestige, a sense of competition, and the marketing advantage that comes from superior outcomes. When data are published, there is always the danger that providers will be more selective about the types of patients they care for. There will probably have to be adjustments for severity along with quality dissemination, which could add elements of inaccuracy to the data.

The fourth issue is that in order to be successful, the evidence-based guidelines, the measurement techniques, and the incentives will have to be universal across most, if not all, patients in all settings. The reason for this is twofold. If incentives and outcome measures differ, this would create a disincentive to reduce variations in care. In addition, a wide variety of outcome and payment standards would lead to increased bureaucratic bloat as well as confusion. So while P4P/EBM both make intuitive sense and appear to have the ability to remedy some of the problems in the health-care system, numerous challenges will make these programs difficult to develop. P4P/EBM programs will not necessarily be well accepted by providers, who may decide that they eliminate autonomy, but they may be seen as an antidote to defensive medicine. Improvement in information technology will facilitate the uptake. Investors will be rewarded if they can identify companies that can solve these significant challenges.

PHARMACOGENOMICS, PERSONALIZED MEDICINE, AND GENETIC VARIATION

Pharmacogenomics is the emerging science of using an understanding of how a person's genetic blueprint affects her response to treatment. The way a person responds to a particular therapy can vary widely depending on her sensitivity to and ability to metabolize a drug. Small genetic variations (differences in genetic sequences) among patients can lead to significant divergences in outcomes of treatment.[7]

Much of medicine uses a one-size-fits-all approach to disease. A disease is identified, a drug is given, and the response and side effects are observed. There is some flexibility in terms of dosage and dosing schedule, but these tools are relatively blunt and require an element of trial and error, even if the pharmacokinetics (the absorption, distribution, and metabolism) of a drug are well known.

The promise of pharmacogenomics is that the response rates and side effects of a treatment can be understood at the individual patient level, which should improve outcomes and reduce the impact of negative side effects. When medicine is tailored to an individual, it is commonly referred to as "personalized medicine." Though this movement is still in its infancy, the concept of tailoring a treatment to an individual is one of the goals of medicine.

From this early stage in its development, there are numerous challenges to getting to the point where personalized medicine is the norm. The technology still has not gotten to the point where medicine understands even a fraction of the available information. Science has yet to begin to grasp biomarkers (indicators of disease or wellness) that lie above the genetic level (proteins, for example). As with many scientific breakthroughs, the pace of the hunt for personalized medicine has been picking up rapidly, and there is little doubt that there will be more research and ultimately treatments to come.[8]

Personalized medicine may be developed incrementally, and discoveries may not all occur sequentially. Data about responses and outcomes will be discovered, catalogued, and used as a preventive or predictive tool, and a treatment will be developed. This will all take time, but there are several therapies on the market today for cancer and HIV that utilize some form of personalized medicine, as they require a diagnostic test to see whether a particular therapeutic agent will lead to an optimal clinical outcome.

Utilizing the variations in the genetic code to develop therapeutic agents could have a wide-ranging impact on the business models of medical products companies. Right now large cohorts are needed to determine if a drug is safe and effective. If there were a way to identify elements of the population that would be most likely to respond safely to a drug, this would enable enrollment in clinical trials to be done more quickly, improve patients' chances of a positive outcome, and speed the therapeutic agent's time to market. Pharmacogenomics may also enable the development of better models, either animals or in silico, for early drug discovery efforts, which could increase the productivity of drug research. Personalized medicine my also increase the variety of drugs on the market. There are drugs that exist in company libraries that would fail when tested on a large population, but that might succeed brilliantly if they were tested on the "right" population. The blockbuster model, or designing therapies that treat the maximum number of patients, was a cornerstone of therapy development in the twentieth century. If companies can develop more drugs that are directed at smaller populations, but for which they can receive premium pricing (for near-guaranteed outcomes), this would alter the blockbuster model substantially.

Personalized medicine also has the potential to alter the way in which health care is delivered and paid for. If the promise of pharmacogenomics as a predictive tool is achieved, providers of care will need to reorient themselves from being deliverers of care to being predictors of future need. This is in stark contrast to the incidence of care procedure-based model that is in place now. Once a disease is detected, there will be more specific treatment paradigms in place, and providers will need to follow these more narrowly defined treatment paradigms. The more accurate a diagnosis and treatment, the lower the cost of delivering care should be, because unnecessary and sometimes counterproductive treatment regimens would not be used. This should allow providers to have better profit margins on the delivery of services. As with therapeutic agents, the higher the guarantee level that a provider can offer for a prospective treatment, the greater the premium price that a provider can command.

From a payer's perspective, wide-scale testing will allow better actuarial predictability in the insured cohort. This will reduce costs and allow insurers to direct patients to the sites of care that have the best outcomes for a particular genetic or disease variant. This will prove positive for the payers' profit margins, as their costs will be reduced because uncertainty is minimized. This change in business model is not without its challenges. The key challenge is seeing that payers do not discriminate against those whose genetic makeup indicates a high probability of significant illness. These are the patients who will need insurance the most and will need to be offset by others in the risk pool.

Health-care reformers are becoming more aware of the challenges and the promise of personalized medicine. Discrimination based on genetic sequences of any kind leads to societal problems and could create a caste of "uninsurables." The bioethics of personalized medicine must be dealt with in some way. The dissemination of genetic information must be handled with great care because there may be privacy concerns that go beyond the individual. Even if a person is willing to have his genetic code available to the public, it may also provide information about near relatives. Reformers will have to deal with the way in which health-care information (both history and genetic information) is made accessible. Whether the genetic code is open source or proprietary will matter in terms of pricing and program design. Both approaches have their problems. Open source increases the chances of invasion of privacy, while keeping data proprietary will slow down science and possibly prohibit patients from "owning" their own genetic information. Given the level of data, it remains to be seen what type of database this information will be relegated to, and that will determine the speed, cost, and efficacy of widespread growth of genetic epidemiology.

Health-care reformers must also focus on developing regulatory pathways that introduce a personalized component to a drug. This would be faster than current timelines because fewer people would need to be enrolled in trials. Personalized medicine does add some technical challenges to proving safety and efficacy, which regulators will have to deal with. Health-care reform must also ensure that reimbursement is sufficient to encourage the development of more sophisticated, successful, and expensive treatments. This increased reimbursement contradicts another of health-care reform's goals: controlling system costs. Reformers will have to reconcile the contradiction of cost and quality. Reformers must find a way to encourage exploration of this field: either direct payments, intellectual property protections, or other types of incentives. Not only will the outcome be better public health but development of new therapies could give the United States a scientific advantage in a world that is growing more competitive.

The investment opportunities derived from personalized medicine are both direct (investing in the technology) and indirect (taking advantage of the impact it will have on the system). Directly, there are life science tools that will allow greater exploration of personalized medicine. As this is an evolving field, it may be difficult to determine the biggest beneficiaries, but a way to anticipate this is to follow the science and see what types of experiments using what types of machinery science prefers. Direct investment in companies that utilize personalized medicine to design therapeutic agents could be an attractive option. Although, as with other types of therapy development, the probability of failure is greater than the probability of success, personalization should improve the odds. As the ability to screen genetics becomes more powerful, a consumer genetics industry may come into being, which may see growth that could follow the trajectory of other high-technology industries, like personal computers, where the market grew substantially as the technology got simpler and less expensive. Acquisition of biological material (blood samples, for example) for archives or libraries will be an important value-creating aspect of any business model, although valuing such assets may be a challenge because knowing a priori if a data set will yield data for a test or a therapeutic agent will be difficult, and there will inevitably be privacy concerns.

Personalized medicine should be a boon for prevention and lead to reduced medical costs. Investors could allocate capital to those companies that would benefit from the improved outcomes and lower costs that personalized medicine might bring. Since personalized medicine is in its infancy, a large-scale positive impact on the system may be some time away. However, if personalized medicine could make the workforce more productive by keeping employees healthy, it could be a boon to all companies and their stocks, not just those in the health-care sector.

DEMOGRAPHICS

Many people are aware of the phenomenon of the graying of America as the baby-boom generation (the largest current generational cohort) begins to reach its peak medical utilization years.[9] In addition to the aging of the population, however, the composition of the U.S. population is evolving, with significant changes in the racial and ethnic makeup of those requiring medical care and services. In addition, the geography of where patients are located is changing, with the population centers moving to urban areas and to the South and the West. At the same time, the health-care workforce is undergoing shifts that closely mirror those of the general population.[10]

These changes will have a significant impact on the pace and structure of reform as well as on the investment opportunities in health care. As the longevity of a population increases, its medical utilization grows substantially. If consumption patterns and physician productivity stay constant, the demand for physicians will increase from 2.8 per thousand in 2000 to 3.1 in 2020.[11] While this may not seem like much in absolute terms, the number of physicians would have to rise from above 900,000 now to more than 1,000,000 in 2020. This problem is compounded by the fact that many physicians are aging along with the general population and will be leaving the workforce, increasing the demand for replacements. The nature of the services older people use are different in type and site from those used by the younger cohort because of the nature of their ailments. Rehabilitation services, cancer treatment, and long-term care facilities are just some of the types of services that older people need more often than younger people.

Minorities have different patterns of health-care use from nonminorities, and given that total patient-care hours spent with minorities could rise to as high as 40 percent of the total in 2020, up from 31 percent in 2000, this could change the way health care is delivered and the types of services and products that are demanded.[12] Although there are probably many reasons for the disparities in care, one of the major drivers is that access to care among this population is reduced—minorities tend to be overrepresented among the uninsured.[13] If the proportion of minorities is growing and access to care is improved, this could substantially increase the demand for medical services. Beyond just differences in ethnic or economic makeup, changes in lifestyle, like diet, stress, and overall economic conditions, can play a role in what type of health care is demanded. As these factors change, they open up challenges for public health authorities and opportunities for investors.

Adapting to the new levels of demand will pose a challenge for both service providers and product makers. Particularly when this is paired with increased demand from emerging markets, the possibility of "supply shocks" exists. Should there be a disruption in the supply chain at either the manufacturing level or the distribution level, a supply shock could ensue. At the manufacturing level, given the stringent safety requirements for these products, any imperfection in raw materials or manufacturing process could render the products unsafe. If there is little spare capacity nationally or globally, any reduction in manufacturing capacity could lead to a shortage, creating a price spike as well as the possibility that lifesaving products may not be obtainable. The same dynamic is in force for other parts of the supply chain: should unsafe or counterfeit products enter the supply chain, the result would be a supply shock, with high prices and access issues.

Logistics also play a role in the supply chain. Should increasing or changing demand put a strain on the medical product transportation complex, the resulting disruption could lead to price shocks or access issues. Regardless of where the weaknesses in the supply chain may be, added demand resulting from changing demographics will tax the current infrastructure and could lead to supply shocks.

Capacity shortages can also take place in the service part of health care. If there are not enough qualified people available to deliver services, these services either won't be obtainable or will be delivered by underqualified personnel or inadequate facilities. The result of personnel shortages is likely to be suboptimal outcomes, increasing variations of care, potential safety problems, and increased cost—all anathema to a reform program. If demand continues to grow at its present rate, the system as a whole runs the risk of being overtaxed in terms of its ability to deliver the required products and services. Supply shocks will have a negative impact on patients' trust in the system and may lead to public health issues in the short run and demand issues in the long run. Those companies that are best able to ensure that the supply chain, from manufacture to distribution, is both safe and consistent and are able to adapt to increased demand in an efficient way should be able to garner a premium and should be looked at as valuable investments, particularly if their competitors cannot offer the same safeguards. Companies with a questionable ability to manage demand changes add an increased element of risk to the investment.

Geography will also play a role in the demand for and supply of medical services. Currently there are many areas that are deemed to have a shortage of physicians, and with a population shift, the supply-demand equation may increase the imbalance further.[14] The types of services required (specialists, for example) in many areas are not in line with the existing supply. These access issues will have to be addressed. In order for a reform plan to succeed, it will have to grapple with the challenges of changing demographics. This will entail increasing the supply of providers of all types and providing them with incentives to practice in places where the demographics call for them. The workforce composition may have to change in order to accommodate the cultural norms of a larger minority population. These changes are all under way already, with movement toward more group practices and toward more minority and female physicians, although these trends are in a very nascent stage.[15]

The nature of employment in the United States is also changing. The economy has been moving and continues to move from a production-based economy to a service-based economy. This change has meant that the types of jobs being created differ substantially from those created in the past. Notably, there has been a reduction in union activity and an increase in independent contracting (freelancing). Although independent contractors' health-care demands are similar to those of employees of corporations, they require different sets of benefits, including portability and the ability to act in some collective fashion with others in order to lower premiums through a reduction in actuarial risk. Because independent contractors are not part of groups, issues like preexisting conditions become more important. Types of work may also have some influence on the types of health care demanded, although it is not clear exactly how this factor will evolve. There may be additional educational requirements for service-sector workers, and this increased education may also alter demand patterns. Good health care has also allowed workers to stay productive at ages historically unanticipated, which will lead to adjustments in demand.

EMERGING INFECTIOUS DISEASES

An emerging infectious disease is defined as one whose incidence has increased in the past 20 years and threatens to increase further in the near future.[16] The range of diseases is quite broad and includes those caused by viruses, bacteria, prions, and parasites. There are also changing vectors (transmission vehicles) of disease, which include mosquitoes, birds, and beef, among others. The threat from emerging diseases has grown.[17] Such diseases as SARS, West Nile virus, avian flu, and HIV, as well as old diseases in new forms, such as treatment-resistant tuberculosis and methicillin-resistant *Staphylococcus aureus* (MRSA), are becoming scourges that have not been seen in the country previously. While the causes of this threat remain a subject of debate, environmental and climate changes and overuse of antibiotics are frequently cited. Regardless of the causes, the fact remains that there are new and dangerous threats that the health-care system will have to deal with in the future.[18]

A key for health-care reform is to develop a system of surveillance that can detect an outbreak of any disease, emerging or otherwise, and early enough to allow public health services to react. Intergovernmental communication, which has not always been effective in the past, will be required to minimize the damage from a potential public health calamity like an epidemic. Another positive step will be to design protocols so that once a new pathogen or vector is detected, a predetermined series of steps is followed to minimize the damage. Since science needs the ability to track and identify any future potential threats, reformers would be wise to include inducements to prevent and treat emerging diseases as part of a health-care reform package. Emerging diseases are also a national defense issue, so other government agencies (like the Department of Defense) may also participate in the development of remedies for new threats. These remedies include bolstering the public health infrastructure, including having plans for first responders and plans to deal with surges in health complaints.

Like any new challenge, emerging diseases offer tremendous investment possibilities. Technology to aid in the surveillance of the health status of large populations has yet to be perfected. Equipment designed to identify previously unknown pathogens is still in its infancy. Vaccine technology and other preventive measures are becoming more sophisticated and more timely. There are many anti-infectives yet to be discovered. Companies that can improve the ability of the health-care system to deal with emerging threats through either surveillance, prevention, or speed to market for new treatments will not only help public health but create shareholder value as well.

ACUTE DISEASES BECOMING CHRONIC

Medicine has been extremely successful in treating very serious disease. HIV, heart disease and heart attacks, certain types of cancer, diabetes, genetic disorders, and mental illness are no longer the killers they once were. The reasons for this improvement are straightforward: better diagnosis, earlier intervention, and advanced therapeutic and procedural approaches. While this development should be applauded, once patients make it past the initial bout with these diseases, they face significant challenges.[19] Some diseases, such as AIDS and heart disease, require ongoing secondary and tertiary prevention efforts, such as medication and more intense observation, to maintain health status.

There are compliance challenges with maintaining health status, as medication often has side effects. There are also challenges with secondary diseases, either caused by the treatment or related to the existing disease, like diabetes, kidney failure, and depression. When combined with the initial diseases, these comorbidities, which otherwise would not have been encountered, lead to complex cases requiring intense medical intervention. Caring for a patient with multiple diseases requires that the diseases be treated in combination, not as isolated issues. Along with the challenges of delivering this type of care in a way that achieves optimal clinical outcomes, dealing with complex cases adds substantial expense to the system. Sites of care beyond the institutional setting, such as caring for the chronically ill at home, and support for primary caregivers will also need to be considered.[20] As medicine will only get more sophisticated in how it deals with acute diseases, we face a future in which more diseases that were formerly fatal become chronic and more types of previously unheard-of sets of comorbidities become commonplace.

For a health-care reform initiative, the challenge in dealing with more diseases becoming chronic is that there will be a larger population of disease survivors requiring continuous or near-continuous intervention. These patients can be more susceptible to comorbidities, which increases the observational challenges. In many of these cases, because these acute diseases have not been survived before, much of the science surrounding the change from acute to chronic is uncharted territory, increasing the medical challenges and demands on the system. It is incumbent upon any reform package to make sure that access to treatment for chronic disease is available, allowing flexibility because of the novelty of these new types of comorbidities, while at the same time managing costs.

From an investment perspective, the increase in chronic disease is a positive. Chronic disease requires continuous intervention, which should increase revenue. A higher level of comorbidities also leads to greater and longer-term revenue potential. Because much of the switch from acute disease to chronic disease is new to much of medicine, the challenges of dealing with side effects and comorbidities will offer new medical challenges. Both public health and the bottom line will be improved as solutions to these issues are found. Since there are no road maps for clinical pathways for dealing with many of these disease states, this offers a greenfield opportunity. There is no existing infrastructure to deal with the coming larger cohort of people with chronic diseases.

MEDICALIZATION OF CONDITIONS

The definition of what constitutes a disease has widened over the years.[21] "Once upon a time plenty of children were unruly, adults were shy, and bald men wore hats"[22]; this is not so anymore, as any problem that can be solved by medicine is considered fair game by much of the medical establishment. The causes of this expansion of what constitutes disease are the subject of some debate, but "medicalization," as it is referred to, appears to be a growing reality for health care. There is no better example of this gray area between disease and normality than lifestyle drugs, which include erectile dysfunction medication, a multibillion-dollar class of compounds. Erectile dysfunction would not appear to lead to fatality, but it is a problem for some people, and there is a medical solution. The same can be said with different degrees of severity about appearance, menopause, attention deficit disorder, anxiety, and reproduction.

Defining what is normal has never been an easy task; in fact, this would appear to be more a philosophical question than a medical one. Medicine is now capable of altering states of being that people want altered. This desire to expand what is "treatable" is a challenge for health-care reformers in terms of both controlling costs and defining what is acceptable to deal with under the umbrella of health care. Medicalization also pits two sides of the health-care sector against each other: the cost-control arm versus the product and therapy makers. Cost-control companies want to rein in the expansion of coverage, while product makers continue to look for new markets or indications. Health-care providers are in a sense stuck in the middle. They may question the medical necessity of a treatment, but if something is a problem for patients, they are under a certain amount of obligation to help. Moreover, if a provider fails to respond to a patient's needs, he risks losing that patient to another provider who is more willing to accommodate the patient's desires. Providers also have the challenge of managing patients' expectations concerning what can reasonably be resolved medically.

Reformers must accede to societal norms within reason and ability to pay, but societal norms and lifestyles may change, in part as a result of the types of therapies that are available. The challenge is to have a system that is flexible enough to deal with societal evolution. Changing dietary norms, changes in other physical health issues (like obesity), and changes in environmental factors (such as pollution) can play a role in the types of products and services demanded. There are also bioethical challenges that need to be addressed in terms of defining what illness is. There will be questions that need to be answered about allocation of resources between medicalized conditions and other health-care needs (lifestyle drugs versus orphan diseases). Society will eventually come to a conclusion about these issues over time, but an ideal solution may not be apparent in the short term. The biggest challenge of the system is that the way society views illness and aging is constantly evolving, which means that patient demand will change commensurately. There is no centralized mechanism to engage in this type of decision making, and many would argue that there should not be. From an investment point of view, expanded use of therapies appears to be inevitable, so there will be opportunities for value creation. Cost-control initiatives may lead to some pushback, so investors must eye the public health value of "medicalized" treatments carefully.

The way society views disease has had some positive effects as well. Speaking in public about certain diseases that were once considered taboo subjects, like mental health, has become more acceptable. Reducing the stigma of any disease should allow those who require treatment to access that treatment more easily, either because the treatment is more available or because the reduced stigma makes seeking treatment more acceptable to the patient, since she does not need to fear social ostracism. Perceptions of cancer, HIV, and mental health, along with other diseases, have undergone shifts in the past, and the advent of Internet communication between sufferers should allow further destigmatization of disease. A reduction in the stigma of diseases is a positive for companies because it opens up demand for products and services and quite possibly lowers costs, as intervention in the disease process may begin earlier in the disease progression if patients seek treatment earlier. Destigmatization of disease also opens up new marketing challenges and opportunities as a dialogue about illness changes.

COST-EFFECTIVENESS

With health-care inflation rising far faster than that for other products, payers and governments have attempted to develop tools to tame the runaway expenses. Some programs have resorted to rationing, but that is a rather unpopular option for the sick. Governments like Great Britain and Australia have taken a less direct route than rationing, preferring instead to create agencies designed to determine the cost-effectiveness of various medical therapies. Cost-effectiveness analysis of medical therapies has an intuitively simple appeal. If a system could sort out the most effective ways to spend its resources, it should be easy to choose the optimal way to allocate capital and control health-care costs. The appeal of this approach has led the trend toward measuring cost-effectiveness to expand worldwide, including in America.[23] As with many things in health care, however, the practical realities are far more complex. While the methodology for measuring cost-effectiveness has gotten more sophisticated over the years, there is no standard set of criteria used across the globe. It is not even clear that the use of cost-effectiveness would be successful in controlling costs.[24] Likely components of a cost/benefit analysis will include functional outcomes like survival and subjective outcomes like quality of life and worker productivity. Other measures will include the actual treatment costs and expectations of longer-term expenditures.

Despite its drawbacks, it appears that the move toward greater cost-effectiveness will continue. The questions will be about the degree and the speed of implementation rather than about whether this tool will be used in cost-control efforts. For reformers, a key to success will be overcoming the political pushback from patients who do not meet a predetermined threshold of benefit. The system has to be adaptive so that as medicine and costs change, so does the cost-effectiveness analysis. Time is a factor in cost-effectiveness also, as benefit curves can change over time, depending on the long-term efficacy of a therapy. The methodology has to represent real-world conditions rather than laboratory-controlled situations—a difficult and expensive undertaking. In the United States, where there is no existing infrastructure to develop cost-effectiveness analyses, there will be the challenge of creating an agency or giving that responsibility to one of the existing agencies. There is also the chance that a heavy reliance on cost-effectiveness analysis could stifle innovation, depending on how onerous regulations are.

Proving cost-effectiveness will increase the challenges for companies, as it will require more data and greater investments of time and capital to obtain results. It is one more hurdle that a product must overcome, in addition to regulatory, clinical, and market acceptance, which not only will increase time to market but could render a product unmarketable, depending on the outcome of the cost-effectiveness analysis. One of the positive effects of this process is that if a product is deemed cost-effective, this would lessen competitive threats because the hurdles facing competitors would be that much higher. Depending on the cost-effectiveness approach, investors may have to apply a discount to products that could potentially have difficulty with a cost-effectiveness hurdle.

CONSUMERISM

Global trends toward consumerism have been in effect for some time. Given the greater amount of information and access, people's desire for greater control over their purchasing decisions is a simple concept. As it relates to health care, consumerism says that individuals should have greater control over decisions affecting their health. A feature of consumerist plans is that of financial responsibility: the patient must bear a greater percentage of the financial cost in return for greater control over what happens to him. The basic premise is twofold: First, greater exposure to costs will eliminate the moral hazard that comes from not paying the bills. Second, patients are better able to determine what is best for them rather than letting the "system" decide for them.

For consumerism to function successfully, some underlying principles need to be in place. First, patients must be able to obtain correct information about therapies and costs and, once having that information, must be able to make the optimal decisions.[25] Consumerism also assumes that the services demanded by patients will be accessible to them. This may or may not be the case. The recent past has brought some changes in health-care access models, like in-pharmacy clinics and mall-based aesthetics clinics.[26] Given the novelty of the approach, there is relatively little information on whether these consumer-driven access points do in fact lead to better resource utilization, cost control, or outcomes. Changes from the traditional "medical home" model where most of the patient's care has historically been delivered could have profound effects on the health-care market. Other consumer-related medical advances, like alternative medicines, will also be a challenge because cost-effectiveness data for many of these products are not in existence. Patients as consumers may also need additional support services (transportation, ease of obtaining appointments) if they are to maximize the benefit. Unlike other consumer areas, there is no availability of recourse (beyond litigation) if patients feel their interests have not been served by the system. Ultimately, to give the patient consumer power there will need to be a better business bureau-like way for patients to adjudicate differences (billing errors, miscommunications) with providers and payers. Over time, it will be incumbent on companies addressing these markets to prove their value proposition.

The challenge for public health authorities will be to make sure that patients are given adequate information, therapies are available, and patients have the wherewithal to control their financial risk. These are difficult factors to keep in balance and will require increased regulation, although this may not be part of a reform package. Some of the concepts in use today that could be expanded are provider report cards, outcomes data, and cost comparisons. It is often difficult to make apples-to-apples comparisons among providers, so report cards have drawn some scrutiny.[27] If the consumerism model is to work, information must be accessible so that people can make informed decisions. Clinical trials to prove the superiority of one modality over another can be difficult to interpret if the data are inconclusive. Nevertheless, until there are better methodological approaches to determine value, both a report card type of information and head-to head comparisons are likely to be features of a consumerist future.

For investors, the challenge will be to find companies that can accurately interpret consumer demand, both offering insurance that fits consumers' needs and offering products where and when consumers need them. Treating patients as consumers has been growing with the increased use of direct-to-consumer advertising for products. There has been liberalization of over-the-counter and behind-the-counter access to pharmaceuticals, which has increased their availability. Though do-it-yourself surgery seems a long way off, it is reasonable to expect increasing movement toward the consumer model. This is a change from the more paternalistic model of medicine practiced over the last century, so investment opportunities will favor those who can adapt. Despite its obvious opportunities, consumerism does open up health-care investors to more cyclical risk than they had been traditionally because they will now be exposed to consumer cycles (economic, sentiment), which will now have to be considered as an investment consideration.

GLOBALIZATION

In addition to being a driver of health-care reform, increasing globalization remains an economic fact of life and will affect the health-care system in ways other than increasing financial anxiety among Americans. The clearest ramification of globalization is that there will be increased competition for resources: scientific, medical, and financial. Over the last century, America has done quite well at being a leader in scientific and medical development. With other economies gaining strengths, however, this scientific and medical preeminence is not a given. The competition may require American-based companies to look outside the country for access to talent in innovative industries, which could change the way in which medical breakthroughs are discovered. At the same time, companies based outside the United States may be competing for the same talent. Americans may have to import labor from elsewhere to deliver some of the care required if the talent is not available domestically.[28] Recruiting and training providers from other places will alter companies' business models and cost structures. An influx of talent from other countries will place new demands on regulators to ensure that credentials and knowledge bases do not vary widely, or there is the possibility that variations in care, one of the banes of the health-care system, will actually increase.

Globalization will also alter the demand side of health care. Countries outside of the United States have different cultures and varying states of economic growth. Successful companies must alter their sales practices and product mix to better tailor their offerings to meet growing global demand if they are to stay competitive. Altering product mix and sales practices will inevitably feed back into the types of services and products available domestically just because of resource constraints at the corporate level. This global feedback loop will need to be mastered if companies are to create value.

Medical tourism is another way in which globalization has altered the demand for health-care supplies and services. In the past, it was not unusual for the wealthy in other countries to travel to the United States to receive care that was not obtainable in their home countries. There has been a nascent reversal of this trend, with Americans who are unable or unwilling to obtain care in the United States traveling to other nations to obtain products and services. The logic is that it is less expensive even when the cost of transportation is added to the cost of the procedure, and the quality of care is the same.[29] It is not inconceivable that if foreign competition continues to maintain a cost edge or quality edge, competition for patients could come from international markets, a factor not foreseen by either reformers or corporations until recently. For the public health system, substantial new competition for patients appears to be some time off; however, it seems unlikely that emerging economic powers will stop striving to improve their health-care systems and attempting to narrow any quality or cost gap (perceived or real), making markets outside the United States more attractive to patients depending on their financial and health-care needs.

HEALTH-CARE INDUSTRY CHANGES

The health-care industry has not remained stagnant in the face of the numerous challenges it has faced. The industry has become more corporate. Although fears of widespread corporatization have been around since the early 1980s, it wasn't until recently that the trend has begun to accelerate.[30,31] The corporatization of health care includes the movement of physicians from single-person practices to group practices, increased concentration of membership among larger managed-care plans, and increased concentration among pharmaceutical companies. Though the move toward more corporate health care does have the ability to improve quality and lower costs, the risks that it might do the opposite are also evident. Regardless of the outcome of the corporatization of health care, the fact that it continues apace raises challenges for companies and reformers alike. The regulatory challenges are to make sure that antitrust, self-dealing, and antikickback laws are followed. There are many regulations already in place, so enforcement may be a more relevant issue than new regulation.

Since the government has the largest market share in health care, it could potentially utilize this share to demand better pricing and other concessions from providers and payers. This, of course, represents a risk to the companies in those industries. Because corporations have become large, government intervention in the markets could have negative effects if it leads to substantial disruption of the provision of care. Politicians, in their own self-interest, are likely to want to keep large-scale disruption to a minimum. The greater cost inflation becomes, however, the more disruption patients (voters) may be willing to put up with in order to obtain price relief.

Concentration of market power is a major issue for corporations. A bigger entity has the ability to increase market share and demand better prices. On the provider and payer side, there has been conflict surrounding the question of pricing based on increases in market share. This trend is likely to continue. Defensible market share is a key competitive advantage, so those companies that can command share at the local, regional, or even national level should create shareholder value. From a product maker point of view, market concentration means less pricing power if it is unable to differentiate its products. Additionally, negotiating with and/or selling products to a small number of bureaucracies is a different business model from negotiating with or selling to a larger number of small entities. Those companies that can successfully adapt to the changes brought about by corporatization should create shareholder value.

Corporatization has yielded another interesting feature in health care: the changing dynamic between big companies and big government, as it relates to health care. A recent example is the competition between a private entity and the government to map the human genome.[32] Ultimately, the human genome was decoded by both entities, but the fact that a company would compete with the government was considered novel at the time. It is likely that there will be more of this type of competition in the future, as companies now have the scale to fund research that was once the province only of government. This changing dynamic is worth investigation by investors, as there could be ample opportunity in those companies that can deploy research dollars and achieve measurable results.

The dynamic is not always competitive. Through the National Institutes of Health (NIH), the government invests a substantial amount of money in scientific research, the results of which will be available to corporations. Besides the obvious benefits to companies, the public does see a return on its investment.[33] It will be incumbent on public health authorities to understand these new dynamics and use their considerable financial and regulatory clout to find a way to optimize the competitive and collaborative relationship with industry. For investors, the challenge is the same: to identify companies with the best ability to manage the same competitive and collaborative dynamic. While a similar dynamic has yet to show up on the payer side, it is not entirely out of the question that one day private industry will compete with the government for treating patients, as private competition exists in countries that have single-payer medical systems.

The changing corporate landscape of medicine also has implications for adoption rates. Assuming that there is market concentration among payers and an incentive to control health-care costs, adoption rates for new technology will almost certainly slow. Cost, legality, time, fear, usefulness, and complexity have all been identified as barriers to technology adoption.[34] Corporations can set their own hurdles in terms of either efficacy, cost, or other measures to determine whether to reimburse for products. The more limited the reimbursement, the slower the adoption of new technology will be. The greater the market share, the greater the impact an entity can have on the fate of medical technology providers in terms of both price and adoption. It is difficult to measure systemwide adoption trends, but it appears that the system probably provides incentives to slow down adoption rather than speed it up. It is incumbent on the public authorities to ensure that new technology, if it is cost-effective, is accessible. For investors, it is the increasing hurdle facing adoption rates that needs to be modeled to determine value creation potential.

INFORMATION AND COMMUNICATION

It is no secret that in the early twenty-first century, the world has undergone an information revolution as a result of the expansion of the Internet. Information technology has the potential for reducing the asymmetry of information and other imbalances that are so prevalent in health care. It will serve as a spur for reform, but it could also have a profound impact on the way health care is demanded and supplied. A critical success factor will be to ensure that public awareness of diseases and resources is adequate. The public can use new communication modalities to interact with the health-care system more effectively. The challenge will be to develop the information if it does not exist, like cost-effectiveness analysis, and make it available to the public in an unbiased way. Some of the information that does exist is kept behind closed electronic doors by scientific journals and others and is either available only for a fee or not available at all. There has been a movement to make this information more accessible, but progress has been slow.[35] While the lack of open sharing of information has undoubtedly slowed medical progress, information providers do need to earn enough of a return to remain going concerns.

There are several considerations involved in expanding public access to information. The location of the information repository would have to be resolved. It costs money to create and update databases. The presumption behind peer-reviewed research is that the writer's peers are most able to judge research, but the final arbiter on what research is important or interesting can often be mercurial. How it is decided what should be published is a question that needs to be answered; otherwise the credibility and utility of any information repository will be limited. When it comes to the question of whether research sponsored by the government should be made available to the public free of charge, members of the public are likely to believe that it should be, since they paid for it once and would not want to pay for it again. There have been cases where a conflict of interest has arisen for the investigator, the trial sponsor, or the journal publishing the data. There is no standard of disclosure, which also decreases the credibility of information. There also is the problem of information overload to deal with. Providers particularly are bombarded with information, and sorting out the important from the unimportant is a challenge.[36] For the public health authorities, increasing and maintaining transparency will be an important determinant of success.

Information and the access to it are competitive weapons for payers, providers, and product makers. Those who are able to gather the most accurate and largest quantity of information can make the most informed business decisions and thus stand the best chances in the marketplace. Of course, it is in a company's best interests to keep this information to itself, setting up a conflict with the rest of the system, which needs information to make its own decisions. Given the advances in information technology, there may be increased regulatory action in this area, although this is not likely to be part of a reform package. Companies that can maintain control of information within the boundaries of the law will be most able to create value for shareholders. Investors can also exploit increasing information as an investment tool to gather information on potential investments. Investors can also invest directly in those companies that either help gather the needed clinical or financial information, interpret the information, or disseminate information. All types of health-care information providers will benefit, as the health-care system of the future will require copious amounts of information in order to function.

In addition to making access to information more accessible, the information revolution has also changed the way participants in the health-care system communicate. There are two routes of communication: one formal and one informal. Formal communications include communications between providers and patients, between payers and providers, between product makers and payers, and between providers and patients. For patients, the ability to communicate with providers electronically could enable better care, as it could facilitate issues like compliance with treatment and follow-up examinations, two issues cited for variances from optimal care.[37] Improved communication, if it leads to optimal patient behavior and clear communication with providers, should improve clinical outcomes. Communication between providers, payers, and product makers should permit more efficient functioning of the system and lower administrative costs over the long term. It is not clear yet whether the full impact of potential cost savings has been felt by the system. It is also not clear how privacy issues will be resolved as this type of communication becomes more common. New communication modalities also allow product makers to reach out directly to patients more easily than before. It allows them to more carefully target those with an interest in a given set of conditions, for example. The danger is that there may be supply-induced demand if patients cannot determine their actual need.

Informal communication is also an important feature of the information revolution. There are now outlets where patients can communicate with one another about diseases, products, providers, and payers. While often anecdotal, this information can facilitate or be a deterrent to the decision-making process, depending on its accuracy. The speed at which information is now being shared means that new ideas can find their way around the globe instantly. As with the decision-making process, speed is helpful only if the information is accurate. The informal network can theoretically help a provider, product maker, or payer if it receives favorable reviews on chat boards and blogs. For public health authorities, the key is to ensure that information, even if it is informal, is accurate and doesn't cause undue harm to the public. Companies, meanwhile, need to engage in reputation management to make sure that they are properly represented. Investors should watch the informal communication networks to determine what both the perception and the reality of a given company may be. Given the anonymity of the informal network, it is always best to verify any information one receives.

NOTES

1. From the Web site of the Centre for Evidence Based Medicine, http://www.cebm.net/.
2. L. A. Petersen, L. D. Woodard, T. Urech, C. Daw, and S. Sookanan, "Does Pay-for-Performance Improve Quality of Health Care?" *Annals of Internal Medicine* 145, no. 4 (2006): 265–272.
3. Timothy J. Mullaney and Howard Gleckman, "A Big Green Pill for Health Care?" *BusinessWeek*, June 29, 2005.
4. See Meredith B. Rosenthal et al., "Pay for Performance in Commercial HMOs," *New England Journal of Medicine* 355 (2006): 1895–1902 and Peter K. Lindenauer et al., "Public Reporting and Pay for Performance in Hospital Quality Improvement, *New England Journal of Medicine* 356 (2007): 5.
5. Jim Jaffe, "Evidence-Based Medicine: Implications for Consumer-Driven Health Benefits," *Employee Benefit Research Institute Notes*, 24, no. 8 (2003).
6. Petersen et al., "Does Pay-for-Performance Improve Quality of Health Care?"
7. Michelle Meadows, "Genomics and Personalized Medicine, *FDA Consumer* magazine, November-December 2005, http://fda.gov/fda/features/205/605_genomics.html.
8. Elizabeth Pennisi, "Breakthrough of the Year: Human Genetic Variation," *Science* 318, no. 5858 (2007), www.sciencemag.org.
9. White House Conference on Aging, Sept. 22, 2005, http://www.whcoa.gov/about/policy/meetings/Sol_forum_agenda/2005_Sep/Dan%20Perry_09_22_05.pdf.
10. "Changing Demographics: Implications for Physicians, Nurses and Other Health Workers," U.S. Department of Health and Human Services, Spring 2003, p. 1.
11. Ibid., p. 5.
12. Ibid., p. 37.
13. Ichiro Kawachi, Norman Daniels, and Dean E. Robinson, "Health Disparities by Race and Class: Why Both Matter," *Health Affairs* 24, no. 2 (2005): 342–352.
14. "Changing Demographics," p. 57.
15. Carol Westfall, "Physician Demographics and Turnover Rates," *Physician's News Digest*, May 2007, http://physiciansnews.com/business/507westfall.html.
16. Wikipedia definition of emerging diseases.
17. "Emerging Infectious Diseases: Review of State and Federal Disease Surveillance Efforts," Government Accountability Office, September 2004, GAO-04-877, http://www.gao.gov/highlights/d04877high.pdf.
18. Anthony S. Fauci, Nancy A. Touchette, and Gregory K. Folkers, "Emerging Infectious Diseases: A 10-Year Perspective from the National Institute of Allergy and Infectious Diseases," *Emerging Infectious Diseases* 11, no. 4 (2005): 519–525.
19. Jane Gross, "AIDS Patients Face Downside of Living Longer," *New York Times*, Jan. 6, 2008.

20. Joel Shalowitz, "Financing Chronic Care Seminar: Chronic vs. Acute Care, Introduction and Macro View," presented at the June 2005 Society of Actuaries meeting.

21. Olavo B. Amaral, "Defining Disease in the Information Age, *PLoS Medicine* 3, no. 7 (2006): e317.

22. Faith McLellan, "Medicalisation: A Medical Nemesis," *Lancet* 369, no. 9562 (2007), 627.

23. "Health Care Economics, Comparison Shopping," *Economist*, Jan. 10, 2008.

24. Anupam B. Jena and Thomas Philipson, "Cost Effectiveness as a Price Control, *Health Affairs* 26, no. 3 (2007): 696–703.

25. Melinda Buntin et al., "Consumer-Directed Health, Early Evidence about Effects on Cost and Quality *Health Affairs* 25, no. 6 (2006): W516–W530.

26. Examples: Barbara Sax, "In-Store Clinics Benefit Pharmacists and Patients," *Pharmacy Times*, Sept. 21, 2006; and Janet Morrissey, "Having a Little Work Done (at the Mall)," *New York Times*, Jan. 13, 2008.

27. David Dranove, Daniel Kessler, Mark McClellan, and Mark Satterthwaite, "Is More Information Better? The Effects of 'Report Cards' on Health Care Providers," *Journal of Political Economy* 111, no. 3 (2003): 555–588.

28. "Nursing Shortage in Critical Stage: Poaching from Overseas?" *60 Minutes*, CBS, Jan. 17, 2003.

29. Krysten Crawford, "Medical Tourism Agencies Take Operations Overseas, *Business 2.0 Magazine*, Aug. 3, 2006, http://money.cnn.com/2006/08/02/magazines/business2/medicaltourism.biz2/index.htm.

30. Paul Starr, *The Social Transformation of American Medicine* (New York: Basic Books, 1982) has a wide discussion on the corporatization of health care.

31. Hoangmai H. Pham and Paul B. Ginsburg, "Unhealthy Trends: The Future of Physician Services, *Health Affairs* 26, no. 6 (2007): 1586–1598.

32. "Breaking the Code," *NewsHour with Jim Lehrer*, PBS, Mar. 16, 2000, http://www.pbs.org/newshour/bb/health/jan-june00/genome_sharing_3-16.html.

33. S. Claiborne Johnston, John D. Rootenberg, Shereen Katrak, Wade S. Smith, and Jacob S. Elkins, "Effect of a US National Institutes of Health Programme of Clinical Trials on Public Health and Costs," *Lancet* 367, no. 9519 (2006): 1319–1327.

34. Paula Garrett, C. Andrew Brown, Susan Hart-Hester, Elgenaid Hamadain, Corey Dixon, William Pierce, and William J. Rudman, "Identifying Barriers to the Adoption of New Technology in Rural Hospitals: A Case Report, *Perspectives in Health Information Management* 3 (2006): 9.

35. Pritpal S. Tamber, Fiona Godlee, and Peter Newmark, "Open Access to Peer-Reviewed Research: Making It Happen," *Lancet* 362, no. 9395 (2003): 1575–1577.

36. Amanda Hall and Graham Walton, "Information Overload within the Health Care System: A Literature Review, *Health Information and Libraries Journal* 21, no. 2 (2004): 102–108.

37. Vincenzo Atella, Franco Peracchi, Domenico Depalo, and Claudio Rossetti, "Drug Compliance, Co-Payment and Health Outcomes: Evidence from a Panel of Italian Patients," Centre for Economic and International Studies Working Paper no. 76, October 2005.

PART TWO

INVESTMENT STRATEGIES FOR THE HEALTH-CARE INDUSTRY

CHAPTER 7

Risks and Rewards of Health-Care Investing

For investors who do not have an in-depth knowledge of health care, an investment in this sector during a period of upheaval may seem like a risky proposition. The investment process in health care is similar to that for other investments, and the same cautions apply when making generalizations. Not all companies and shares are created equal. Valuations of different companies in the same industry can and do vary widely, and this will have a significant impact on returns. Management teams differ in their ability to execute. Products and services may be superior or inferior. Cost structures and accounting can deviate widely among companies. Health care is a broad industry and can accommodate most investors, no matter what their investing or trading style, valuation metrics, market capitalization requirements, or risk profiles. However, with health-care investing, particularly in an era of change, one should understand certain nuances that are specific to the industry before deploying capital.

Health care can support almost all possible investing and trading strategies; however, the industry itself is different from other industry groups. Investors need to appreciate these differences because the investing process for health care is different from that for other industries. Perhaps the most important differentiating factor between health care and other industries is that it has been the subject of almost continuous large-scale reform efforts. Few other industries have seen any wholesale reform, let alone almost constant calls for change.

Few others are subject to the impact of government to the degree that health care is, which makes understanding the levels of profit, levels of autonomy, and government appetite for reform so important to investors.

Reforms or attempts at reform have been a feature of health care since the early 1900s. Cost pressures and lack of access, the same drivers of reform as in the past, are still with us and are still encouraging change. Some of these reform efforts (Medicare) have resulted in major changes and a substantial opportunity. Others, like the Balanced Budget Amendment of 1997 (BBA 97), offered risk to investors but provided reward to those who shorted the stocks affected (bet that the stock price would go down). An in-depth understanding of the health-care reform process will allow investors to reap the ample opportunities from stock mispricings that change will bring to the industry.

Beyond the external changes foisted upon the health-care environment by reform efforts, the industry is built upon innovation. The magnitude of reform may fluctuate, but the industry is continuously attempting to put itself out of business in that value-creating changes always target a reduction in either disease or cost. Anathema as this may be from a public health perspective, the worse the disease and the greater the costs, the more helpful it is to the industry's financial performance. It is better to own the innovators and not own or short the noninnovators, but sorting out the two is a major challenge for health-care investors. Few other industries can have such a wide dispersion of outcomes or can see major business model or delivery changes in a relatively short period.

The government's role in health care is also a differentiating factor for investors. While other industries have the government either regulating them or being their primary client, health care differs in that government plays both a regulatory and a payer role. The government itself can be a mercurial factor, as there are elections every year and rapid changes in philosophy can occur that can significantly alter the way government approaches either its payment or its regulatory function in dealing with health care. It is imperative that health-care investors have an understanding of the government's position. Because the government's role in health care is so overarching and the details are extremely complex, there is the danger that investors will get lost in the minutiae. If there is a government-related risk, investors must understand whether the valuation takes the risk into account. If the valuation of a company does not offer enough of a margin of safety in the event of a major government shift, investors should avoid its shares.

Science plays a significant role in health-care value creation. This is important in the development of advanced pharmaceuticals, biotechnology, and medical technology. If a company is successfully innovating, this science will be cutting-edge, with no other comparable types of information available because the science is novel. Understanding and quantifying ideas that have never been tried before is a challenge for health-care investors that is rare in most industries. Given the high level of failure in science, investors should be particularly skeptical when it comes to early-stage scientific developments. By the time a company reaches the public markets, some of the science has usually been vetted by early-stage (venture) investors, but not always. Investors should pay particular attention to the idea of proof of concept—there must be a reason why the science should work, at least in theory.

Products that work in theory may not work in practice, so the greater the amount of work that has been done on practical applications, the easier it will be for investors to quantify possible outcomes. "Snake oil salesmen" have been around for some time, and in modern days there have been cases in which fictitious magic elixirs have been turned into corporations. As with other investments, if the outcomes seem too good to be true, they probably are, and evidence of success is the best predictor of future success. Investors should not necessarily avoid early-stage projects completely; however, with early-stage companies, analysts should pay special attention to the design of trials; the statistics underlying the trials; whether the output of the trials is meaningful in terms of a cost, clinical, or access advantage; and whether the results are reproducible by independent sources. These "story stocks" often require substantial amounts of capital and time before they can produce tangible results, so an investor must demand a substantial discount to future growth to compensate for the risk and time required for the endeavor.

Health care also has a catalyst-driven component to it that differs substantially from other industries. A catalyst, in investing parlance, is an event that can change the value profile of a company instantaneously. Most investors are familiar with quarterly earnings reports, which can change the underlying value of the company or the perception of that value. Health care offers numerous types of information and events beyond simple earnings reports. Such catalysts include the releases of data from clinical trials, approval by the FDA or other regulatory agencies, and reimbursement decisions by the government or other payers. Also referred to as "binary events" because they are often an all-or-nothing proposition, these catalysts can have a profound impact on a company's share price. In terms of value creation, share price action around the time of these information releases can be quite volatile. Even after a product or service is on the market, ongoing clinical trials or other information can come to light that, when released, can change either the value creation or the perception of value creation. Often the postapproval issues are safety-related and predominantly negative, but occasionally experimenting will find novel uses or indications for a product, which can be positive.

From an investing perspective, binary events present a challenge because most valuation measures assume some predictability in revenue, earnings, or cash flow, and catalysts can cause extreme shifts in these results. Investors need to be aware when a binary event is possible and prepare themselves in terms of overall portfolio risk. Generally, companies disclose that trials, regulatory processes, or reimbursement processes are ongoing. Although it is often difficult even for the companies to tell exactly when such results will be available, some window of time within which the event is likely to occur can be estimated. The investor must then apply the appropriate discount to the stock. The amount of the discount is dependent on existing data (outcomes for similar products) and the philosophy of the regulatory or reimbursing body. It is also imperative that investors attempt to understand what discount the market itself is placing on the stocks, often referred to as what is "priced into" the stock. This involves listening to the commentary on the event provided by other analysts or industry experts. If what is priced into the stock differs significantly from what the investor believes is the likely outcome, the investor could benefit if his forecast is correct.

Health care is an industry that is beset by a push and pull between cost pressure and innovation. While cost pressure is well understood in other industries, because health-care inflation has been so pronounced and its economic effects so profound, actions taken to forestall future cost increases have sometimes been extreme. At the same time, medicine has made tremendous strides in improving clinical outcomes for a broad swath of disease states through the development of innovative products and services. The tension between cost control and innovation is unique to health care, since in other industries, other factors would relieve the pressure: either increased competition, availability of substitute products, or government intervention. In other industries, competitors can come to market quickly; in health care, the entry of competitors and the cost deflation that often accompanies it are slower because of regulatory hurdles, limited availability of substitute products, and intellectual property rules. While these hurdles to competition can benefit the health-care investor, they do differentiate the industry from most others.

Health care is also highly interconnected in terms of business relationships between its various subsectors. The various subsectors cannot exist without each other, and to date there has been relatively little horizontal integration—e.g., payers buying product makers— in part because of antikickback and other regulatory issues, but also because the skill sets, infrastructures, and capital needs are so different that integration would have a substantial probability of failure.

This tight interconnection presents both risks and opportunities to health-care investors, but interdependence with other sectors of the industry needs to be considered before deploying capital. Reliance on other entities represents a risk that is outside the companies' control. Though companies have attempted to gain more control of their destinies through such means as direct-to-consumer advertising, exogenous factors that are not directly related to a corporation's business conditions can lead to shocks. If investors understand the interconnectedness of industry subsectors, they can quantify how successful a company's products, services, or payment profile is by watching other subsectors in the group. Choosing the correct subsector or individual company to watch can allow the investor to second-guess the management of her investment.

Health care is not as cyclical as many other industries. It is not as tightly bound to the economy as cyclical industries. Although health care will not have the significant growth in share price that can come from catching the movement from trough to peak for a cyclical company, the health-care investor avoids the risk of misforecasting the economy because an error will not be as detrimental to share price returns as it would be in cyclical industries. The advantage of the lack of cyclicality is that when the economic variable is removed, forecasting earnings and sales can become easier because they are more predictable, and this predictability reduces the possibility of a major shortfall. Predictability should garner a premium valuation in the market, and the reduced volatility that comes with less volatile results should lower an investor's overall portfolio volatility.

Health care is not a commodity, and its profits are not driven by a commodity. Some industries are dependent upon the cost of a commodity, either because they derive profits from selling it directly or because it is a major cost and thus has an impact on profits. In order to make sound health-care investments, investors do not also need to forecast the price movement of a commodity. As with economic cyclicality, the removal of a variable in forecasting for health-care stocks allows the health-care investor greater precision in determining outcomes over the long run. The disadvantage is that a health-care investor misses out on the great returns that can be achieved when a commodity moves in his favor. Health care may one day be commoditized like some parts of the financial system. There are structured products that surround life insurance, so it is not out of the question that creative financial product designers could tailor derivatives contracts to health care. If these structured health-care financial devices are ever constructed, they may give investors more tools with which to use their health reform knowledge.

Innovation in health care, when it has happened, has been rapid (and the trend, if anything, looks as if it will accelerate). The rapid growth rate of some companies' revenue has given rise to the hyper-growth stock. Health care is different from most industries because most industries have a relatively slow pace of development and thus a moderate growth pace. The investment challenge with a hyper-growth stock is how to properly value companies whose products are growing at many times the rate of overall GDP, since clearly the opportunity is not infinite. At some point growth will have to decelerate; the challenge is to determine when that deceleration will occur. This is easier said than done. By focusing on the saturation point and applying some discount to it (the bigger the discount, the more conservative the forecast), the analyst can determine a set of parameters for the valuation. If the company still has many years to go, valuation is less of a concern than if the saturation point could be a near-term event.

Health care is not a utility. Although health can be considered a public good, there are significant roadblocks to pricing the goods and services provided by the industry the way the outputs of the public utility industry are priced. These differences include the wide variations in demand that patients have and the fact that future demand is hard to quantify, given changes in utilization and potential changes in therapeutic regimens. The lack of transparency in pricing does make a utility pricing scheme attractive in some instances; for example, numerous private payers use either Medicare or Medicaid pricing as a starting point for setting their own reimbursement rates, and numerous providers accept these rates. Thus, to some degree, the government is involved in rate setting. Unlike in the utility industry, however, where a state commission or some other regulatory body often sets rates, Medicare and Medicaid rates are set using formulas that are often complex and are difficult for citizens and investors alike to easily comprehend.

There is always the possibility, although it is somewhat unlikely, that some type of agency could set prices in an overt way, and if that were to happen, it would alter the analysis of health-care stocks. Until that happens, investors should make the assumption that no sea change is imminent. In the recent past, information technology has allowed for greater transparency, and although rates paid and contracted for are a competitive tool for providers and payers alike, visibility is likely to increase over time. Companies that can adjust to a new paradigm of greater transparency in rates are likely to have a competitive advantage over those that cannot.

Health care has a moral and ethical component that is lacking in most other industries. It affects both the quality and the duration of life. Because of this impact on life, moral and ethical dilemmas that do not exist in other industries often arise. The importance to life of building an industrial factory is quite different from that of building a hospital in terms of perception, for example. Morality and ethical considerations are things that a health-care investor must contend with because of the nature of the industry. The health-care investor must realize that there are strong opinions on many health-care issues that do not respond to purely economic factors. Euthanasia, end-of-life care, abortion, and stem cells are just some of the moral and ethical dilemmas that companies in this sector face. Given this, it is paramount that the returns expected from any product or service should be discounted appropriately if it has the potential to be derailed by nonfinancial considerations.

WHAT MAKES A GOOD HEALTH-CARE COMPANY?

Health-care companies have their own nuances, which can affect their success or failure. They are companies first, however, and thus investors must first impose some requirements concerning the type of franchise they wish to invest in, as they would with any other industry or company. While there is some disagreement among the many researchers, there are some generally agreed-upon standards of how to define a "good company." A definition of a good company is a company that returns capital at a level above that which is invested—basically getting more out than an investor puts in. A company with a sustainable competitive advantage is considered promising. A competitive advantage is any way in which a company is better than its competition, and this list could be infinite. The more obvious competitive advantages are better products, less expensive products, a better research and development organization, and a better sales organization.

The ability to maintain these advantages over the competition is in itself a competitive advantage, as this can create longer-term shareholder returns, and coming from a position of strength in the industry can make it easer for the company to adapt should the corporate environment change (which in an era of health-care reform is almost a given). Because of the way the industry is oriented, in an era of reform, the most important differentiating advantage that a health-care company can have is either to improve the quality of care, improve the cost of care, or improve the access to care. Companies that show an ability to do any of these three things (preferably all of them) and do so in a sustainable way are likely to create shareholder value.

Good markets are another important factor in looking for superior companies. Despite any competitive advantage a company may have, if its markets are in decline or otherwise lackluster, it will be more difficult for that company to drive increased shareholder value. Although difficult to define, a good health-care market is one in which there is ample present demand and the opportunity for future demand for a product or service. In good markets, there is demand at prices that allow a company to make profit. In an optimal market, competition will be limited, although in reality an above-average profitable market will eventually draw in new entrants. Health care is made up of numerous submarkets, some of which are very good and some of which are quite poor in terms of this definition. There are some health-care submarkets that have yet to be created, depending on the pace of innovation. For a health-care investor, it is incumbent that she understand the market opportunity and market dynamics (competition, substitution potential, and demand) in order to appropriately determine the viability of a given market.

Management is yet another component that is often used to differentiate a good company from a bad company. Defining good management, like many other areas of company analysis, is more subjective than quantifiable. As in other subjective areas, there is no firm agreement on what makes a good management team, but there are some general features that a good management team should have. It should have the ability to set goals that will lead to profitable actions and successfully execute on those goals. It should be able to make good decisions on business questions where judgment is required. It needs to motivate employees and communicate effectively. A good management team should be able to develop a culture that rewards success. It should always be looking for ways to improve the business and be willing to make changes when they are called for. It should be able to identify potential risks to the franchise and act accordingly. It should have a vision for what the franchise, the industry, and the overall market environment will look like in the future and a strategy to take advantage of the changes. For health-care companies, the ability to explain complex clinical concepts to investors is an important characteristic. Managing highly technical people like researchers in an effective way is a core competency. A management team that understands public health, regulatory, and reimbursement issues is a must for health-care companies.

Determining whether a management team is able to accomplish these goals is often difficult for an investor; however, a history of accomplishing some of these goals should be evident in the success of the business and the growth in the value of the company. While investors should be rightly skeptical about future plans, a history of achieving goals should give investors some confidence. For health-care investors, because change is so important to the health-care industry, a vision and a strategy along with the ability to execute are the most important capabilities. An investor with an understanding of health-care reform can compare her vision of the future with that of the management team to see if the two are in sync; if they are, there is potential for value creation.

Conservatism is another important factor in distinguishing a solid company from inferior companies. A high-quality company takes a conservative approach to accounting. Accounting rules give companies significant latitude in terms of recognizing revenue and costs and of valuing assets. From an investment point of view, the more conservative (assuming the least benefit to the company) the stance the management takes, the more likely it is that there will be a positive outcome for investors. An aggressive accrual policy and other such accounting approaches are associated with underperformance of share price.[1]

Conservatism in the way the company sets investor expectations is another way in which a more tempered approach can aid investors. Expectations can involve earnings- and sales-related issues (growth or actual results), timelines for certain corporate events (product launches), or other corporate outcomes (cost cutting). Missed expectations (particularly earnings) are a driver of share price underperformance, particularly for growth stocks.[2] Missed expectations are not a guarantee of future underperformance, however; sometimes the issues that lead to the missed expectations are temporary, and the company can recover from them. However, the more conservative the company's approach to setting investor expectations, the less likely it is that these expectations will be missed. Investors can raise their expectations on their own without management's participation, but a conservative management is likely to take steps to make sure that investors' expectations are realistic and can be exceeded if conditions warrant.

The opposite of conservatism in expectations is the notion of the "too promotional" company. There are companies that spend more time selling their potential than they spend actually executing on the core fundamentals. Generally, these companies appear to be managing the price of the stock rather than managing their business. Investors need to be wary of companies that overpromise and underdeliver when it comes to results. Because health care is so often catalyst-driven, and in an era of reform is going to be change-driven, conservatism in both accounting and future performance will be paramount. Within a certain margin of error, expectations can be set that are conservative, and health-care investors should focus on those companies that have shown an ability to be conservative in both their accounting and their ability to forecast expectations and achieve them.

Being shareholder-minded is another characteristic that distinguishes superior companies from inferior companies. Because all companies are subject to the same principal-agent conflicts found in health care, it is incumbent on investors to identify the more shareholder-friendly companies, as they are the more likely to drive shareholder return. Corporate governance is a component of shareholder friendliness whose principles include compensation for managers based on performance and the ability of shareholders to make changes in management or corporate direction. The more a company considers shareholders in the decision process, the better it can be considered with regard to being shareholder-friendly. Corporate governance drives positive returns, with more shareholder-friendly companies outperforming.[3] Communication with shareholders is a way in which companies can evince shareholder friendliness. The more open the communication, the better able shareholders will be to properly understand the business and place a value on it. There are certain prohibitions, both legal and competitive, that explain why complete transparency is probably unachievable, but despite that, the more shareholder communication there is, assuming that the companies are accurate in their comments, the better off investors will be. Because health care is a changing industry, frequent updates on the altering landscape will be helpful in making capital deployment decisions, so the more communicative a company is, especially in the context of good corporate governance practices, the more likely it is that investors will see positive returns.

Loss-making companies, although they can be good investments, offer significant financial risk if they cannot alter their loss-making trajectory. Profitable companies give investors confidence that they will not cease to be going concerns as a result of foreseeable near-term financial issues. Also important in understanding the financial situations of companies is the visibility with which investors and the managements themselves can anticipate financial results. The more accurately a management is able to forecast profits using both sales and costs as inputs, the more likely it is that it will be able to avoid surprises, plan for the future, and design a strategy.

For investors, the better their ability to verify a company's financial performance, the more confidence they can have in deploying their capital in that investment. Companies with good visibility and lower earnings risk should be given a premium. Superior companies require modest amounts of external capital, if any, to fund their business operations. The need to raise external capital can dilute the holdings of the existing shareholders, puts the company at financial risk if it fails to raise capital, or at a minimum limits the company's ability to execute if capital is unavailable. Health-care investors should pay special attention to profitability; in addition, current profitability may not be as important as future profitability, particularly for innovative companies, given how high margins on successful therapeutic agents can be. Current profitability and whether a company needs to raise future capital are important considerations, particularly for less mature businesses in the health-care sector.

The key value drivers of superior health-care companies will be those that have a positive impact on cost, quality, and access under a shifting reform paradigm. Therefore, not only will the superior company's products have to be able to improve the system, but management will also require an understanding of the changing landscape.

Patient referral patterns are a factor that may determine the success or failure of a health-care product or service. Companies must understand how patients access their product or services and who drives the patient flow. Since the use of services and products is generally driven by third parties (often physicians), it is incumbent on companies to understand these channels: who provides the care, who refers the patient to the care, and what types of systems or services are required to accompany the product. Understanding the referral channels can lead to better strategy, as well as to the ability to alter sales practices to optimize the existing infrastructure. It is incumbent on investors to understand how these referral channels operate in order to determine whether a company is addressing the channel successfully and to quantify the earnings streams from a given business line.

As the payment sources for health care are highly fragmented, successful companies will understand the reimbursement sources for their products or services. Those companies that receive the majority of their reimbursement from the government need to act in one way, while those that receive most of their reimbursement from private payers may have to operate in another way. Generally speaking, reimbursement from private payers is higher than that from government sources. The government has numerous payers (Medicare, Medicaid, and the Veterans Administration), each of which has its own remuneration systems. The process of having their products or services accepted for reimbursement by the various payers is also something that service providers and product makers must understand. There are different thresholds for acceptance across the wide spectrum of payers. All payers have specific rules about performance standards, and those companies that can best stay within the guidelines are the best positioned to maintain good contract standing. The most successful companies will understand who their reimbursement targets are and optimize their strategy to reach the greatest number of those that provide the highest reimbursement. For investors, it is critical to identify those companies with the best ability to maximize the opportunity from the byzantine reimbursement system.

Health-care companies must also be cognizant of what their service areas are. Although this may apply more to provider and payer companies, product companies are not completely immune from geographic issues, especially with regard to logistics. There are wide variations in practice patterns and health-care demand patterns across different geographic areas. Understanding what is happening in a particular geographic area, in terms of utilization or competition, is the key to developing a profit-maximization strategy. From a logistics point of view, some areas require more resources dedicated to logistics in order to improve corporate performance. Areas may face differing levels of competition and, depending on market share, may or may not qualify as targets of new market development or continued market presence. The companies that best understand service area dynamics have a strategic edge, as they can deploy their resources more efficiently and gain a competitive edge. Much of this information can be accumulated and analyzed through the use of technology, so those companies that can use technology effectively have an edge. Companies with a proven track record of understanding service areas the best are worthy of investment consideration.

Health care is a heavily regulated industry, with issues ranging from safety to marketing to antikickback regulations, and eventually to outcomes and pay for performance. The companies that create value for shareholders will be those that are able to deal with the wide-ranging compliance issues that will inevitably crop up in the course of doing business in the sector. A superior company will be proactive in reducing potential negative compliance outcomes before they happen. The problem with dealing with compliance issues after the fact is that doing so usually results in at least increased legal fees and possibly financial penalties and has possible negative market ramifications ranging from bad public relations to actual market nonacceptance because other players do not want to deal with a company that is perceived to be "out of compliance." The ability to comply with regulation can separate superior companies in the sector.

Health care is delivered at a wide variety of locations. These sites of care can include hospitals, outpatient procedure centers, physician offices, retail-based clinics, and even homes. Health-care companies need to understand where their product or service is being delivered and how to optimize the assets at these sites of care to maximize profits. Some sites of care may be inefficient for some types of services, and moving care to better sites, from either an outcome or a cost point of view (e.g., from a hospital ER to a physician office), makes sense. Those companies that can match sites of care with products delivered most successfully are more likely to add to shareholder value. For investors, the most important question to ask is if the companies are actually maximizing the efficiencies at the various sites of care.

In an era of reform, health-care companies will face an environment that will place an emphasis on cost-effectiveness, or proving that their product or service delivers some pharmacoeconomic benefit over other options. Few other industries will see their products and services scrutinized as much by the public, the government, and private payers. Pharmacoeconomic benefit is difficult to define and may require studies that are expensive and logistically difficult to complete. Shareholder value will accrue to companies that can prove that they offer significant benefits to the system. Those companies that can facilitate the illustration of that benefit (research organizations or laboratories, for example) could also see added value. The superior companies understand that pharmacoeconomic benefit is a differentiating factor from both a marketing standpoint and a premium reimbursement perspective. Investors should focus their efforts on those companies that have a proven track record of displaying pharmacoeconomic benefit from their products and services.

Superior health-care companies also have a consistent ability to achieve returns on their R&D investments. Although this statement is true across many industries, it is among the most critical success factors that an innovative health-care company can have. Intellectual property rules allow competition for compounds to appear after a finite amount of time, and without a continuous stream of new products, companies producing therapeutic agents can find themselves with significant declines in revenue. Medical technology companies, which also see competition, need to build a better mousetrap and overtake their competitors in an industry where the pace of innovation seems to be accelerating. R&D productivity is difficult to measure and also difficult to encourage. Advances in R&D are made through "eureka!" moments rather than by designating a certain percentage of revenue for R&D. Companies that allow researchers scientific freedom, with no penalties for failure, and that have a research management that is proficient in allocating resources to successful programs and killing failures early in the process tend to do better than those that do not. One of the ways in which investors can judge if a company is capable of consistent R&D growth is to look at its track record of success with organic (not acquired) new product development. Those companies with superior R&D, particularly for novel products and services that deliver pharmacoeconomic value, will also create shareholder value.

HEALTH-CARE-SPECIFIC RISKS

Accompanying the health-care-specific nuances are risks that are specific to the health-care industry. The development of clinical projects has a high failure risk.[4] Given that clinical events are often all-or-nothing propositions, higher discounts are required for clinical projects, particularly those involving novel diseases or novel therapeutic classes. Health care also faces very intense regulatory scrutiny, both before and after the product or service is on the market. What a regulator deems to be safe and effective may differ from what a company believes is safe and effective. Failure to receive approval is an ever-present danger for companies, as the approval of many different agencies across the globe is required. A clinical trial is usually conducted under somewhat unusual circumstances vis-à-vis the real world. Clinical trials usually enroll small populations of people under tightly controlled circumstances. The performance of a product in the real world, where it is exposed to larger populations and noncontrolled circumstances, can be markedly different from what is seen in the trial setting. Therefore, even after a product is on the market, regulatory risk is an ongoing factor.

Once a product is on the market, payers of all stripes will have a say about its value. Companies can set any price they want for the product, and, depending on its pharmacoeconomic value, they often get a price somewhere near what they ask for. However, reimbursement agencies, in an effort to control costs, can differ with the innovator about the value of a product and reimburse accordingly. Reimbursement availability can contribute to a product's success. If a product or service fails to be accepted for reimbursement, the commercial opportunity could be severely curtailed. Investors must understand the risk that some products and services may not be paid for at any price, depending on what else is available across the wide range of products and services. For service providers and payers, reimbursement risks take a somewhat different form than for products. These companies' concerns are that reimbursement exceeds the cost of providing care in the short term (in the longer term, it is easier to offset increased costs by raising prices). If costs rise more quickly than expected, or if reimbursement declines, there could be a significant loss; therefore, forecasting both short-term reimbursement revenue and costs is paramount.

Like products and services in other industries, health-care products are subject to market risk. However, the final user of the product or service (the patient) is often not the party who is responsible for choosing that product or service. Therefore, market adoption has a great deal to do with successfully creating demand on the part of intermediaries. Investors must be cognizant of this type of adoption risk.

Because health care is changing rapidly, obsolescence risk is always a possibility for products. Like adoption risk, because of the third-party decision-making element, obsolescence risk can be fast or slow, depending on the specialty and the pharmacoeconomic advantage. Health care is an innovating industry, so many products will eventually be surpassed by superior products because the understanding of the disease process increases over time.

Intellectual property risk is yet another issue for health-care investors. Health care can be a capital-intensive industry that requires specialized knowledge to develop innovative treatments. Once the resources—financial, human, and intellectual—have been deployed to create an innovative product or service, in all likelihood that product or service will be easily duplicable. If it is duplicated too quickly, the investment will not be able to deliver a positive return because an entity that did not have to invest capital will be able to underprice the innovator and still make an economic profit. Because health care is expensive and there are areas of the globe that do not have the wherewithal to make such investments, free-riding on intellectual property is a risk that could endanger investment returns. At one time, intellectual property was considered somewhat sacrosanct; however, in an era when information is as free as it is now, the health-care analyst must price some intellectual property risk into the investment.

NOTES

1. Konan Chan, Narasimhan Jegadeesh, Louis K. C. Chan, and Josef Lakonishok, "Earnings Quality and Stock Returns: The Evidence from Accruals," Feb. 15, 2001; available at SSRN, http://ssrn.com/abstract=259691.
2. Douglas J. Skinner and Richard G. Sloan, "Earnings Surprises, Growth Expectations, and Stock Returns: Don't Let an Earnings Torpedo Sink Your Portfolio," July 1999; available at SSRN, http://ssrn.com/abstract=172060.
3. K. J. Martijn Cremers and Vinay B. Nair, "Governance Mechanisms and Equity Prices," August 2003; Yale ICF Working Paper No. 03-15; NYU Center for Law and Business Research Paper No. 03-09; AFA 2004 San Diego Meetings.
4. Mark P. Mathieu (ed.), *Parexel's Bio/Pharmaceutical R&D Statistical Sourcebook 2007/2008* (Waltham, Mass.: Parexel International Corp., 2007), p. 212.

CHAPTER 8

Fundamental Techniques for Picking the Right Stocks

While there is a seemingly infinite number of ways to pick stocks (and investments in other asset classes, for that matter), one of the most common methods is fundamental analysis. Fundamental analysis involves looking at the business conditions of a company or industry to determine whether these conditions will lead to positive returns. There are two ways to conduct fundamental analysis. One is top-down, looking at macro-economic factors, market conditions, asset classes, broad industry groups, regions, and styles to determine their potential for growth. Bottom-up analysis involves looking at an individual company's unique characteristics to determine whether it can drive returns. The goal of any analysis is to identify hidden (or not well observed by the market) value, growth, or risks of a potential investment and invest when the price of the company diverges from the value.

Profiting from changes in the prices of health-care company shares that are related to health-care reform is an example of using fundamental top-down investing. In this approach, investors will be looking at macro- and microtrends to determine where future profit exists. Because companies that are direct competitors can vary widely in terms of their quality and return potential, many analysts also use analytic techniques with company-specific information to determine the true underlying value of individual companies. There are some basic techniques that fundamental analysts use in making a decision to buy or sell shares in a company. These techniques are applicable to a wide range of companies, including companies in the health-care industry. In some cases, these techniques need to be adapted to accommodate analytical challenges that are specific to the health-care industry.

IDEA GENERATION

Idea generation is often the starting point for the analysis that an investor must do in order to identify target companies for investigation to determine if there is return potential. There are a number of ways to determine whether a company is worth investigating, although some seem to have better success rates than others. Thinking about health-care reform in advance of an actual announcement or initiative is a useful way to anticipate (before the market does) how the reform program will play out. The next step is to invest in companies that will benefit, then wait for the information cascade to bring the herd (the majority of investors) to the same conclusion.[1] This approach does require the analyst not to try to outsmart the market by being *too* far ahead of it, as this can lead to negative returns, especially for those with shorter time horizons. This approach also requires some vision, as the analyst must look forward and imagine the future.

In addition to anticipating which sectors may benefit from health-care reform, quantitative screening is another way of iden-tifying investable ideas. This requires an analyst to establish a set of parameters (usually financial); if a company moves below or above a predetermined level of a variable (valuation or growth, for example), the analyst can then conduct further research on the company. Yet another method is to determine whether a company is seeing a major change in its business, often referred to as an inflection point or catalyst. A major change can signal that there will be a major change in valuation. Companies that are undergoing individual change as a result of a major secular change like health-care reform may be worthy of further study. Inflection points can also be identified by changes at competitors, suppliers, or customers. Changes at other points in the health-care channel can signal that alterations will be felt elsewhere in the system in the future.

Unusual price action in a company's stock, either up or down, may also indicate to an analyst that the company is worthy of future investigation. Sometimes companies' shares are unfairly punished or rewarded as a result of market factors or other issues that are not related to long-term company or industry fundamentals. If there is a significant move in a stock, an analyst may want to research the company to determine whether the move is justified; if it is not, there may be a positive return possibility. An analyst may be able to identify stocks with positive return potential by staying in the information flow of an industry. During a process of health-care reform, staying current with the news or industry information can be of value in identifying winners and losers. The risk is that the analyst becomes overloaded with information and cannot distinguish value-added insight from misinformation.

FINANCIAL STATEMENT ANALYSIS

Once an idea has been selected for further investigation, the starting point of a company analysis is usually to review a company's financial statements. These are documents that public companies are required to file that discuss the company's financial performance in some preceding period. Understanding how to interpret the various financial statements gives the analyst significant insight into the operations of the business. The analyst can then verify the data about the company's business that he is getting from other sources, including management and other industry sources such as suppliers, customers, and competitors.

At the highest level, investors should expect the financial statements to paint an accurate picture of the company's business. Investors expect that companies will generally be honest in reporting their financials. However, since companies do have latitude in certain areas of accounting, such as accruals, their decisions in these areas can have an impact on their reported information.

Overly aggressive accruals can be predictive of underper-formance,[2] but there are numerous other indicators of potential financial statement quality problems as well, including, but not limited to, aggressive revenue recognition, using one-time events to boost results, recording costs improperly, and the use of off-balance-sheet entities.[3] Other financial statement categories, such as management compensation, related-party transactions, and legal proceedings, should also be monitored for potential risk factors affecting the business. Changes in inventories, accounts receivable, gross margins, selling expenses, capital expenditures, inventory methods, and labor and sales force productivity have been predictive of abnormal future returns.[4] Therefore, these items should be investigated to make sure that there are no significant changes. An analyst should have enough familiarity with corporate accounting techniques to understand when accounting is being aggressive and make sure to discount her level of return accordingly.

Once the analyst has established that the financial statements are an accurate reflection of the business reality, he then needs to look for trends in business conditions. When an analyst detects that a company's financial condition is heading in a certain direction and can verify that this trend is either decelerating or accelerating, this merits further research. There is a danger with extrapolation, as many unforeseen events can affect results and make the future different from the past, so it is incumbent on the analyst to risk-adjust any extrapolation of prior trends. The closer a forecast of future performance can be to the ultimate reality, the more likely it is that the investor will be able to achieve positive returns, all else being equal.

Investors can get a sense of how successful previous management decisions have been by looking at the financial statements. If management made good choices, then the capital it deployed was able to generate returns in excess of what the company invested. If management made poor business choices, that should be evident from an evaluation of the financial statements as well. If there are untapped assets or other capital that could be deployed, but is producing suboptimal results, that is also worth observing, as another management team might be more willing or able to monetize this capital. In addition to using financial statements as a management evaluation tool, investors should look at them to see if they have been predictive of future results in the past. If prior period results have in fact been useful in determining future period results, that should raise investors' confidence in the predictive capability of financial statements, although, as alluded to earlier, the caveat is that the future is not predictable with any certainty.

Financial statements should also be able to offer clues as to whether the company's current performance is sustainable or whether there may be a change coming in the future. In this case, it is a question of determining what is driving performance. Driving sales by offering below-cost prices is not sustainable, whereas increasing demand by opening new markets may in fact be sustainable. Understanding the sources of performance should be able to offer the investor some hints about the sustainability of that performance. The more sustainable a business, the more likely it is that it will be a successful investment.

Another way to use financial statements is to compare a target company's financial results with those of other members of its industry group. Different companies use different accounting methods and often do not have exactly the same business models, product mixes, or geographic presence, and this can make apples-to-apples comparisons difficult. Wide variations in growth rates or margin rates among companies can be meaningful and are worthy of further exploration by the investor. Even if the numbers are not exact, if the business trends seen by the various companies in the industry are similar, this can increase the investor's confidence that these trends are industrywide and not company specific. Industrywide trends are easier to quantify than company-specific trends because there are far more data points and data sources to access in order to verify the trend's existence and quantify its impact.

With respect to health-care reform, many financial statements have a section in which management discusses what it sees in the current operating environment. Investors should monitor this section to see if management understands the nature of health-care reform and if it is developing a strategy for dealing with this. Investors should also evaluate any section that discusses interaction with government agencies, as reform will almost certainly have a government component to it. A change in the regulatory framework could represent risk for companies that are not equipped to deal with it, as any regulatory error is likely to be disclosed. In addition to sales and earnings growth and asset utilization, which are important for all companies, product makers need to see returns on their R&D investments to ensure a steady stream of future growth drivers. For service companies, which tend to have lower margins than product makers, costs are extremely important, particularly for companies, like HMOs, that take on financial risk and thus can see substantial losses if costs rise above plan.

FORECASTING

Once a company's baseline financial condition has been established using its financial statements, the next step is forecasting (sometimes referred to as modeling) the future performance of the firm. The goal of modeling is to attempt to draw as accurate a projection of the future of the firm as possible because the more accurate an analyst's assessment of a company's financial success (or failure), the more accurate he will be in placing a value on the shares in the present. The end result is to arrive at a point where it is possible to determine whether the share's current price is justified by the current and future profitability of the firm and the future business conditions, or whether the share price under- or overstates the value. If a mispricing can be identified, the investor can see a positive return when the market eventually recognizes the mispricing and reprices the shares accordingly. However, predicting the future is a subjective matter that relies on extrapolating from the past and using analytic judgment to incorporate the anticipated future events or trends that will alter a firm's financial picture.

There are some issues to be aware of when forecasting financial performance. The investor must determine what attributes drive performance. Some companies are driven by sales growth, while others are driven by how efficiently they utilize their assets. The analyst must match the forecasted variables with the business drivers if the forecast is to be an accurate assessment of the company's value creation. A mismatch of forecast and value drivers will render the model unillustrative. Predictability is another important character of a forecast. More predictable firms often outperform less predictable firms.[5] This is especially true for earnings and revenues, but any unpredictable line item is likely to cause uncertainty for investors, and investors tend to reduce the value they place on a company in uncertain situations.

In addition to earnings visibility, the sustainability of performance is also important. Financial performance generally reverts to the mean.[6] It is important to judge whether future changes in financial performance are temporary in nature or whether there are secular changes in certain factors that will allow the altered level of performance to continue over the longer term. Many companies go through a life cycle, during which financial performance can vary depending on whether the company is in the early stages of its growth or whether growth has stopped because of the maturing of the company or its markets. Using longer-term trends can help smooth out temporary factors and identify changes in the company's growth profile.

The output of any forecast is a function of its assumptions, so analysts need to pay attention to what types of factors they are using to drive the model. No model is foolproof, and overreliance on any one model for decision making is risky. A model is, after all, an idealized version of reality, and is only as good as the quality of information that goes into it, the accuracy of assumptions made within it, and the ability to analyze the output. An optimal approach uses assumptions that are achievable and predictable in their own right. Sensitivity analysis is the process of running the assumptions using a variety of possible scenarios to see if they are feasible. The most conservative approach would be to assume the absolute worst-case scenario. If the assumptions still hold, the forecast is viable. As the forecast moves away from the worst case, the risk increases, as a worst-case scenario, even one that is unforeseen, always remains a possibility. Assumptions should be able to stand up to a basic commonsense test. If the assumptions are unreasonable, they will produce a forecast that is not predictive. It is also imperative that the analyst understands the potential level of error embedded in her assumptions. The larger the potential errors, the less predictive the forecast will be. If the analyst has a good idea of the limitations of the forecast, then she can probably adjust the model and may be able to increase its predictive value.

The time frame also plays a role in the model. Near-term forecasts tend to be more accurate because changes in many business factors take time, so near-term visibility is usually greater than that for longer-term forecasts. Forecasts with very short time frames (months or weeks) can have their own elements of volatility embedded in them, such as temporary disruptions and changes in order patterns for big-ticket items. Interpretation of the output of a model is another factor that the analyst must attend to. The analyst must be able to place the forecast in the context of Wall Street expectations as well as being able to place a value on what the model projects.

Many public companies issue their own projections of the future, which are referred to in Wall Street parlance as guidance.

The time frames over which companies issue such guidance can vary, but investors often use guidance as a tool for making future projections of future performance. The analyst can then use the company's ability to perform in accordance with its guidance to evaluate the success of its performance. One would assume that companies would be able to forecast their own performance, but it often happens that a company uses faulty assumptions of its own. It is incumbent on the analyst to develop assumptions independent of the company to determine if the company's management is being realistic, conservative, and accurate. The financial community relies fairly heavily on the company in setting expectations, particularly with regard to the quarterly earnings report. So if expectations are exceeded or missed, there will be a reaction as well as some drift in the direction of the performance.[7] Companies that are consistent in their ability to achieve the results set out in their initial guidance are generally rewarded with a premium even if their short-term performance is not indicative of their longer-term ability.

By convention, many Wall Street financial models are sales-driven. This means that once sales are forecasted, the other financial measures (cash flow, inventory turns, earnings) can be derived from that number. While there are other potential starting points, forecasting sales has an intuitive appeal because it is relatively simple compared to other forecastable metrics and because revenue in and of itself can be a useful valuation measure.[8] To derive sales, the first step is to determine a maximum market. For a health-care company, the number of markets and market sizes can be estimated with some precision, at least in the United States, because of the number of databases of diseases and population kept both by the government and by private entities. Then the task becomes one of forecasting adoption rates or market share capture. These rates will vary depending on competition, pharmacoeconomic value, and the company's effectiveness in the sales process, among other things. The analyst must then take costs into account, and those will vary by company. Other than at hyper-growth firms, most company metrics should not move a great deal over short periods of time. If they do, it is at least an analytic yellow flag to determine why this substantial movement has occurred. Over the long term, analysts should focus on modeling the rate of change of various metrics.

As with other modeling assumptions, the rate of change should be reasonable in the context of what is achievable from the business.

Beyond financial metrics, health-care companies present other forecasting challenges. The outcome of any reform plan will clearly play a role in any financial forecast, as it will affect the volume of goods and services sold, and potentially the cost or price of those goods and services. Even without reform, the health-care industry regularly sees changes in reimbursement rates, so the analyst needs to forecast the timing and magnitude of those changes as well. The clinical component of health care also needs to be forecasted, and it is important to recognize that a change in a treatment paradigm caused by the approval of a new therapy developed either by a company or by one of its competitors can substantially alter a financial forecast.

Competition can come from generic versions of a product (after product patents expire) or from companies with "me-too" similar products—possibilities that are not often found in other industries. Again, the entrance of potential competition needs to be a component of a forecast. Because health care has a significant regulatory component, the timing of regulatory actions can have an important impact on a company's financial performance, and the investor should be cognizant of this. Some health-care companies are not financially driven, but rather are catalyst driven; these can include smaller therapeutic companies that are paid fees for achieving certain goals in clinical development, referred to as milestones. With those companies, the analyst must be aware of the timing of such payments and the probability of the company's receiving them.

The extremely fast-growing company is another type of entity found in health care. Since nothing grows forever, the analytic challenge is determining when the rate of growth will ultimately slow. For innovative products, this is a challenge, particularly if a product can address more than one discrete market. In addition to modeling using adoption rates, statistical techniques such as the Verhulst equation can be used to anticipate adoption rates, but care should be taken, as investor expectations around hyper-growth companies can often get ahead of what the company is reasonably able to accomplish in a short period of time. A key to developing a revenue and earnings model for a hyper-growth company will be to forecast the point in time when the product will reach its saturation point and at what volume level that will be.

There is a seasonal factor in health-care forecasting as well; the summer tends to be a slow time for elective procedures (particularly in Europe), while the flu season in late fall and winter and the tendency for companies to buy medical capital equipment at year end raise utilization. Modeling a product or service's pharmacoeconomic value is also a challenge, but determining its true worth to patients and the system is a key to anticipating demand. This is a function of the product or service's ability to alter the cost, quality, or access for health care. Determining this is not simple, but it is necessary in order to determine the ultimate success of the product or service. The market may offer some clues to the value of the product, as the earlier and faster the adoption of a product or service, the more likely it is to be of pharmacoeconomic value to the system.

VALUATION

Since the goal of investing is to buy stocks that go up and to short-sell or avoid stocks that go down, the price at which one purchases a security is probably the most important factor in determining returns. The purpose of valuation is to determine the intrinsic value or worth of the company. If the company's worth (intrinsic value) is not reflected in the price of the stock, then there ought to be opportunities to take advantage of this information. This concept rests on the fact that the market is somewhat efficient, but that it occasionally misprices a stock relative to its true worth. The market's level of efficiency is a highly debated topic, but there is some evidence that the market is semiefficient, and that is enough to justify the use of fundamental analysis to seek out gains.[9]

There are essentially three things an analyst can value when it comes to stock selection: assets, current earnings, and future growth. There are also a number of techniques an analyst can employ to determine whether the business characteristics (financial strength, profitability, asset value, growth potential, and risk) are properly reflected in the public market valuation of the stock. There is relative valuation, where a company is compared to its peer group or to its own history using some measure of share value, like price, and a financial metric, like earnings. There is private market valuation, where the company is assessed in terms of what a strategic or financial buyer would pay for the assets. There is also absolute valuation, where a company's future cash flows are discounted to determine a proper present value. Each of these approaches has its adherents, and successful investments have been made on the basis of many types of analysis.

Converting a financial forecast into a valuation rests on the analyst's ability to select the proper valuation approach that suits the type of company, time frame, and risk involved. There are no hard-and-fast rules for defining what valuation method to use, when to use it, or what types of inputs lead to the optimal valuation. Some general guidelines are useful, however. The intuitive approach is to seek out the sources of value for a given company (how the company currently or potentially will make the majority of its money) and place a value on those items first, before going on to place a value on the rest of the franchise. Companies with assets and relatively predictable and slow-growing earnings streams are amenable to asset analysis or cash flow analysis. Companies in innovative industries, with limited assets and a value that is predicated on their potential, are more amenable to relative valuation or private market valuation.

MULTIPLES

Multiples, usually developed by comparing the price of the shares to a financial metric like earnings, can be used either to compare a company to other companies, to compare a company to its historical valuation, or to evaluate a company based on forecasted fundamentals. The attraction of using multiples is that they are easy to calculate and readily available. They are commonly used and are often the basis for investor expectations and Wall Street price targets. Low price/earnings ratios, price/book ratios, and dividend yield (dividend to price), among others, are associated with outperformance.[10]

There are some cautions that need to be considered when using multiples. Companies can use different accounting methods, which sometimes make even comparisons between companies in the same industry difficult. Different industries and subindustries are often evaluated with different metrics,[11] so using one metric across multiple industry groups may not be predictive. It is important that when an analyst is choosing comparable companies, she chooses those with similar businesses, business models, and accounting standards; without this, the ratio analysis may not be illustrative. When using multiples based on forecasted values, if the forecast is incorrect, the ratio will also be incorrect, so discounts must be applied to multiples used in this way. Some discounts include the errors around predictability, time horizon of the forecast, and volatility of outcomes of the forecast.

Multiples are particularly useful when forecasting the performance of growth companies with high but changing rates of growth, as the multiples can be adjusted dynamically to suit both a short- and an intermediate-term time horizon and adoption rate. Given their ease of use and ability to be adapted to different types of companies, multiples can be applied across a wide variety of health-care industries and companies. Multiples given to a company's assets, earnings, or growth are not static and can expand or compress over time, given factors like competitive challenges, new market features, or changes in predictability, among others.

PRESENT-VALUE MODELS

Dividend discount models and discounted cash flow models are examples of combining a projection of future cash flows with a terminal value discounted back to the present to determine the value of a company. The important factors with this approach are determining what the cash flows will be, when they will occur, and what the terminal value will be. There is a wide variety of measures of cash flow, time horizons, and terminal values. This can often make present-value models complex. As with the multiple approach to valuation, the output of the model is a function of its assumptions, so the better the assumptions, the closer the approximation to the true value or worth of the company. Because of their complexity, these models can easily convey a "false sense of precision,"[12] so care must be taken to ensure that this approach is used with the right type of company and that the assumptions are within the realm of reason. In general, this type of valuation approach is useful with larger companies like health-care distributors that do not see much change in their cash flows over a relatively long period of time or health-care service companies with similar profiles. For companies that are subject to wild swings in profitability as a result of the development of new products or companies whose fortunes may be altered radically by reform, this approach may not be appropriate.

PRIVATE MARKET VALUATION

Analyzing companies from a potential acquirer's point of view is another way to approach valuation. Acquisitions have been common in the health-care industry, so this method is one that health-care investors should focus on. Most companies will not be acquired, so using this method gives the analyst a range of values that the company might be worth rather than a pinpoint value as the market may perceive it. The first consideration is what type of buyer may be making the purchase. A purchaser who is simply seeking a positive financial return (a financial buyer) will approach valuation differently from a strategic buyer, for whom the assets and growth may fit more synergistically. Buyers of franchises use valuation approaches similar to those used by equity investors to determine what price to pay for the franchises. There is usually a record of recent acquisitions in the sector on which an analyst can base his assumptions concerning discount rates and multiples paid. The issues with this method are that the multiples paid for companies can change depending on the financing climate, the scarcity value of the asset, and the strategic fit for a buyer.

Companies are not completely comparable, either as businesses or as strategic assets, so caution should be used. The strategic buyer is also considering the notion of reproduction costs—that is, what value the buyer would place on the company if it needed to build a replica of the company. That determination has a great deal to do with the current cost structure and capabilities of the strategic buyer. A sum of the parts analysis is the way to develop a reproduction value. With this technique, an analyst attempts to value a company by separating it into different parts and valuing them independently, with the goal of adding them up to determine the overall franchise value. Although this method can be effective, it requires the analyst to have detailed segment data and often good comparables for the segments, which are not always available. Using private market values can be useful when looking at companies that are not earning any profit or revenue or companies that may add value to a larger entity.

GROWTH

While it is potentially the most difficult aspect to value, future earnings (sales and cash flow) growth is possibly also the most important item for analysts anticipating health-care reform that will alter growth rates. The problem with valuing potential growth is that it will take place in the future, and predicting the future with a high degree of certainty is impossible. There are some considerations to keep in mind when placing a value on future growth. The first is the degree of visibility of this growth. Does the company have good visibility, either through long-term contracts or through some other assurances that predictions of growth can be made with some accuracy? The more measurement precision there is, the higher the premium that the growth stream deserves.

The rate of change of the growth rate and whether the growth rate is accelerating or decelerating are important considerations in valuing the growth potential. Accelerating growth rates deserve more of a premium than decelerating rates of growth. The sustainability and duration of growth are also important considerations. Since it appears that very few companies can grow at rates much higher than market rates (GDP, population growth) over long periods of time, determining how sustainable a company's growth is and how long the company can continue to grow are also essential. The longer the growth can continue, the higher the valuation that is warranted.

The sources of growth are also important in determining the value of the growth stream. Is growth mostly derived from internal sources (organic growth), or does it come from outside sources, either acquisitions or some other exogenous entity? Organic growth has the virtue of being more easily controlled by the company and deserves a premium, while reliance on outside forces for growth adds an element of uncertainty to the valuation and merits a discount. The number of threats to growth in the form of competition or other forces, such as regulators, lowers any premium valuation given the growth. The growth rate should get more of a premium valuation if there are many opportunities for future growth; however, unrealized opportunities should be probability adjusted to reach a proper valuation.

The same type of analysis that was used for growth can also be applied to existing earnings power, except that the data are less subject to variability. Valuation of any type is subjective, and the risk is that the analyst will overvalue potential and undervalue what exists. The analyst should always assume the worst case, and if the company still merits consideration, there is a good potential for positive returns.

QUALITATIVE RESEARCH

Qualitative research is among the most important techniques in a fundamental analyst's tool kit. It is also among the most difficult to define, but it involves taking in information and making judgments about that information in order to come to an investment conclusion. The advent of technology has automated a good portion of the other fundamental techniques (financial statement analysis, forecasting, and valuation), but no way of automating the gathering and interpretation of data that have yet to become apparent in a company's financial results has yet been found. These data may be used to help model future changes in a company's financial performance. Data may also increase an analyst's confidence in her investment decisions. Conversely, if information emerges during the process that contradicts the analyst's initial thesis, she may be able to eliminate the position before the negative consequences of a change in business conditions are felt in the share price.

The important data will vary by company, but any data that shed light on ether the business environment (e.g., competition, reimbursement, regulatory, or market changes) or company conditions (e.g., new products, changes in cost structure, or strategy shifts) will be helpful in developing an analytical picture of the company. In response to some of the issues that emerged during the Internet stock bubble of the late 1990s, the government passed Regulation FD (Fair Disclosure), which prohibits company insiders from selectively disclosing important (material) corporate information to small groups of investors. This leveled the playing field, and now investors without corporate contacts are able, through diligent research, to obtain the same amount of information as those with extensive corporate contacts.

Even before Regulation FD was issued, it was important for an analyst to do fieldwork to determine the current and future business conditions in which a company operates. The reasons for this are threefold: to evaluate the company's performance relative to the forecast; to evaluate the environment, which may have an impact on future changes in the business; and possibly to identify other investments. Stylistically, analysts vary in how they conduct fieldwork, but in general it involves some combination of speaking with suppliers, customers, competitors, and the company itself to develop a picture of the business environment. The interconnectedness of the health-care sector allows numerous checks on the business operations of companies, as service companies can inform investors about product companies and vice versa. Because health care has so many constituents, including patients, physicians, and the government, data can be gathered from those sources as well.

Anecdotal information and the opinions of well-informed, unbiased sources can help the analyst draw value-added conclusions. The analyst must use some imagination in order to determine what questions to ask in order to evaluate the current business conditions and to identify the optimal sources of answers to these questions. Once the analyst has the data, she must interpret them correctly in the context of other data points. If all of the data points seem to be pointing in the same direction, it should give the analyst confidence that the picture is correct. If there are conflicting points of view, then the analyst should revisit her sources and questions to get a sense of the correct direction. There may not be an absolute answer, and the analyst should be aware of this. In addition, the analyst should be aware of the echo chamber effect. Sometimes a common theme takes over the discussion of a business; even if it is incorrect, it can become the conventional wisdom if it is repeated often enough. The analyst should always attempt to find data points that disagree with her initial opinion to stress-test her current thinking. In terms of the numbers, it is hard to define how much information the analyst needs to have and how many sources she needs to cultivate. More information is usually better, but the analyst runs the risk of having too many sources, which could muddy the picture. Sometimes one opinion (the right one) is all that is needed to determine a company's business conditions.

As part of qualitative research, the analyst should also put himself in the position of customers and competitors to anticipate what actions they will take. Understanding what factors are important to customers will allow the analyst to determine the strengths and weaknesses of the company's products and services. Understanding customers can aid the analyst in anticipating future demand, and if a company is capable of addressing future demand, the investment has upside potential. The same method can be used with competitors. Analysts can put themselves in the shoes of competitors and anticipate strategic competitive responses. If the set of responses does not represent a substantial threat to the franchise of the investment, there is opportunity.

In an era of health-care reform, there will be many opinions, some informed and some uninformed. Much of the data on reform and its impact may be shaded (spun) by those with vested interests. The analyst needs to be prepared to deal with a wide variety of opinions and always stress-test any information against a reasonableness standard as well as against other sources of information. Qualitative analysis is not a one-time event; it is an ongoing and adaptive process of developing new information, because as the business environment changes, so will the information.

GAINING AN EDGE

Success in fundamental investing rests on the ability to determine outcomes better than the market can. In Wall Street parlance, this is described as having an edge. There are four broad areas in which an investor can have an advantage over the Street, informational, analytical, behavioral, and executional.[13] Within these areas, there are subspecialties in which an investor may be able to develop skills superior to those of the rest of the market. It is unlikely that even the savviest investor will be able to have an edge in everything at all times, so it is important for the analyst to understand his own strengths and weaknesses and know the circumstances under which he can get an edge. When those circumstances arise, the analyst must be prepared to allocate his capital because having an edge by its very nature allows for a greater possibility of positive return.

Information

Information is power on Wall Street. Getting information about a company, product, or market faster than the market can allows the investor to make informed decisions ahead of the crowd and leads to outsized gains. Since investment decisions are often made with incomplete information, any incremental data an analyst has will have direct impact on investing returns. However, information can be difficult to come by in a timely manner. Companies do not like to share information for regulatory or competitive reasons, and large numbers of investors are also seeking similar information. Technology has been a tremendous boon to analysts seeking out information. A key to developing an information edge is first knowing what information is most important for making an investment decision. The next step is to determine who or what entity would have this information and would make it available to the analyst. Once the information is obtained, it must be placed in the context of what the analyst already knows. The better the fit of the new information into already verified information, the more confidence the analyst can have in her investment choices. The analyst then must assume that this information will eventually make its way into the market and project the reaction of current or future holders of the shares.

Because there is so much information available about all manner of subjects, one way to develop an informational edge is to build up an area of specialization. It can be as broad as health-care reform itself, or it can be a subsector, such as the impact of health-care reforms on medical technology. With a specialization, the analyst will be able to understand what is important and place it in context. Specialization can also help the analyst locate the most accurate and reliable sources of information. Specialization does not help in diversification, however, and this is something that an analyst must consider in the course of portfolio construction. Another issue to be aware of in developing an information edge is not to be overwhelmed with voluminous amounts of data (missing the forest for the trees), but to know how much information is required and make sure that the information gathered is relevant to the creation or destruction of value for the company.

Verification of sources is paramount, as bad information will not lead to an edge. Maintaining an informational edge is an adaptive process that requires the continuous seeking out of new data points.

Analytical

The analyst can also develop an analytical edge. To achieve this type of edge, the analyst must take existing information and derive better decisions from it than the market at large does. As with other edges, developing an analytical advantage is difficult because there are many other market participants who are attempting to do the same thing. Developing a particular area of expertise can help the analyst develop an edge. Good analysis entails placing information in the proper context, so having the proper perspective can lead to an advantage for the analyst. Pattern recognition is another edge that can come with specialization. There are a finite number of strategies that a health-care company can deploy, and an analyst with good pattern recognition skills can determine whether a strategy will be successful based on past experience and invest accordingly.

The ability to judge what the market has priced into a stock can be an edge, especially if it varies from what the analyst believes is the true business condition of the company. In addition to context and pattern recognition, honing forecasting and valuation skills can lead to outsized gains if an analyst is familiar with either analytic techniques or specific industry irregularities. Knowing how to model specific industries takes some effort, but it will be helpful in analyzing specific companies or the industry as a whole. Knowing the industry rules of thumb, an analyst can develop a more accurate model relative to the amount of effort expended. Knowledge of "where the bodies are buried" when modeling business performance can be helpful in reducing modeling errors. Recognizing areas where possible company failures may be located is much easier for analysts with sector expertise than for others.

What applies to modeling also applies to valuation. Certain industries and even products or services within industries need to be valued in certain ways. Often valuation skills that are appropriate for one industry are not useful for another because of variations in revenue or cash flow patterns. Determining what is "reasonable" better than the market at large can be a source of analytical advantage. Experience may be the most important part of developing an analytical edge, as it takes time to hone analysis skills, so the investor should start by allocating small amounts of capital until she gets comfortable with her analytic edge.

Behavioral

Analysts have biases; there are situations in which they do not make optimal decisions (such as when they are under stress) and situations and/or markets in which they do make optimal decisions. Since all investors come equipped with maladaptive situational responses and biases, understanding one's own shortcomings can give the analyst an edge over other investors who don't have this insight because he won't make the same mistakes. Productive behaviors include an investor's ability to take a loss early enough to maintain capital, to be able to learn from past mistakes, not to trade excessively. Adhering to predefined risk limits (i.e., stop losses), understanding the environment in which he operates most successfully, understanding when he has some type of an edge, and not becoming overconfident about his abilities are other behavioral points to keep in mind. Because the market can be noisy (with stock movements often being unrelated to the fundamentals of the underlying company), the analyst should not let the market dictate his investment strategy, but should let the facts drive the decision-making process.

For an analyst, having a behavioral edge means that he does not respond in the same counterproductive ways as the market. Being able to keep a cool head (acting in a rational, fact-based manner) in a market that is acting overemotionally can be a way to take advantage of temporary market or stock dislocations. Knowing under which circumstances he makes his best decisions will allow the analyst to place himself in situations where the outcomes are more favorable. Developing a behavioral edge takes self-exploration to understand one's own makeup; understanding oneself can then lead to improved discipline and patience in the investment decision-making process.

Executional

Having an executional edge means that the way an investor goes about the investing process is in some way superior to what is done by others in the market. This is often structural in nature and can depend on the type of organization the analyst works for. The ability to achieve the best prices on trades through either trading skills, algorithms, or trading styles is one way to get an executional edge. Risk management is another executional edge in that being able to quantify the risk of both an individual stock and an entire portfolio can lead to capital preservation, which can allow the analyst to invest at a time that is more conducive to her investment style.

Portfolio management is closely related to risk management. Understanding how the parts of the portfolio fit together and which parts deserve what percentage of capital is an advantage to those who are good at it, as it allows for outsized gains through good decision making. Portfolio management also entails determining which asset classes are most conducive to returns at a particular time. Sometimes stocks are not the optimal approach. Given the current information, an investor with a portfolio management edge will seek out the best asset (bonds, options, derivatives) for achieving her investment goals. Access to information is another execution edge; the ability to gather information quickly and inexpensively can give an investor an advantage over the competition. This edge is related to gaining an informational edge, but obtaining and interpreting information smoothly can lead to outsized gains. Incentives and time frame are other potential execution edges. If an investment requires a certain time frame to play out, but the investor is unable to wait that long, there will be a mismatch, and the opportunity will be lost. The same is true for incentives; if the analyst is given incentives to do something she is not good at (e.g., trading rather than investing), solid opportunities will be lost. Being forced to be fully invested even when opportunities are not available is another wrong incentive that could derail returns. An executional edge in trading costs, information access, risk management, or portfolio management is often overlooked as a source of potential return, but developing an edge in any of these areas can lead to gains. Solid criteria for trade entrance, exit, and timing; position sizing; portfolio correlation; and market view can also provide an execution edge.

WHAT CAN GO WRONG

In theory, equity research is easy, but executing it in practice is something completely different. No discussion of equity research is complete without discussing the errors that analysts can make or traps they can fall into when coming to investment conclusions. For every type of research methodology and technique, there is usually some way in which it can be misused, leading to the wrong investment conclusion and potentially an investment loss. Analysts should always begin their analysis with an understanding of the limitations of their approach and adjust the probability of various outcomes accordingly. With financial statement analysis, missing accounting signals or assuming that temporary conditions will prevail over the long term can lead to poor investment outcomes. In forecasting, wrong assumptions and time frames and failing to account for foreseeable events can lead to negative investment conclusions. In terms of valuation, there is a wide variety of mistakes that an analyst can make, including not adjusting discount-rate calculations for riskiness, making calculating errors in cash flow, making calculating errors in residual value, missing inconsistencies and conceptual errors (applying to multiples, among other things), making interpretation errors, and making organizational errors.[14] For qualitative analysis, not identifying the right information to seek out, overreliance on an information source (particularly if it is company management), and ignoring information that disagrees with the initial thesis but that is accurate are issues that can lead to poor investment outcomes.

Not responding quickly enough to a changing environment that is indicated by the available information, even when the analyst has included that information in her analysis, is a potential mistake. Not acknowledging that business conditions can and often do change is another error in qualitative analysis. Assuming that because a stock is up over some short time frame, the investment thesis is correct is another typical error that a fundamental analyst can make. A stock price is a reflection of supply and demand at a particular point in time and may not necessarily reflect correct assumptions about future performance. The same is true for styles and segments; at times an entire industry may be in or out of favor, and analysts should ensure that the share price performance of a sector is consistent with fundamentals rather than being based on other market factors. An investor should not confuse a good company with a good investment. Sometimes a company's "good" fundamentals have already been priced or overpriced into the shares, reducing the return potential, whereas a company with lackluster corporate potential may have solid share price return potential because the market has underpriced the fundamentals.

Health care as a sector adds an additional series of possible mistakes for fundamental analysts, particularly in an era of reform. Analysts may err by assuming that their political or ethical views are ideologically correct and that the market will agree with them. The market may or may not in fact do so, and thus it is important for the analyst to deal with health-care reform in terms of "what is" rather than what she believes "should be." If an analyst turns out to be incorrect, she may generate a negative investment outcome. The market is often subject to rumor or innuendo, known as chatter. With a transformative event like health-care reform, there is likely to be a great deal of noise from parties with vested interests, either investors or companies. Much of the chatter is likely to be opinion masquerading as fact. The health-care analyst should stick to what is verifiable in reaching her investment conclusion. If the analyst feels that the price action in the shares is not predictable based upon the fundamentals as she understands them, she should revisit the thesis and perhaps reduce the amount of capital invested, but do so based on fundamentals, not on chatter. Occasionally companies will take advantage of temporarily high levels of reimbursement. Though it may look to the uninitiated that these are permanent, if in fact the reimbursement is inefficient for the system eventually the system will fix it. Investors should not confuse advantageous reimbursement with genuine sustainable improvements to health outcomes.

Another health-care industry error is to extrapolate future revenue or cost performance into the future without adjusting for the very large swings that health-care reform or other industry factors can bring about. Health care is a dynamic industry, and straight long-term extrapolation is probably the least likely scenario. Health care is also the subject of frequent fads. Physician practice management companies and genomics are just two of the many areas of health care that were once touted as the "next great thing," only to peter out in the harsh light of future reality. Investors should avoid fads, if possible. Knowing a priori whether something is a fad is difficult, but a significant increase in corporate finance activity in the form of public offerings of stock or venture capital investment in a sector should at least raise a yellow flag to investors. Given that health-care shares are highly interconnected from both a business perspective and a share price perspective (stocks in similar groups are often indexed together), the analyst could hold a portfolio of companies whose stocks are correlated with one another (autocorrelation). If one of the companies were to have a failure, leading to underperformance, this could have ripple effects across the entire portfolio if it is not diversified enough. Analysts should be aware of both overt and informal relationships to ensure that a health-care portfolio is not overly risky.

Failure to distinguish between clinically interesting findings and clinically meaningful findings is another mistake analysts can make when it comes to evaluating product makers. Sometimes a product can lead to activity in a disease state (like a reduction of hair loss) but may not be meaningful to the outcome of that disease state (like survival). In order to be successful, especially in an era of health-care reform, products will have to demonstrate that their efficacy will also result in improvements that patients, physicians, and the system deem important. Health-care analysts may become dazzled by the science behind a product and fail to recognize that interesting science does not always lead to profits. While a discovery can be an important starting point for other discoveries, moving a product from the science stage to the point of commercialization takes time, capital, and a substantial number of steps, inducing formulation, manufacturing at scale, and verification of the product's safety and stability, at each of which it can fail. The flip side of overreliance on science is a lack of patience. Developing products takes a significant amount of time, so expecting instantaneous returns is unlikely outside of groundbreaking clinical trial results; therefore, the analyst must adjust his time frame suitably to meet the development timetable of a therapeutic agent.

NOTES

1. See David A. Hirshleifer and Siew Hong Teoh, "Herd Behavior and Cascading in Capital Markets: A Review and Synthesis," Dice Center Working Paper No. 2001–20, Dec. 19, 2001; available at SSRN, http://ssrn.com/abstract=296081, for more information on herding.

2. Konan Chan, Narasimhan Jegadeesh, Louis K. C. Chan, and Josef Lakonishok, "Earnings Quality and Stock Returns: The Evidence from Accruals," Feb. 15, 2001; available at SSRN, http://ssrn.com/abstract=259691.

3. Ibid. See also Howard M. Schilit, *Financial Shenanigans: How to Detect Accounting Gimmicks and Fraud in Financial Reports* 2nd ed. (New York: McGraw-Hill, 2002) for more detail on aggressive accounting.

4. Partha S. Mohanram, "Separating Winners from Losers among Low Book-to-Market Stocks Using Financial Statement Analysis," April 2004; available at SSRN, http://ssrn.com/abstract=403180, or DOI, 10.2139/ssrn.403180.

5. Jeffery S. Abarbanell and Brian J. Bushee, "Abnormal Returns to a Fundamental Analysis Strategy." August 1997; available at SSRN, http://ssrn.com/abstract=40740.

6. Mark T. Soliman, "Using Industry-Adjusted DuPont Analysis to Predict Future Profitability," February 2004; available at SSRN, http://ssrn.com/abstract=456700.

7. David A. Hirshleifer, James N. Myers, Linda A. Myers, and Siew Hong Teoh, "Do Individual Investors Cause Post-Earnings Announcement Drift? Direct Evidence from Personal Trades," March 2008; available at SSRN, http://ssrn.com/abstract= 1024046, or DOI, 10.2139/ssrn.299260.

8. Shiva Sivaramakrishnan and Lynn L. Rees, "Valuation Implications of Revenue Forecasts," Texas A&M Working Paper, June 28, 2001; available at SSRN, http://ssrn.com/abstract=275490.

9. Robert J. Shiller, "From Efficient Market Theory to Behavioral Finance," Cowles Foundation Discussion Paper No. 1385, October 2002.

10. Jonathan W. Lewellen, "Predicting Returns with Financial Ratios," MIT Sloan Working Paper No. 4374–02, August 2002; available at SSRN, http://ssrn.com/ abstract=309559, or DOI, 10.2139/ssrn.309559.

11. Jing Liu, Doron Nissim, and Jacob K. Thomas, "Equity Valuation Using Multiples," August 2000; available at SSRN, http://ssrn.com/abstract=241266, or DOI, 10.2139/ ssrn.241266.

12. Stephen H. Penman, "Handling Valuation Models," *Journal of Applied Corporate Finance* 18, no. 2 (2006): 48–55; available at SSRN, http://ssrn.com/abstract= 943542, or DOI, 10.1111/j.1745-6622.2006.00087.x.

13. For more information on edges, see Jason Zweig, "Bill Miller: What's Luck Got to Do with It?" *Money Magazine* interview, July 18, 2007, http://money.cnn.com/ 2007/07/17/pf/miller_interviw_full_moneymg_/index.htm.

14. Pablo Fernández, "Company Valuation Methods: The Most Common Errors in Valuations," Feb. 28, 2007; available at SSRN, http://ssrn.com/abstract=274973, or DOI, 10.2139/ssrn.274973.

CHAPTER 9

Other Investment Considerations and Techniques

Health-care stocks do not exist in isolation. They exist in the context of a broader market for stocks of companies across a wide variety of industries, sizes, regions, and other asset classes. There is robust literature on analyzing stocks with the goal of seeking out methods for determining a priori outperformance (stocks that create greater value than would be expected from the market as a whole). By its very nature, health care lends itself well to a wide variety of characteristics studied by researchers. It can fit into most style boxes, size boxes, life-cycle boxes, and business-cycle boxes. Almost any category of stocks or types of companies is likely to include at least one health-care company. Health-care stocks are amenable to a wide variety of stock-picking methods, including discounted cash flow valuation, relative valuation, and private market valuation. Investors can also apply quantitative tools, behavioral finance tools, technical analysis, and options analysis, and they can sell stocks short or own stocks for the long term. Among the most important considerations for health-care investors is using the proper context in which to analyze the investment, both by itself and also as part of a broader portfolio. Understanding where a particular health-care company fits into the broader investment picture and one's own investment philosophy should help lead to positive returns. Not understanding what techniques to apply, how to apply them, and when to apply them opens up the investor to risk.

TIME FRAMES

It is hard to prove conclusively that investing time frames have gotten shorter. However, with the increasing number of entities that provide incentives for shorter-term performance (hedge funds) and a reduction in transaction costs because of the use of improved and more efficient technology, the preponderance of the evidence suggests that this may be the case. In general, volatility is helpful to shorter-term investors because rapid short-term movements can lead to outsized gains in a short amount of time.

Among the more obvious investing targets for those with short-term time horizons are the catalyst-driven companies that tend to populate the product side of health care, most notably small-cap biotechnology and medical technology companies. In these cases, the success or failure of a product, either in clinical trials, regulatory acceptance, or market acceptance, can significantly alter the value proposition. The more reliant the company is on any individual product (the smaller the follow-on pipeline is), the more the success or failure of that product will matter. Since catalysts usually occur at a finite point in time that is determinable, investors will not have to wait a long time to see a payoff if they invested correctly.

Another type of company that may appeal to investors with a shorter time horizon is emerging growth companies in products or services. These companies are generally smaller and are bringing something relatively new to the health-care industry, either a new product for an existing indication, a product for a new indication, or a service that is unlike others that are currently available. Again, the more reliant the company is on a small number of products or services, the more dependent it will be on the success of those products or services. For those with short-term horizons, market acceptance or failure will be observable within a relatively short time frame—either the use of the product or service is growing or it isn't—allowing investors to know whether they have made the right choices. This leverage works in both directions; if a product or service should fail, there could be significant downside risk to the investment. Moreover, even if the product or service succeeds, the larger the company gets as a result of its initial success, the more difficult it will be for the company to maintain significant returns. Therefore, even investors in successful companies need to be mindful of the sustainability of the business model, which entails an understanding of the future pipeline of products or services and whether the company can either maintain or accelerate returns. In addition, though this is somewhat rare, a successful smaller company could become an attractive acquisition candidate for a larger company that is looking externally to accelerate its own returns.

Health care also offers opportunities to longer-term investors. This is particularly true for investors who are looking at reform as a growth driver for stocks. It's possible that the announcement or implementation of reform programs may lead to near-term volatility in these companies' shares. However, generally speaking, macro factors like reform take time to evolve, and so do the business models of the companies that will be able to create the most value out of the change. For investors who can successfully interpret the future of reform, a longer-term horizon makes value judgments quantifiable because analysis becomes a matter of comparing a company's current and future capabilities with the market demand created or destroyed by a reform plan.

Longer-term investors can also benefit if they can recognize companies that need to change their business models. These turnaround situations often occur when a company's franchise cannot accommodate change that has been foisted upon it by outside forces. Once a company fails, it is likely to be neglected by investors, as investors in general seem to have little patience with a lack of success. Neglect can lead to attractive valuations, and if a management team can alter the franchise or if the business operating environment reverts to one that makes the company's franchise viable again, investors can see significant returns. These changes take time and are likely to happen in fits and starts, and so they are more accessible to investors with longer-term time frames. The changes caused by health-care reform have the potential to render some current business models inoperable. It is important to understand the possible long-term failure potential, as investors can monetize this failure by selling shares short or avoiding a short-term failure to capture the longer-term upside.

A longer time horizon also allows investors to benefit from the R&D efforts of the various industries. Certain companies in the sector, like pharmaceuticals, biotechnology, and medical technology, have long lead-time R&D cycles where it can take many years for an R&D investment to deliver returns. Investors with a longer-term vision of where a given therapy may go may be more able to capture the upside than shorter-term investors.

The same is true for the evolution of service companies. There are numerous macro trends that are changing the way in which health care is supplied and demanded. These macro trends will take time to reach a critical mass where companies are able to drive returns. Investors with a longer-term vision will give these companies the time required for these macro trends to play out. Companies like managed-care organizations and other service companies that are able to take advantage of megatrends by investing capital now for the longer term may not see immediate returns, but they will see significant returns in the future. Those investors who can determine which companies are making the correct investments—in terms of both the right choices and the optimal level of risk—and who have the time horizon to wait for returns on investments will benefit by taking the long view.

VALUE VERSUS GROWTH

Investors often differentiate themselves into two categories, value and growth. While both seek to generate a positive return, their focus tends to be on different elements of a business. Value investors want to buy stocks for less than they are worth today, measured either by their assets or by their current ability to make a profit. Generally, these investors are looking for stocks that are trading at a low ratio of share price to assets (price/book ratio), a low ratio of share price to earnings, or some other metric geared toward showing the value of a company. The value investor tries to purchase shares when these ratios indicate that the true worth of the business is undervalued by the market. Eventually the market will recognize the true worth of the business, and the value investor will see investment returns.

Growth investors, while being aware of existing earnings and assets, focus more on taking advantage of future potential. Growth investors are willing to pay higher ratios of price to earnings and price to assets than value investors if they believe that the market is underpricing the potential of the business. Growth investing relies somewhat more on vision than value investing does because the future is unknowable with perfect certainty. Also, higher valuations do raise the risk of overpaying for future returns. If growth investors forecast potential correctly, however, they can see a significant upside.

Health care and health-care reform will provide both types of investors with opportunities that meet their criteria. Both philosophies rely on identifying some type of mispricing of shares relative to the value of the business in order to be successful. Both philosophies require some type of change that will lead the market to recognize its previous mispricing. Health-care reform offers the potential for both mispricing and eventual recognition of the true value of the franchise. Value investors may prefer some of the larger companies that focus on realizing returns from their substantial assets in an era of reform, like distribution companies and large pharmaceutical companies. Growth investors may prefer early-stage companies whose products are dedicated to taking advantage of the new paradigms in health care.

OTHER ANALYSIS TECHNIQUES

There has been significant research into the factors that lead either stocks or companies to outperform. The list is long, and some items on it are somewhat controversial because they cannot always be replicated. Moreover, research into stocks can be subject to data snooping and other biases, which can make the results less than absolute. Additionally, once a factor that can lead to outperformance is identified, it is possible that others will arbitrage that factor to the point where it is no longer successful in driving positive performance—essentially the observer effect, where the mere observation can alter what is being observed.

The more thoroughly researched and agreed-upon anomalies (characteristics that lead to share mispricings) include low price/book ratios, low price/earnings ratio, small size, profitability, accruals, momentum,[1] noise,[2] earnings surprises,[3] price to cash flow,[4] stock repurchases and insider activity,[5] earnings whispers,[6] investor sentiment,[7] reversion to the mean,[8] and style and sector rotation.[9] Health care, because it includes a wide variety of companies, has stocks that can offer all kinds of anomalies. As health-care reform emerges, some of these anomalies may play a greater role than others and must be considered by investors. While quantitative factors like price ratios are important, particularly with regard to generating positive returns, they may not be as important in an era of significant change as the more qualitative factors like sentiment, noise, and momentum.

Once the direction of a health-care reform plan becomes clear, investors are likely to congregate in those stocks that appear to be the largest beneficiaries of the change. It is important for investors to distinguish those that will truly be beneficiaries from those that the herd believes will benefit. Ultimately, if a company is not a long-term beneficiary, its profit and its share price could in fact decline substantially, leading to losses. After any major reform, there may be an opportunity to utilize quantitative techniques to screen for companies that, by virtue of being wrongly positioned for reform, may become inexpensive relative to their core businesses, so that an investment at that point in time may lead to significant subsequent returns.

Technical Analysis

There are a wide variety of analytical techniques and trading strategies that investors and traders employ when they are trying to achieve positive returns. Technical analysis is a forecasting method that uses share price movements, volume measures, and sentiment to anticipate future share price action. It is predicated on estimating the indicators of supply and demand of items (in this case, stocks) in a given market.[10] Technical analysis has been used as far back as the eighteenth century, when Japanese rice traders used candlestick patterns to forecast changes in rice prices. It assumes that there is knowledge in price and behavior. One of technical analysis's virtues is the ease with which it can be applied, given the now wide availability of price charts and volume metrics, and there is academic evidence that it has practical applications in real-world settings.[11] It is widely practiced on Wall Street. Health-care analysts must be aware of technical analysis because it is in widespread use and because it can add to returns. There is ample literature on the subject, but the main cornerstones of technical analysis are that trends exist, that longer-term trends influence shorter-term trends, and that changes in volume (in terms of number of shares traded) are an important indicator of where the crowd believes the price action will go in the future. Two of the key features that the technical analyst tries to evaluate are sentiment and momentum (trends).

Sentiment

Sentiment indicators estimate trader and investor attitudes about the market in general or about specific stocks in terms of return potential. They are related more to expectations than to actual return potential (cash flow changes, for example). Events like the "Internet bubble" show that sentiment can overwhelm fundamentals at times. Sentiment plays a role in the performance of health-care stocks, as concern over governmental action can sometimes lead to mispricing, as it did in the early 1990s, when pharmaceutical stocks were sold off out of fear of the Clinton health-care reform package rather than because of any cash flow changes the stocks may have faced. Sentiment also plays a role in the speculative stories, as a scientific discovery by one company can spur price reactions in other companies, even if their science is unrelated. It appears that small-cap stocks that are higher in volatility and have a growth component to them are more subject to investor sentiment than other types of companies.[12] These characteristics (small cap, speculative) describe a broad swath of health-care companies, so sentiment, particularly as it relates to health care, should be monitored closely, especially in terms of the rotation of investment sentiment from one health-care sector to another (from pharmaceuticals to managed care, for instance) or from another industry into health care (from technology into health care, for example). For analysts, the key to keep in mind is that sentiment can change the discount rate, at least in the short term. The analyst should also bear in mind that sentiment may not reflect fundamental reality, or, as John Maynard Keynes was purported to have said, "The market can stay irrational longer than you can stay solvent." There are some guideposts that are often used to track sentiment; these include liquidity (trading volume), stock issuances, closed-end fund discounts, mutual fund flows, option volatility, company insider trading activity, and investor surveys.[13]

Momentum

Although there are data supporting contrarian strategies—buying losing stocks and selling winning stocks in a shorter-term time horizon (3 to 12 months)—there is also evidence that stocks that are trending in one direction tend to continue going in that direction.[14] Research has yet to determine a reason for this anomaly with certainty, although the possibility that large investors like mutual funds buy past winners and sell past losers and the tendency of sell-side analysts to recommend high-momentum stocks may be part of the reason.[15] Window dressing and closet index benchmarking are charges that have been leveled at mutual funds and hedge funds, and although such charges are difficult to prove, this phenomenon cannot be ruled out as a cause of the momentum effect. Moreover, there are well-documented issues with the sell-side process, so again, the explanation is not out of the question. Regardless of the causes, despite having been observed for more than 15 years, this phenomenon does not seem to have been arbitraged out of the system.[16] For health-care investors, the implication is that the amount of time required to put a reform plan into action will matter, as stocks that are perceived as benefiting (or as being harmed) are likely to retain the resulting share price trajectory until the reality of the situation is borne out. Recall that it took the government about two and a half years to enact and implement Medicare Part D, so investors should assume that it will take at least that long to pass a larger reform package. If a reform package takes longer than two years, the momentum effect is likely to diminish, and share prices will revert to the mean, either because of a contrarian reaction or because of the company's fundamentals reasserting themselves.

Noise

Noise in the stock market refers to share price movement that is not related to trends, cash flow, or business conditions. The stock market can be noisy in general, with transitory components accounting for a standard deviation of between 15 and 25 percent and accounting for half the variance in monthly returns.[17] A reform program has the potential to increase the noise level through whispers (informal communication between investors with often unverified information) and changes in investor sentiment. It is important that the investor put the chatter around a stock in the proper context. Getting the context correct can allow the investor either to take advantage of temporary downside mispricing resulting from stock price movements that are unrelated to business fundamentals or to avoid (or short) those stocks whose prices are temporarily inflated by unnecessary chatter and feedback trading. There is evidence that individual investors can move stocks irrespective of the underlying cash flow characteristics. Noise trading can sometimes be used to forecast future returns, at least in the short term.[18] This factor is especially important in an era of health-care reform, as the market should be particularly noisy as small investors react to media reports, pronouncements from government officials, comments from corporate executives, and Wall Street "whispers." Since most individuals have direct experience with at least a portion of the health-care system, this experience may encourage them to invest faster than they would in the more arcane industries. There has been shown to be some correlation among small traders in terms of impact caused by attention-grabbing events.[19] Investors should not overlook this effect, even if they disagree with the premise of the announced event—"Don't fight the tape" in Wall Street parlance. Rather, "informed" investors should acknowledge that these dislocations will happen and take appropriate steps either to minimize the risk before an event or to take advantage of a dislocation after the fact.

Behavioral Finance

Much of traditional finance has operated under the assumption that investors are completely rational and that mispricing of stocks (or other assets) is rare because as soon as the mispricings are detected, they will be arbitraged out. Behavioral finance assumes that investors often act irrationally, and that not all situations can be arbitraged out. Given these two assumptions, predictive models can be designed to understand the phenomena and perhaps lead to outperformance.[20] For investors, the more important thing about behavioral finance is the framework of beliefs and preferences. Some of the counterproductive beliefs that this area of study has identified are overconfidence, wishful thinking, representativeness, conservatism, belief perseverance, anchoring, recency, loss aversion, limited attention spans, assumptions about patterns, inertia, and differences in preferences.[21,22,23] Moreover, the assumption that all investors are completely rational at all times seems more applicable to theory than to the reality of the market, given the often high levels of volatility. In an era of reform, the analyst should understand where he is vis-à-vis these psychological constructs. The investor should also understand that the market may be operating on the basis of these psychological dynamics; this perspective may give him an extra tool for understanding the sometimes unusual price action that will come with potential radical change in the underlying fundamentals of many companies affected by health-care reform.

Selling Shares Short

Failure is a fact of life in corporate America. Another unpleasant fact is that sometimes stocks go down, either as a result of a corporate failure or because investors have mispriced the value of the business franchise or business environment. Selling shares short (shorting) can be a way to profit from falling stocks or of hedging market risk on long positions. The mechanics of selling stocks short are that the investor borrows the shares, sells the borrowed shares, and then buys them back at a lower price and captures the difference. This assumes that the shares are available to be sold short (borrowed) and that the stock goes down. Short selling can be difficult because the market has tended to go up over time, taking the majority of stocks with it. Also, shorting stocks tends to be a bit antithetical to American optimism, which is why corporate managements occasionally complain about short interest in their shares. Short selling may not be appropriate for all investors, but understanding what makes a stock go down as well as up is important for all investors. Moreover, short interest has been shown to be predictive of poor future performance in some cases, so investors should monitor that factor for changes.[24] An obvious reason for a stock to go down is a recognition on the part of investors that the price of the shares is not justified by the fundamentals. What can bring about this revaluation? Either performance is not equal to what the financial community is expecting, previous results were misstated or misinterpreted, or the business environment has changed in such a way that many stockholders' reasons for owning the stock are no longer operational.

Because of its rapidly changing nature, health care has always attracted a fair amount of short interest as, at least for informed short sellers, negative changes can be forecasted. In an era of health-care reform, where change is inevitable, some companies will fail, and investors should be attuned to those, either as short-selling candidates or as stocks in which to avoid taking a long position. Obviously, the companies that fail will be those that cannot improve either cost, quality, or access, especially if they have competitors that can do so. Generally, these companies will have decelerating growth, accelerating costs, or declining cash flows, among other attributes. Analysts should be wary of companies where these conditions will possibly emerge should a health-care reform program become tangible. Market neutral is a strategy that uses an equal amount of long and short stock to hedge market risk. Health-care investors can use this strategy of buying good companies and shorting bad ones to maximize both financial and social returns.

Options

Options are financial instruments that convey the right, but not the obligation, to engage in a future transaction in some underlying security. The contract usually specifies at what price, in what time frame, or both the operation must be executed. Options can serve as an investment vehicle on their own, with the investor speculating that the price of a stock will reach a certain price point by a certain point in time, or they can be used in combination with equities to either hedge a position or derive additional capital from it. Options also have been shown to predict future equity returns under certain circumstances.[25] Options can be especially useful in an era of health-care reform, as they offer equity investors some loss protection in times of substantial change. Moreover, options give an investor an opportunity to make substantial returns on investment because they require the investor to put up relatively little capital for the amount of stock she ultimately could control. So if an investor believes that she understands what a stock or an index of health-care stocks may do and in what time frame, options provide significant opportunities. Options, like stocks, can be mispriced, so the analyst must be sensitive to pricing methodologies with this asset class (Black-Scholes is a frequent valuation methodology). Options can also be helpful if the analyst believes that there is an imminent corporate change coming but is unsure of the direction in which the stock will move. There are numerous option strategies to accommodate all situations, and there is substantial literature on the subject. Even if the analyst does not intend to use options as a tool, she should be cognizant of changes in option volatility (a measure of price) and option volume, as the options may be transmitting information about future returns that cannot yet be seen in the stock itself.

Insiders, Repurchases, and Activists

Following insider transactions and changes in institutional ownership is another approach commonly used in stock analysis. The presumption is that insiders and/or large institutions may have information that is unavailable to the general public. There is literature that has indicated that there is some predictive value to observing insiders.[26] The sources of this asymmetry of information have not been identified with certainty, but the argument has been made that insiders are in a better position to understand intangible values, particularly of R&D.[27] It makes sense that insiders have the opportunity (though not always the ability) to evaluate intangible assets like R&D, intellectual property, and reputational issues better than outside investors. If insiders are correct in their assessment, they should be able to reach a value conclusion with more accuracy than an analyst. Analysts can use this information as a proxy to aid them in their own valuation efforts. Changes in share buyback, head-count, or dividend policy may also be clues about R&D. Evaluating R&D is particularly important for health-care product makers, so the more insight an analyst can glean on the value of R&D productivity, the more precise he can make his forecasts and valuations.

Changes in large institutional holdings can also be a signal of potential positive returns.[28] There are two potential mechanisms by which this may be the case. First, large institutions may have access to research capabilities or information that an individual analyst may not have. Second, large institutional holders can advocate for a different strategy or other corporate changes (shareholder activism) if they see a potential for upside from such a change. At a minimum, having activist investors among the larger shareholders indicates to management that there are holders who will attempt to compensate for the principal-agent problem so often found in investing.

NOTES

1. Eugene F. Fama and Kenneth R. French, "Dissecting Anomalies," CRSP Working Paper No. 610, June 2007; available at SSRN, http://ssrn.com/abstract=911960.
2. Brad M. Barber, Terrance Odean, and Ning Zhu, "Do Noise Traders Move Markets?" EFA 2006 Zurich Meetings Paper, September 2006; available at SSRN, http://ssrn.com/abstract=869827.
3. Jonathan W. Lewellen, S. P. Kothari, and Jerold B. Warner, "Stock Returns, Aggregate Earnings Surprises, and Behavioral Finance," MIT Sloan Working Paper No. 4284–03, February 2003; Simon School of Business Working Paper No. FR 03–05; AFA 2005 Philadelphia Meetings.
4. Brian J. Bushee and Jana Smith Raedy, "Factors Affecting the Implementability of Stock Market Trading Strategies," April 2005; available at SSRN, http://ssrn.com/abstract=384500, or DOI, 10.2139/ssrn.384500.
5. John E. Core, Wayne R. Guay, Scott A. Richardson, and Rodrigo S. Verdi, "Stock Market Anomalies: What Can We Learn from Repurchases and Insider Trading?" July 31, 2005; available at SSRN, http://ssrn.com/abstract=533323, or DOI, 10.2139/ssrn.533323.
6. Mark E. Bagnoli, Messod Daniel Beneish, and Susan G. Watts, "Whisper Forecasts of Quarterly Earnings per Share," March 1999; available at SSRN, http://ssrn.com/abstract=74369, or DOI, 10.2139/ssrn.74369.
7. Malcolm P. Baker and Jeffrey A. Wurgler, "Investor Sentiment in the Stock Market," Feb. 12, 2007; available at SSRN, http://ssrn.com/abstract=962706.
8. Jonathan W. Lewellen, "Temporary Movements in Stock Prices," Texas Finance Festival, March 2001; available at SSRN, http://ssrn.com/abstract=307339, or DOI, 10.2139/ssrn.307339.
9. Yul W. Lee and Zhiyi Song, "When Do Value Stocks Outperform Growth Stocks? Investor Sentiment and Equity Style Rotation Strategies," EFMA 2003 Helsinki Meetings, January 2003; available at SSRN, http://ssrn.com/abstract=410185, or DOI, 10.2139/ssrn.410185.
10. Charles D. Kirkpatrick and Julie R. Dahlquist, *Technical Analysis: The Complete Resource for Financial Market Technicians* (Upper Saddle River, N.J., FT Press, 2006), p. 3.
11. Andrew W. Lo, Harry Mamaysky, and Jiang Wang, "Foundations of Technical Analysis: Computational Algorithms, Statistical Inference, and Empirical Implementation," NBER Working Paper No. 7613, March 2000.
12. Baker and Wurgler, "Investor Sentiment in the Stock Market."
13. Ibid.

14. Werner F. M. De Bondt and Richard H. Thaler, "Does the Stock Market Overreact?" *Journal of Finance* 40 (1985): 793–805.

15. Narasimhan Jegadeesh and Sheridan Titman, "Momentum," University of Illinois Working Paper, Oct. 23, 2001; available at SSRN, http://ssrn.com/abstract=299107.

16. For more details, see "Beyond Reason: The Strange Existence of Market Anomalies," the Buttonwood column, *Economist*, Feb. 23, 2008, p. 90.

17. James M. Poterba and Lawrence H. Summers, "Mean Reversion in Stock Prices: Evidence and Implications," NBER Working Paper 2343, July 1989.

18. Barber, Odean, and Zhu, "Do Noise Traders Move Markets?"

19. Brad M. Barber and Terrance Odean, "All That Glitters: The Effect of Attention and News on the Buying Behavior of Individual and Institutional Investors," EFA 2005 Moscow Meetings Paper, November 2006; available at SSRN, http://ssrn.com/abstract=460660, or DOI, 10.2139/ssrn.460660.

20. Nicholas Barberis and Richard H. Thaler, "A Survey of Behavioral Finance," September 2002; available at SSRN, http://ssrn.com/abstract=327880.

21. Ibid.

22. Robert J. Shiller, "From Efficient Market Theory to Behavioral Finance," Cowles Foundation Discussion Paper No. 1385, October 2002; available at SSRN, http://papers.ssrn.com/sol3/papers.cfm?abstract_id=349660.

23. Robert J. Bloomfield, "Behavioral Finance," Johnson School Research Paper No. 38-06, October 2006; available at SSRN, http://ssrn.com/abstract=941491.

24. Ekkehart Boehmer, Charles M. Jones, and Xiaoyan Zhang, "Which Shorts Are Informed?" AFA 2007 Chicago Meetings Paper, Feb. 4, 2007; available at SSRN, http://ssrn.com/abstract=855044.

25. Xiaoyan Zhang, Rui Zhao, and Yuhang Xing, "What Does Individual Option Volatility Smirk Tell Us about Future Equity Returns?" June 15, 2007; available at SSRN, http://ssrn.com/abstract=970088.

26. Core, Guay, Richardson, and Verdi, "Stock Market Anomalies."

27. David Aboody and Baruch Lev, "Information Asymmetry, R&D and Insider Gains," *Journal of Finance* 55, no. 6 (2000).

28. Jacob Oded and Yu Wang, "Large Shareholders' Activism and Corporate Valuation," Mar. 1, 2005; available at SSRN, http://ssrn.com/abstract=676998.

Investing in Pharmaceuticals

Pharmaceutical manufacturers have come a long way since the days when they were originally founded as chemical makers. The pharmaceutical industry is now the largest of the health-care sectors in terms of market capitalization. The branded industry alone accounts for more than $1.5 trillion in value. The large-capitalization companies are among the best known and most widely held companies in the investing world. The small-capitalization pharmaceutical companies can represent the cutting edge of science, while the generic companies are aiding in the effort to control runaway health-care cost inflation.

A common definition of pharmaceuticals is drugs or medicines that are prepared or dispensed and used in medical treatment. The business model of pharmaceutical companies is to develop new drugs and sell them; in practice, this is extremely challenging. The definition of a pharmaceutical has changed somewhat over the years with the development of new technology. The line between traditional pharmaceutical products (small-molecule pills) and large-molecule biotechnology drugs (injections or infusions) has been blurred by the movement of companies that were once considered either distinctly pharmaceutical or distinctly biotechnology into the other area of research.

The business model of an individual enterprise depends on the size of the company (large or small) and whether the company participates in the branded (novel drug development) sector or competes in the commodity generic industry. Some companies cross over the multiple types of businesses. Each of the different pharmaceutical business models has its own investment challenges and can appeal to different types of investors. Because of the diversity of the companies in the sector, it is important for investors to carefully match the investment decision process with the right type of company. Each segment has its own individual nuances. Companies also have their own company-specific issues (pipeline, new products, patent expiration), so given this heterogeneity, investors need to spend at least some time using a bottom-up approach. In an era of reform, sentiment can influence the whole group, and this may have an impact on multiples and short-term share price performance because of the high correlation between stocks in the group. Longer term, if a company does have solid underlying fundamentals, it should be able to overcompensate for at least some macro headwinds. Failure to acknowledge that companies have different fundamentals and are affected differently by macro factors can lead to a negative investment outcome. Given the return consequences of big sentiment shifts, the analyst must be cognizant of these connections. As with other investments, time horizon, risk profile, and return potential will all play a role in pharmaceutical industry investing preferences.

LARGE PHARMACEUTICAL COMPANIES

Large pharmaceutical companies are the bellwethers of the industry. There is no official dividing line between big and small pharmaceutical companies, but a ranking in the top 20 on sales or sales of more than $1 billion a year is often used as a benchmark. Generally large pharmaceutical companies have multiple products and sell them on several continents. They tend to spend significant amounts of capital on research and development and to have sizable workforces, including substantial sales forces. Since patients are exposed more directly to drug prices through out-of-pocket expense than to the costs of other areas of health care, and since it is the part of the system that they interact with most (drugs for chronic conditions are lifetime propositions), it is one of the parts of health care that consumers pay the most attention to. Because of patients' awareness of this area, the size of these companies, and their name recognition, the big pharmaceutical companies are among the more obvious targets of public scrutiny and political reform efforts. If reform is on the horizon, investors should look to big pharmaceuticals as a sector that could be dramatically affected. These changes need not be uniformly negative, as expanded insurance coverage could help the financial performance of companies in this sector if other reform issues, such as price reductions and regulatory changes, are not overly detrimental. The changes resulting from reform will bring about mispricings in shares as a result of uncertainty, which will lead to opportunities; however, investors must still be able to evaluate the merits of specific pharmaceutical companies. The ability to innovate and the ability to sell the resulting products will have a direct impact on a pharmaceutical company's success.

Innovation

The key value driver for branded pharmaceuticals is innovation. There are still significant unmet medical challenges that are amenable to drug therapies, which means that there is abundant opportunity. Innovation and discovery is an expensive proposition, with the cost of bringing the average drug to market being more than $800 million.[1] A portion of the costs arises from the difficulty of finding drugs and running preclinical and clinical trials. A portion of the costs comes from the large number of drug failures that have to be written off against the relatively few successes. Drug development is a high-risk endeavor. Only 1 in 1,000 drugs makes it from discovery into clinical trials.[2] Furthermore, of every 100 compounds that enter clinical trials, roughly 90 do not make it to market.[3] And for some clinical indications, the success rate is even lower—there are still no cures for many diseases. Drugs take a substantial amount of time to develop, often requiring eight to ten years to reach the market.[4] This long time frame can create a mismatch between financial investments and both clinical and share price results.

Compounding the difficulty of innovation is the fact that drug discovery cannot be a one-time event if a company is to remain successful. New competition from other compounds, other drug classes, and other therapeutic modalities as well as patent expirations mean that in order to continue to create shareholder value, pharmaceutical companies need to continue to develop new compounds. If companies fail to continue to do this, they will ultimately fail as going concerns because cost pressures (from generics) or competitive pressures (from new therapies) will ultimately push most old products into obsolescence.

Not all research and development is created equal. Some companies have been more successful than others in bringing new products from discovery to the market. Different types of compounds for different diseases manufactured by companies of different sizes and types can have a wide diversity in both time to market and success rates.[5] Investors need to factor all of these variables into their models when anticipating and valuing the outcomes of clinical development. As with other aspects of valuation, there are no definitive rules for determining the likely outcomes or timelines of products. Investors should realize that higher-risk compounds tend to be aimed at diseases where there is still a limited understanding of the physiology involved.

There is not a linear relationship between R&D output and the amount of capital (either human or financial) deployed. Drug development has an element of serendipity, sometimes referred to as "eureka" moments, that is difficult to quantify. Such drugs as penicillin, certain chemotherapy agents, and erectile dysfunction drugs, among many others, were found accidentally.[6] It could very well be that the companies that spend the most on developing new drugs will fail because of the lack of a eureka moment. Investors should focus on the types of structures that make it possible for researchers to have flashes of insight rather than attempting to quantify serendipity.

Drugs frequently fail during the research process. As with any other R&D process, this is to be expected, as it is unlikely that any entity can be completely successful when it attempts to develop novel therapies to meet unserved medical needs. Beyond the overall difficulty of bringing new products to market, inability to innovate can be related to numerous factors; failure of management to understand the science, conformism among scientists and managers, lack of leadership, too many mergers (leading to confused infrastructure), a focus on blockbuster drugs (rather than successful drugs that target smaller markets), and poor resource allocation (continuing to fund failures while shelving possible successes) are all possible hindrances to R&D productivity in pharmaceuticals.[7] Drugs can fail for numerous reasons: safety, efficacy, formulation, pharmacokinetics (PK), bioavailability, toxicology, commercial factors, cost of goods, or failure to prove that the drug is better than something that is already on the market.[8]

One measure of success is a company's ability to continue to innovate. If a company has a continuous or near-continuous stream of novel compounds, investors can infer that the company at least has an infrastructure that is conducive to further future development. Companies that successfully create one or two new compounds and then fail to continue to innovate require increased investor wariness. Determining as early as possible which compounds have the best potential to make it to market and which do not is a key to successful resource management. The sooner a management team realizes that a product is likely to fail, the better off that team will be if it terminates the project and redirects its capital elsewhere. Like investors, however, managements can be reluctant to take a loss on a project when substantial resources have been invested in that project. "Failing fast" is an important competitive advantage (assuming that the company has other projects in the pipeline).

Because drug development takes a substantial amount of time, a drug that is put into clinical trials can unintentionally (or intentionally) end up being the second or third drug of its type on the market. Such drugs, often referred to as "me-too" drugs, have been viewed in a negative light by payers and regulators. They represent both a threat and an opportunity for pharmaceutical companies. While creating a me-too drug is probably easier (although no drug development can be considered easy) than building a novel compound from scratch, in an era of reform, it will be imperative for pharmaceutical companies to show the value proposition of these follow-on drugs. The existence of these types of drugs has reduced the marketing exclusivity of innovative drugs.[9]

Companies often show data at clinical conferences or otherwise make data on trials available to the public. Investors should be cognizant of both the timing of data releases and the types of results needed if a clinical trial is to be considered a success. Data releases can be potential catalysts for share price performance if the products are important to the company's future. Other important clinical trial considerations include the size of the trial (the bigger the trial sample size, the better the chances that data from the trial will hold up in later-phase trials by limiting issues like the placebo effect). The type of endpoints, what the trial is attempting to measure, and the clinical meaningfulness of endpoints are all important considerations for anticipating the success of a trial. How the endpoints stack up against what is already on the market and against the company's target audience requirements are also major considerations. Whether the types of patients allowed into the trial are representative of those with the disease and the duration of the trial are also important considerations, as diseases that require longer trials can have a higher failure rate.[10] Having a number of backup compounds (compounds that are similar in action to the drug that is currently being tested, but that differ in some other characteristics) that may be better than the drug that is currently being tested is also important in the event of the failure of the original drug. More information about clinical trials is now being disclosed as a result of changes in regulation and information technology both from companies and the FDA,[11] and there could be consequences such as misinterpretation of the data and competitive threats. Figure 10-1 provides an overview of the clinical trial process.

Among the most important parts of research is target selection— what to conduct early-stage research on. There are no definitive rules for selecting a target. Some considerations include strategic importance to the firm, existing products on the market, length of time and cost of the therapeutic class,[12] and overall market opportunity.[13] Other considerations include the state of the science behind the compound, the company's abilities in the given therapeutic class, reimbursement, complexity of manufacturing, and potential speed to market. A disease need not have enormous market opportunity in terms of incidence to be a solid target. In the United States, the Orphan Drug Law was enacted to encourage companies to develop drugs for diseases affecting fewer than 200,000 people. If a company is successful in creating a drug for an underserved population, it receives favorable intellectual property treatment and less pressure with regard to reimbursement. Investors should understand how a company arrives at its target selection; this should give them a sense of how management thinks about the science as well as enabling a better assessment of the probability of success.

F I G U R E   10-1

Clinical trial overview

Source: FDA Web site.

Dealing with regulators is a competency that separates superior big pharmaceutical companies from inferior big pharmaceutical companies. Regulators have their own priorities, and these are not always in sync with the pharmaceutical companies' priorities (emphasis on safety versus speed to market, for instance). Since regulators have the final say on most major pharmaceutical product requirements, timelines, and approvals, a company needs to understand and satisfy regulatory demands if it is to be successful. If a company does not understand what regulators require, it could face significant setbacks in its development program. As clinical trials become more global as a result of countries with an emerging middle class wanting trials conducted on their populations, regulators are going to require an increasing variety of information. This will place increased importance on a pharmaceutical company's ability to deal with regulators, as changes in the system could create even larger competitive advantages.

Once a drug has been successfully brought to market, it must be marketed, sold, and distributed. The priority for pharmaceutical companies is to reach peak sales (the maximum potential) in as short a period of time as possible and to maintain those sales. The ambition of the sales force is to attain blockbuster status (sales of $1 billion or more). However, relatively few compounds address markets this large. Many companies are happy to achieve sizable returns on their R&D and sales investments, regardless of what the ultimate level of peak sales is. There are many factors that affect the adoption curve and the ultimate sales level of a product. Among these are the size and productivity of the sales force, the price of the product, competition in the drug class, the size of the drug class, the type of payer that dominates in the region and its reimbursement requirements, where in the clinical treatment paradigm the drug is placed (first line, meaning that it is used initially, or second line, meaning that it is used after something else has been tried first), formulary tiering, clinical guidelines, clinical practice, label and indications of the product, availability of generics, stage of the life cycle, proportion or share of new prescriptions relative to existing prescriptions, the type of physician that prescribes the drug, and the site of care at which it is prescribed.

The traditional pharmaceutical sales model is to employ a large sales force to "detail" the health-care providers in order to get them to prescribe the drug. This model, often referred to as "share of voice," relies on ensuring that the brand is as widely known as possible, leading to increased prescribing. The traditional business model also incorporates marketing in trade journals and other professional awareness channels, which can include honorariums for thought leaders.

In 1997, the federal government changed the law to allow pharmaceutical companies to advertise directly to the public (DTC), and this dramatically changed the way pharmaceutical companies conduct business. Despite being a relatively small part of the overall pharmaceutical promotional spending,[14] DTC is the segment of pharmaceutical advertising that consumers know best. Aggressive sales tactics have been shown to be effective;[15] had they not been, this strategy would probably have been dispensed with in favor of other forms of marketing, including the use of new media that are also at the companies' disposal. Sales channels can also be used in a defensive way in counterdetailing by pointing out the weaknesses of competing products.

The sales process takes place in a broader context, and this needs to be considered when attempting to forecast the growth curve of a given compound. At the highest level, the sales process will be affected by who decides what compound to use. This decision is also influenced by what type of entity is responsible for payment. The United States is a mostly physician-centric and payer-centric model, in which physicians make the decisions on what drugs to prescribe, taking into consideration what payers will pay for. Other areas have different models in which the deciding factor could be the government, the pharmacist, or even the consumer himself.

The increasing power of payers has required pharmaceutical companies to retool their business models to focus on business development with those payers that have the largest market share. By virtue of their size, large payers often have more information about cost and outcomes than individual doctors or patients do. The large payers can reduce the asymmetry of information between innovators and prescribers, but payers' incentives may not necessarily be aligned with those of patients or providers, and there will always be cases where a paradigm for drug prescribing fails; given the heterogeneity of any given population, prescribing can often be a case-by-case proposition.

The tools that payers use to drive demand are mostly financial and include increased copays, tiering (making more expensive drugs less financially appealing), staging (requiring that less expensive drugs be tried first), and outright refusal to pay for a drug that they deem unnecessary. While a patient can still pay for drugs out of pocket, a financial disincentive can be a deterrent to using a given drug, especially if there are substitutes. Superior pharmaceutical companies will be able to navigate an environment in which one or more big payers dominate a market by clearly defining a value proposition for their products. In addition to showing the value of the product, this may involve strategies such as rebates in exchange for a payer's guaranteeing a level of sales. To the extent that a health-care reform plan alters the payer structure, companies need to be equipped to adapt to a new landscape.

The sales process also takes place in the context of a dynamic clinical landscape in which prescribing patterns can change as more knowledge is gained about the way a disease responds to treatment. Prescribers (predominantly physicians) have significant latitude in deciding on the optimal course of treatment. The prescriber can be influenced by both awareness of current guidelines and the drug's label. The label lays out the indicated uses of a drug, along with prescribing information (dosing, for example) and contraindications (conditions in which the drug should not be used). A goal of pharmaceutical companies is to expand the label to include as many eligible patients as possible. This is done by conducting additional clinical trials (label expansion trials) to show the drug's efficacy either in other patient cohorts (e.g., expanding the age range), at a different point in the disease development (e.g., moving appropriate usage earlier in the disease process), or in different diseases altogether.

Not all drugs are amenable to wide usage, so it is incumbent on the company to allocate its resources carefully in order to receive a return on its product expansion activity. Given the latitude that physicians have in prescribing drugs, they often prescribe drugs in ways that are not indicated on the label. This phenomenon, referred to as off-label prescribing, presents both challenges and opportunities to pharmaceutical companies. The danger of using a drug in a setting for which it is not intended is that the risk/benefit trade-off is not favorable, leading to negative clinical outcomes and financial repercussions for the company and its shareholders. The opportunity is that physicians may discover that a drug is efficacious against a condition for which it was not tested. Companies can conduct their own comparative trials, with their products competing against other compounds in the treatment paradigm to help identify optimal therapy. If reform ultimately requires proof of cost-effectiveness, studies of this type will become commonplace, although who will conduct them and how they will be conducted may have an impact on the outcome. Companies that can best balance the risks and rewards of possible off-label experimentation with drugs would obtain a competitive advantage. The same dynamic applies to evolving changes in clinical practice guidelines, where companies need to optimize sales without creating a situation in which the risk of adding an additional patient is higher than the clinical and financial reward.

There are also sales challenges in addressing different segments of prescribers. Different medical specialties have different prescribing patterns, often driven by guidelines and by the level of understanding of a particular disease. Specialists and generalists may have different prescribing patterns for the same disease, given the physicians' level of experience with a disease or their personal preference. Even within the individual cohorts, there are likely to be varying levels of prescriptions written for different drugs in different disease classes. Pharmaceutical companies have tended to target the "high-decile" prescribers, as these offer the best return on marketing investment. In recent years, however, physicians have not been as amenable to direct sales information, and some local governments have taken steps to curtail direct sales activity, as they view this sales practice as one that may lead to malincentives vis-à-vis patients. Different sites of care (e.g., hospital versus office-based practice) can also influence prescribing patterns.

The companies that best understand the disease processes and where their products fit into the treatment paradigm will see a competitive edge. Reform plans, recognizing that there is no standardization in drug prescribing rules and that this could lead to variations in care, may target prescribing activity so that it better reflects clinical guidelines. Companies that recognize that health-care reform may alter the information flow on their products and are able to react to changes are more likely to see marketplace success than those that do not.

Branded drugs, like many non-health-care products, go through a life cycle: they are launched, grow, then plateau, and eventually decline. Unlike other products, when a pharmaceutical's patent has expired, it is very likely to face competition from a generic version. Although the level of competition rests on factors like the size of the branded product and the potential for existing competition, the trend is for compounds to see their market exclusivity period declining.[16] There is significant pressure on the part of the health-care system to reduce costs, and an expiring patent represents an opportunity for cost savings, as a premium product is replaced by a commodity. The upside is that a patent expiration allows more cost headroom in the system for other new compounds without a change in overall spending. The downside is that the company that makes the branded product loses a substantial amount of revenue.

Pharmaceutical companies have developed strategies for dealing with patent expirations, such as manufacturing their own generic products (branded generics); adding new features to the original product, such as extended release formulations, new delivery methods, or slightly different drug forms (different isomers); and adding another compound to the initial drug to form a fixed-dose combination pill. Making a compound available in an over-the-counter form, as has been done with allergy medication, is another strategy that has been employed to maintain the revenue stream. Although regulatory bodies can influence whether any of these strategies are feasible, life-cycle management techniques have been useful in the marketplace.[17] Companies that master life-cycle management can add to shareholder value, but in a potentially restrictive cost environment, only those companies that can show the value proposition behind their extended-life-cycle products will garner an upside and an advantage over those that do not.

External development efforts have traditionally been a hallmark of large pharmaceutical company business models. These activities have consisted of four strategies: mergers, acquisitions, in-licensing compounds or partnering (with companies or universities), and disposition of products or businesses that the company no longer considers part of its core operations. Mergers among large pharmaceutical companies are the events that draw the most media attention, but they have become rarer as the industry has become more concentrated. Acquisitions of smaller companies, along with in-licensing or partnering, are more common than large acquisitions because they are logistically easier to accomplish, are less expensive, and have relatively lower risk. The target company tends to see immediate gains in terms of market value, while the larger company presumably will see value creation over a longer time frame.

Investors need to take several factors into account in determining whether the external activity will lead to longer-term value creation. Motivations for external development can include economies of scale or a less expensive or logistically easier way of gaining an asset. They can be a response to slowing growth or to a managerial desire for a larger entity. Other factors that can affect value creation include the price paid, the strategic fit, and the potential for a regulatory roadblock like the Federal Trade Commission. Deal structures like outright acquisitions have higher risk profiles than licensing, although the return profiles are also different—another factor that investors must weigh when anticipating the potential for value creation. Investors should use the most conservative assumptions when analyzing whether corporate activity will create shareholder value, as there is scant evidence that it does. In fact, the evidence appears to be to the contrary, and there is a possibility that such actions, particularly larger acquisitions, may be a signal of slowing growth or excess capacity.[18] Divestitures are also not a guarantee of positive shareholder returns. The key will be whether the divestiture really does allow the company to better utilize its existing assets and whether the capital gained from any divestitures can be deployed in a way that generates higher returns than the divested assets did. Even if an investor's holdings are not directly affected by the external corporate activity in the sector, the analyst should pay attention to the outcome and the valuation because it can provide some insight into the current market price of the assets that the investor does hold and because these deals can happen in waves,[19] so an analyst's holdings may be next.

GENERIC MANUFACTURERS

In 1984, Congress passed the Waxman-Hatch Act, which reduced the regulatory burden on the production of generic pharmaceuticals. Prior to this act, the manufacturer of a generic drug had to go through a process similar to that required of branded manufacturers to get a drug approved—a time-consuming and expensive undertaking. The act called for manufacturers to prove bioequivalence to the branded drug rather than mandating that the product go through trials. The generic industry accelerated substantially after that.[20] Beyond the value creation that ensued, investors should be aware that reform legislation can lead to dramatic changes in the industry, and Waxman-Hatch is an example of this.

The primary reason for the development of generics is to reduce the cost of medications. As an inducement for developing new generic compounds, the act allowed the first generic on the market exclusivity for six months, leading to near-monopoly profits.

Even after other entrants are allowed on the market, the first mover generally still maintains significant market share.[21]

As with other commodity products where there is little differentiation, cost is the key advantage for manufacturers of generics. Companies in this sector can gain a cost advantage by having access to less expensive raw materials, more efficient manufacturing operations, or a more effective supply chain. In a more global era, this may mean that raw materials and manufacturing may take place in different geographic locations, even though there are increased regulatory costs that accompany this form of less costly production. Scale in terms of breadth of products and ability to produce significant quantities confers a certain advantage as well. It is worth pointing out that in less developed economies, generic products will be preferred to branded drugs because of a lack of resources.

Where generics diverge from the traditional commodity business model is in the legal component of the pathway to regulatory approval. Given the stakes in the launching of a generic drug, innovative companies and generic companies are likely to engage in aggressive tactics to tilt the outcome to their benefit. Patent disputes are the most common disagreement between branded and generic manufacturers. There are three types of strategies that a branded company can employ to defend itself against a generic and that a generic company will have to overcome. The branded company can create new features, like extended release formulations or new types of isomers, to extend the life of the patent. It can use legal or regulatory strategies to keep the generic off the market, like citizens' petitions, for example. The branded company can also enter into an agreement with the generic company covering when a generic can come to market. Generic companies that can successfully navigate these potential roadblocks created by innovative companies stand the best chance of creating shareholder value.

Difficult-to-manufacture generic drugs are another area in which generic companies can differentiate themselves. The manufacture of certain compounds, notably biologic drugs, but also those compounds using nontraditional delivery methods like aerosols or topical creams, can demand a higher level of expertise than small-molecule generic manufacturing. Companies that can obtain these skills will be able to create shareholder value, as more complex drugs are becoming more common and will ultimately see patent expirations.

SMALL-MARKET-CAPITALIZATION PHARMACEUTICALS

Below the top 20 pharmaceutical manufacturers are a number of small pharmaceutical companies; this group is referred to on Wall Street as specialty pharmaceutical manufacturers. Although this is a bit of a misnomer, it relates to the fact that smaller pharmaceutical companies have tended to specialize in a particular therapeutic area, geographic area, or some other strategic niche rather than attempting to be a multiline, multigeography pharmaceutical company. As with bigger pharmaceutical companies, the key driver of this group is innovation. Those companies that can develop new therapies are likely to create shareholder value. There are some hindrances for specialty pharmaceutical companies: given their more limited resources, it can be difficult for them to adequately invest in infrastructure (R&D and sales force), and therefore they are often reliant on the capital markets or partnerships with larger entities.

Recent advances in science and the advent of contract research organizations have leveled the playing field somewhat between small and larger companies, yet there is still a divide in capabilities caused by scale. In this regard, small pharmaceutical companies are more similar to smaller biotech companies than to large pharmaceutical companies. However, like larger pharmaceutical companies, they have to deal with patent expirations and also risk overreliance on key products. Beyond developing new drugs, those companies that can reduce their reliance on outside forces for the success of their products are more likely to create shareholder value. Such strategies include developing a sales force, marshaling financial capital or assets, or investing in an R&D franchise. Developing an R&D infrastructure is particularly likely to give these companies an advantage when it comes to partnering with larger entities.[22] Given their size and specialization, smaller pharmaceutical companies can have a different shareholder base from the larger companies, which can make their share prices react differently and be subject to moves based on catalysts and availability of capital.

REFORM RISK

Investors instinctively become concerned when any type of change is announced. Much of this has to do with the uncertainty discount that is built into stock prices. With health-care reform, there is at least one natural experiment that can be used to quantify the impact: the Clinton health-care reform proposal in 1992–1993. Under the shadow of that reform effort, larger pharmaceutical companies declined by an average of 38 percent, and smaller stocks also saw significant share price declines.[23,24] Though the reaction to it eventually proved to be overdone, it was related to a great extent to fears about the actions the government might take with regard to pharmaceutical pricing. Since consumers are most exposed to price, and since drug price inflation had been running substantially ahead of general inflation for some period before the Clinton health-care plan was proposed, drug prices (and affordability) were an obvious target, both for political expediency and as a relatively easy way to reduce system costs. Of course, drug costs are a relatively small proportion of the overall system spending,[25] so in the longer term, it is questionable whether reducing drug prices would be enough to rein in overall health-care spending.

Drug pricing may not be the only target of a health-care reform plan, but a reduction in price flexibility can hurt R&D efforts[26] and can lead to reallocation of pharmaceutical capital to lower-return activities such as political action.[27] There is a recognition on the part of the government that price controls in other countries have hurt the pharmaceutical industries in the countries that have enacted them.[28] Tools such as reduced approval times through mechanisms like the Prescription Drug User Fee Act have both helped the pharmaceutical companies and increased the social good, and such tools might be a carrot to use in a reform plan to counteract a price stick.[29] The government may not have the appetite to hurt an industry that is important to the United States' standing around the globe.

If pharmaceutical reform is consistent with the goals of improving quality, access, and cost, there are other reforms that may also be included in a reform package. Such a package may deal with the sales process and address issues like direct-to-consumer advertising, pharmaceutical advertising to doctors, off-label advertising, doctors' conflicts of interest with regard to pharmaceutical company honorariums, and the capture of physicians' prescribing habits. A reform program may put into place risk-sharing arrangements with pharmaceutical companies, where the company is paid only if the drugs actually reduce health-care expenditures.

Intellectual property issues may be altered, making it either easier or more difficult to extend a patent's life. A reform package may change the regulatory process, making it either less costly and time-consuming to move a drug to market or the converse. There may be mandates for comparative studies or cost-effectiveness studies, which may create an additional burden on some manufacturers. A reform package may provide incentives for innovation, including changes in the tax code or access to government-sponsored research such as that from the National Institutes of Health (NIH). A government program may take a cue from the private sector and offer drug manufacturers market share guarantees in exchange for discounts. The plan may also mandate patient assistance programs to help those who need drugs but can't afford them gain access to them. Mandates that companies disclose more of their clinical trial information might become the standard, and this, because the information would be subject to the interpretation of the marketplace, could lead to misinterpretation and gyrations in the share prices. Investors will need to evaluate the varying levers that the government chooses to pull.

It is incumbent upon investors to anticipate potential changes. Investors generally have time to anticipate consequences, as news is diffused into share prices relatively slowly.[30] Companies that foresee changes and can adapt their business models to accommodate a postreform environment are likely to create shareholder value and will see better returns than those companies that are unable to adapt. It is almost inevitable that fear will rule the day early in the reform process, as it has done in the past, and that pharmaceutical stocks will be weak, but profit will go to those analysts with enough vision to forecast the longer-term value creation and recognize that a package will not be completely one-sided.

FUTURE OPPORTUNITIES

There are opportunities that are not associated with reform that the industry may be able to avail itself of. Pharmaceutical companies have begun branching out into areas beyond their traditional small-molecule formats and moving into larger-molecule products that require infusions or injections. These large-molecule, traditionally biotechnology-derived drugs that have been the purview of smaller more specialized companies have become attractive because they tend to receive premium pricing. Biotech drugs have tended to have a lower attrition rate.[31] It is unclear whether a reform plan would affect price, but given that technology has allowed more drugs of these types to move to the market and that pharmaceutical companies have not been operating in this therapeutic class, it offers the pharmaceutical companies a new growth opportunity.

Pharmacogenomics, the expanding science of understanding how an individual reacts to certain compounds, offers pharmaceutical companies another growth driver. This should allow clinical trials to be less expensive and of shorter duration because the pharmaceutical manufacturer will know a priori in which patients the drugs will work. Pharmacogenomics may also allow pharmaceutical manufacturers to tailor drugs to individual patients to reduce the occurrence of serious adverse events. Companies may be able to receive premium pricing for these compounds because of the guarantee of efficacy. Even in an era of health-care reform, it seems unlikely that a plan would refuse to pay for a product that reduces costs and improves outcomes. Though the science is early in its development, it does have promise for improving pharmaceutical R&D, which should lead to value creation.[32]

New technology may also allow the development of vaccines to address previously unmet needs. Many pharmaceutical companies had abandoned this therapeutic class as a result of an inability to derive positive returns. These companies now have the potential to develop high-value vaccines and add another growth driver to their portfolio. Certain diseases, such as cancer, have become potential targets of vaccines. Should the technology advance further, either from the manufacturing side or in terms of the types of diseases amenable to vaccine technology, the potential return could be significant. This is particularly true for emerging markets, where vaccination is one of the first steps a population takes to reduce the disease burden.

As globalization takes hold, developing economies represent another opportunity for pharmaceutical companies. As the populations of these countries become wealthier, they will seek greater levels of health care. Included in this health-care demand will be a requirement for increased access to prescription pharmaceuticals. Though much of the demand may be for generic products, branded manufacturers will also benefit, as a premium will be placed on supply chain integrity and name recognition. As economies gain wealth, the types of disease they face may change as well, with an increase in chronic diseases like cardiac disease and diabetes and a decrease in infectious diseases like malaria. Intellectual property disputes will play a role in emerging market development, as will the idea that some of these economies are "free riding" on U.S. innovation. Differential pricing among countries can probably be made to work under the right set of circumstances.[33] Access to less expensive raw materials and labor outside the developed world may be an issue, but safety and quality issues must be resolved.

VALUATION

Valuation of pharmaceutical companies is difficult because so much of their future value is embedded in the pipeline, and the outcome of products in the pipeline cannot be known with a high degree of certainty, given the high attrition rate. The analyst can make some assumptions about ranges of valuation for pipelines, which, along with a valuation of current earnings power and assets, may allow him to get a sense as to whether the shares are under- or overvalued. At the very highest level, firms that conduct more R&D tend to outperform less R&D-intensive firms.[34] All else being equal (though it seldom is), companies with more aggressive R&D programs should receive a higher valuation than those that do not. The analyst should be suitably assured that the company has a well-developed R&D franchise, particularly when it has had some successes, as more successful R&D tends to receive higher valuations.[35] Determining what types of compounds are in the pipeline and their stage of development is an essential element of pipeline valuation. This is not always an easy task, as disclosure approaches vary by company. For larger companies, there will be a variety of programs across a variety of clinical areas at different levels of development, from preclinical to postmarketing.

There are several approaches to calculating the value of the projects in the pipeline that are relatively similar to approaches to valuing stocks; these include looking at projects as options,[36] net present value calculations for individual projects, and re-creation value. The basic premise behind all these approaches is to attempt to adjust the probability of the ultimate returns from a project for risk, time, and capital expenditures. As with equity valuation, a lot depends on the assumptions that go into the valuation. Re-creation value is intuitively more simple than the other, more mathematically oriented approaches, as it requires only knowledge of current prices for projects involving different compounds in different phases for different types of buyers. Since investors do have some general cost parameters, time parameters, and success parameters for drugs[37] and some knowledge of the potential market for a drug, they can get a general valuation metric for an individual compound. An analyst may get a sense of the importance of a product by looking at the level of patent citations it receives.[38] The analyst can then go through the pipeline and sum up the re-creation value of the individual compounds. In general, later-stage products are worth more than earlier-stage products because their chances of success are higher, and an early-stage compound with solid results directed at a significant unmet need can be worth a significant amount as well. Because pipeline valuation is an inexact science at best, analysts should use wide error bars and conservative assumptions, and also refine their models frequently to accommodate any new information. If the pipeline still appears inexpensive with conservative assumptions, the shares of the company may be undervalued.

There are numerous factors that affect adoption rates, including the novelty of the product, the price of the product, the pharmacoeconomic value of the product, the competitive environment, the sales effort behind the product, physicians' knowledge of the disease state, physicians' willingness to change prescribing habits, information diffusion, and payer acceptance. Depending upon the product, some of these factors may be of greater importance than others. The shape of the adoption curve is likely to be more important than the ultimate peak sales, as the sooner after the launch the growth comes, the higher the longer-term returns will be.

Merck

In the summer of 2004, the shares of Merck had been holding up after an inline second-quarter report. Late in that summer the FDA presented a study which showed that Vioxx had a higher risk of cardiovascular side-effects than other compounds that treat osteoarthritis. The results spurred several large insurers to reevaluate the placement of Vioxx on the formulary, and some even removed the drug from the list of drugs that would be reimbursed. For a stock analyst, the removal of Vioxx from formularies foreshadowed an eventual decline in sales and should have set off some warning bells. The removal also foreshadowed the eventual withdrawal of the drug from the market due to negative cardiovascular effects in certain populations, although this was clearer in retrospect. Merck's shares declined precipitously (over 44 percent) after the withdrawal on fears that litigation risk would overwhelm the company. The company ultimately settled with plaintiffs for a multibillion-dollar sum. In the intervening years, the shares recouped much of their lost value on the strength of innovative vaccines and diabetes products, many of which were first in their respective classes. There are several lessons that investors can draw from the Merck example. Even without specialized knowledge of the class of drugs (like the Cox-2 class to which Vioxx belonged) and its potential side-effects, watching actions of the payers who can drive much of the sales activity can offer clues to future growth. Under certain types of reform, a Vioxx-like problem would not have the impact as it did, because there may be more cost-effectiveness data available, and there may be more careful monitoring on sentinel events like cardiovascular disease, which may point out problems with therapies earlier. Ultimately, a robust R&D effort with drugs that address genuine public health needs can create value, and a careful analysis of a pipeline, especially when shares are depressed, can lead to a profitable investment.

NOTES

1. Christopher P. Adams and Van V. Brantner, "Estimating the Cost of New Drug Development: Is It Really $802 Million?" *Health Affairs* 25, no. 2 (2006): 420–428.

2. Christopher P. Adams and Van V. Brantner, "New Drug Development: Estimating Entry from Human Clinical Trials," FTC Bureau of Economics Working Paper No. 262, July 7, 2003; available at SSRN, http://ssrn.com/abstract=428040 or DOI, 10.2139/ssrn.428040.

3. Mark E. Mathieu (ed.), *Parexel's Bio/pharmaceutical R&D Statistical Sourcebook 2007/2008* (Waltham, Mass.: Parexel International Corp., 2007), p. 212.

4. Rosa M. Abrantes-Metz, Christopher Adams, and Albert D. Metz, "Pharmaceutical Development Phases: A Duration Analysis," FTC Bureau of Economics Working Paper No. 274, October 2004.

5. Adams and Brantner, "New Drug Development."

6. For more details on eureka moments, see Morton A. Meyers, *Happy Accidents: Serendipity in Modern Medical Breakthroughs* (New York: Arcade Publishing, 2007).

7. Pedro Cuatrecasas, "Drug Discovery in Jeopardy," *Journal of Clinical Investigation* 116, no. 11 (2006): 2837–2842; available at DOI, 10.1172/jci129999.

8. *Parexel's Bio/pharmaceutical R&D Statistical Source Book 2007/2008*, p. 213; see also Maria Gordain, Navjot Singh, Rodney Zemmel, and Tamara Elias, "Why Products Fail in Phase III," IN VIVO, April 2006.

9. Joseph A. DiMasi and Cherie Paquette, "The Economics of Follow-on Drug Research and Development: Trends in Entry Rates and the Timing of Development," *PharmacoEconomics* 22, suppl. 2 (2004): 1–14.

10. Abrantes-Metz, Adams, and Metz, "Pharmaceutical Development Phases."

11. The FDA Web site has more information on clinical trials: http://www.fda.gov/oashi/clinicaltrials/default.htm.

12. Adams and Brantner, "New Drug Development."

13. Jonathan Knowles and Gianni Gromo, "Target Selection in Drug Discovery," *Nature Reviews Drug Discovery* Vol. 2, January 2003.

14. Paul H. Rubin and Adam Atherly, "The Cost Effectiveness of Direct to Consumer Advertising of Prescription Drugs," Emory Law and Economics Research Paper No. 08–28, February 2008; available at SSRN, http://ssrn.com/abstract=1092164.

15. The Kaiser Family Foundation report, "Impact of Direct-to-Consumer Advertising on Prescription Drug Spending," June 2003.

16. Henry G. Grabowski and Margaret Kyle, "Generic Competition and Market Exclusivity Periods in Pharmaceuticals," *Managerial and Decision Economics* 28 (2007): 491–502.

17. David Reiffen and Michael R. Ward, " 'Branded Generics' as a Strategy to Limit Cannibalization of Pharmaceutical Markets, " May 2005; available at SSRN, http://ssrn.com/abstract=724401.

18. Patricia M. Danzon, Andrew Joel Epstein, and Sean Nicholson, "Mergers and Acquisitions in the Pharmaceutical and Biotech Industries, Organizational Economics of Health Care Conference, September 2003.

19. Ibid.

20. David Reiffen and Michael R. Ward, "Generic Drug Industry Dynamics," FTC Bureau of Economics Working Paper No. 248, October 2002; available at SSRN, http://ssrn.com/abstract=390102, or DOI, 10.2139/ssrn.390102.

21. Sachin Gupta, Yu Yu, and Rahul Guha, "Pioneering Advantage in Generic Drug Competition," Johnson School Research Paper Series No. 37-06, August 2006; available at SSRN, http://papers.ssrn.com/sol3/papers.cfm?abstract_id=925346.

22. Ashish Arora, William B. Vogt, and Jiwoong Yoon, "Does In-house R&D Increase Bargaining Power? Evidence from the Pharmaceutical Industry," 2004; available at SSRN, http://ssrn.com/abstract=670304.

23. Sara Fisher Ellison and Wallace P. Mullin, "Gradual Incorporation of Information: Pharmaceutical Stocks and the Evolution of President Clinton's Health Care Reform," *Journal of Law & Economics* 44, no. 1 (2001): 89–129.

24. Joseph H. Golec, Shantaram P. Hegde, and John A. Vernon, "Pharmaceutical Stock Price Reactions to Price Constraint Threats and Firm-Level R&D Spending," March 11, 2005; available at SSRN, http://papers.ssrn.com/sol3/papers.cfm?abstract_id=685121.

25. National Center for Health Statistics, *Health, United States, 2004, With Chartbook on Trends in the Health of Americans*, (PHS) 2004-1232 (Hyattsville, Md.: National Center for Health Statistics Press, 2004); GPO stock number is 017-022-01575-7.

26. Golec, Hegde, and Vernon, "Pharmaceutical Stock Price Reactions."

27. Sara Fisher Ellison and Catherine D. Wolfram, "Pharmaceutical Prices and Political Activity," MIT Department of Economics Working Paper No. 01–30, August 2001; available at SSRN, http://ssrn.com/abstract=281391, or DOI, 10.2139/ssrn.281391.

28. Joseph H. Golec and John A. Vernon, "European Pharmaceutical Price Regulation, Firm Profitability, and R&D Spending," August 2006; available at SSRN, http://ssrn.com/abstract=932989.

29. Joseph H. Golec, Randall Lutter, John A. Vernon, and Clark Nardinelli, "FDA New Drug Approval Times, Prescription Drug User Fees and R&D Spending," AEI-Brookings Joint Center Working Paper 06–21, September 2006; available at SSRN, http://papers.ssrn.com/sol3/papers.cfm?abstract_id=931153.

30. Ellison and Mullin, "Gradual Incorporation of Information."

31. Adams and Brantner, "New Drug Development."

32. John A. Vernon and W. Keener Hughen, "The Future of Drug Development: The Economics of Pharmacogenomics," NBER Working Paper no., 11875, www.nber.org/papers/w11875.

33. Patricia M. Danzon and Adrian Towse, "Differential Pricing for Pharmaceuticals: Reconciling, Access, R&D, and Patents. *International Journal of Health Care Finance and Economics* 3, no. 3 (2003): 183–205.

34. Louis K. C. Chan, Josef Lakonishok, and Theodore Sougiannis, "The Stock Market Valuation of Research and Development Expenditures," June 1999; available at SSRN, http://ssrn.com/abstract=195488, or DOI, 10.2139/ssrn.195488.

35. Rebecca Toppe Shortridge, "Market Valuation of Successful versus Non-successful R&D Efforts in the Pharmaceutical Industry, *Journal of Business Finance & Accounting* 31, no. 9–10 (2004).

36. Eduardo S. Schwartz, "Patents and R&D as Real Options," *Economic Notes* 33, no. 1 (2004): 23–54; available at SSRN, http://ssrn.com/abstract=551803.

37. See Adams and Brantner, "New Drug Development"; Abrantes-Metz, Adams, and Metz, "Pharmaceutical Development Phases"; and DiMasi, Hansen, and Grabowski, "The Price of Innovation" for quantified parameters of cost, time, and success rates.

38. Mark Hirschey and Vernon J. Richardson, "Are Scientific Indicators of Patent Quality Useful to Investors?" *Journal of Empirical Finance* 11, no. 1 (2004).

CHAPTER 11

Investing in Biotechnology

As an industry, biotechnology is young. In 1953, James Watson and Francis Crick identified DNA (deoxyribonucleic acid).[1] The discovery of recombinant DNA technique by Stanley Cohen and Herbert Boyer in 1973 and the creation of the monoclonal antibody by Georges Köhler, César Milstein, and Niels Kaj Jerne in 1975 accelerated the development of the industry.[2] The Bayh-Dole Act of 1980 and the Supreme Court ruling in *Diamond v. Chakrabarty* set the stage for additional growth of the industry, as these milestones allowed federally funded universities to license technology to private entities and allowed the issuance of patents for microorganisms, respectively. Discoveries like recombinant DNA and monoclonal antibodies captured the imagination of investors at the time, although their financial benefits were not felt until later. In an era of reform, a change in laws like Bayh-Dole becomes more likely, and investors should be aware that seemingly small changes in legislation could lead to significant value creation in the long run.

Like that of pharmaceuticals, the business model of biotechnology is to develop and sell new therapeutic agents. Unlike traditional pharmaceutical firms, biotech firms have historically focused exclusively on deriving compounds from living cells rather than from chemicals. Traditional pharmaceutical products are derived from inorganic chemicals. Biotechnology companies have also historically focused on large molecules instead of small molecules. Generally, the dividing line between a big and a small molecule is that a molecule is considered big if it cannot gain entry into a cell easily and must act from the outside through receptors. A small molecule can enter the cell and make changes in its machinery to bring about a therapeutic change. Some biotechnology companies do not attempt to develop therapeutic agents; instead, they develop technologies that other companies can use to either manufacture or produce therapies.

Given the expense and complexity of developing and manufacturing a biologic compound, biotechnology companies have tended to focus on more acute and higher-value areas like oncology, where they have been able to charge very high prices. Biotechnology has given medicine some of its most important and most costly advances. Given the cost of these novel therapies, only insured patients have been able to afford the most advanced biotechnology treatments.

A number of biotech companies have achieved financial results that are on a par with those of the pharmaceutical industry, and now the industry boasts companies with market capitalizations equal to or greater than those of traditional pharmaceutical companies. In terms of quantity, these larger profit-making companies are outnumbered by the smaller discovery-stage entities. As with pharmaceuticals, the analytical challenges differ somewhat depending on the size and financial characteristics of the firm. As firms grow and mature, their financial metrics start to become more quantifiable and thus become more important determinants of value.[3] Smaller, unprofitable companies are often judged using other metrics.

The therapy development model of the biotech industry has generally been to pursue basic science discoveries such as genetic sequencing, monoclonal antibodies, genomics, proteomics, and high-throughput screening and translate them into medicines that can treat human diseases. This approach has led to numerous blockbuster drugs directed at a variety of different disease states. Pharmaceutical companies have in the past been slow to adopt new technologies, in part because there are many technologies and it is difficult to determine which, if any, of them will bear fruit. Investors face the same conundrum as the large companies as they try to determine where to place their investment dollars and at what valuation.

There are differences in business models between traditional pharmaceutical companies and traditional biotech companies, and these have implications both for investors and for the impact of health-care reform. The R&D cycle for biotech drugs is a little longer than that for small-molecule products, although the out-of-pocket costs are somewhat lower and the success rates are somewhat higher.[4,5] Some of the differences may be a function of the types of diseases that are amenable to biotech therapies, but the differences may also be attributable to biotech drugs themselves in terms of their ability to be more targeted than systemic small molecules.

The manufacturing process for biotechnology drugs also differs from pharmaceutical manufacturing. Manufacturing biotechnology drugs often entails the use of recombinant DNA technology, which means that the genetic sequence of a cell is altered so that it produces a required substance. Blood proteins, human hormones, immune modulators, and vaccines have all been produced this way.[6] The cost of this method of production is high because of its level of complexity. Quality control is also important, as even small variations in genetic sequence can alter the formulation of the drug. The difficulty of scaling up production can even lead to drug shortages.[7] Although there are shortages of pharmaceuticals on occasion, their less complex manufacturing process can allow the companies making them to scale up fast and move production between facilities relatively easily if necessary.

The delivery mechanism is another factor differentiating biotech drugs from small-molecule pharmaceuticals. The size and chemical composition of large-molecule products mean that these treatments are generally not amenable to absorption into the bloodstream via the gastrointestinal tract like small-molecule pills. The result is that in order to be effective, these drugs need to be injected or infused into the body. The implication is that they often either have to be administered by a health-care provider at a special medical site or require special patient training. This delivery approach creates an additional financial hurdle as well as a logistical burden. The reimbursement process is also different for small- and large-molecule products. Given the often high price of biotech drugs, they are frequently reimbursed through specialized divisions of health-care insurance companies. The government also reimburses companies for these types of drugs differently, often paying for them through the Medicare Part B program.

There is some benefit to a company from a more difficult drug administration pathway or disease state, as the drug is usually prescribed by a relatively small number of specialists. This smaller number of specialists means that a smaller sales force is able to address the market, which implies that the company's costs will be lower. Despite the lower sales force costs, however, the manufacturing and delivery of biotech drugs tend to make them significantly more expensive than a small-molecule equivalent (generally speaking), and this presents challenges for the health-care system. With the increasing number of biologic drugs coming on the market will come rapidly increasing costs.

CONVERGENCE

Because of the similarities between biotechnology and pharmaceutical companies, it should be no surprise then that these industries are starting to converge. Pharmaceutical companies, seeing greater life-cycle lengths, better intellectual property protections, and higher reimbursement, are moving toward developing biotech drugs.[8] Biotech companies, seeking to diversify their product offerings so that they are less reliant on a few technologies or therapeutic classes, and also looking for a way to better utilize their expertise in clinical areas,[9] are moving toward small molecules.

Convergence has both practical implications for the companies and investment implications. Practically, it requires companies to enter businesses with which they may not be familiar. Entering an unfamiliar line of business engenders a higher level of risk than expanding an existing line of business. For example, the sales process differs in terms of end market users (different types of physicians) and different reimbursement processes. Drug development, regardless of whether it is biotech or pharmaceutical, is subject to high attrition rates, and experience with a therapeutic class seems to be associated with positive outcomes.[10] For analysts, biotech companies have different return profiles from pharmaceutical companies. Also, biotech companies and pharmaceutical companies have tended to have different types of holders with different risk tolerances and return requirements.

ALLIANCES

The complexity and novelty of biotech drugs, along with the time and financial resources required to develop them, have made collaborating with bigger pharmaceutical companies and licensing products to them a part of the biotech business model as well. A small company may not have the substantial resources required to move a project through the development process from preclinical to market. The clinical cycle can take nearly a decade[11] and sometimes more, and this is a long time to spend on a product with a high probability of failure before it comes to fruition. If a company is reliant on a single product, the risk of outright failure for the franchise is extremely high in an industry with high attrition rates.

Because of the duration of a clinical project, biotech companies often rely on alliances to provide them with capital.[12] There is a reduction in developmental risk when two companies partner to develop a compound. Each of the partners has less financial risk, and the smaller biotech company can access a larger company's greater experience and research capabilities to augment its own. If the smaller biotech company has more than one compound to be developed, it may well be unable to develop all of these compounds without the aid of a larger company. In addition, if the product is successful, the smaller company must either develop manufacturing and sales capabilities or rely on a larger company that already has these capabilities.

The value of an alliance is highly variable and depends on many factors, some of which are the same factors that investors must consider when valuing a company for equity investment. The stage of development of the product, the number of products being developed, and R&D expenditures[13] can alter the value proposition for the partners. The clinical category, the chances of success for that product, the competitive environment for the product, and the product's importance to the larger alliance partner will also play a role in the value of the franchise. Access to capital may affect alliance valuations.[14] A small biotech company's experience with alliances also has an impact on valuation, with less experienced companies often receiving a discount.[15] As with the smaller pharmaceutical companies, a greater R&D capability and more clinical and business options give small biotech companies leverage in negotiating an alliance.[16]

For a larger company, the benefit of an alliance is that the company may gain access to pipeline products that it cannot create because of intellectual property or other barriers or gain access to them in a less costly manner than creating them from scratch. Depending on the terms of the deal, the larger company may even be able to mitigate much of its own development risk. In-licensed compounds often have a higher success rate than compounds developed organically.[17] Collaborations with universities or academic research are also an important part of biotechnology development; although the initial expenditures are often small in size, they may lead to greater royalty sharing upon the success of a product. Companies that can successfully navigate academic collaborations can bolster their development prospects.

VALUATION

As with pharmaceutical companies, the challenge in valuing biotech companies is to place a value on intangible assets like intellectual property and early-stage clinical trials. For larger companies, the task is made easier by the existence of tangible assets and measurable financial metrics such as sales, earnings, and cash flow in addition to pipeline valuation. For development-stage companies, the task is more difficult because these companies lack assets and earnings power. For these companies, investors need to rely on proxy measures of value. One method is to determine the quality of the company's science,[18] but given that much of the science is novel to investors and many researchers, there may be some difficulty in evaluating science quality directly. Some metrics used to determine science quality are the presence of star scientists (well-published researchers who are known in the field) on the staff, the number of patents granted, Small Business Innovation Research (SBIR) grants to the firm,[19] and number of patent citations.[20] As the number of patent citations grows, there is the potential for significant increases in valuation; this can be expected especially when a low ratio of price to number of citations is combined with more traditional valuation metrics associated with future performance, such as a lower price/earnings ratio.[21]

Harder variables such as equity value, cost of sales, and R&D expenses should not be ignored, as they contribute to stock returns in biotech just as they do in other industries.[22] Biotechnology firms derive most of their future success from their R&D efforts, and R&D intensity in early-stage development companies can be associated with stock returns, although the effect seems to diminish as firms mature.[23] Other factors that need to be considered are the capital-raising environment, as not only does this influence decisions regarding alliances,[24] but a difficult capital-raising environment can also be detrimental to share price performance.[25] Capital is the lifeblood of developmental biotech because developing drugs is a time-consuming and capital-consuming process. Smaller companies can also use capital as a competitive weapon, both to receive better deal terms and to access technology and additional experimental compounds.

Investors should be aware that there are times when the capital market is "open" and firms can raise money; at those times, the analytical challenge is to make sure that existing investors' ownership is not diluted materially. For companies that have existing products on the market or have products that are due to be launched in the near term, the same factors that come into play in the pharmaceutical adoption analysis heuristic apply to biotechnology: novelty of product, price, pharmacoeconomic value, state of disease knowledge, diffusion of information, and willingness of providers to shift their prescribing habits.

As with pharmaceuticals, the shape of the adoption curve may be more important than ultimate peak sales, as the earlier the product generates growth, the higher the total return on the product will be and the better the near-term performance of the company will be. Although relative valuation may not be the ideal way to value the sector, given the occasional bursts of irrational behavior that overcome speculative stocks and the wide diversity of stages of development and biologic targets, it can be useful as a guidepost during those times. Quantitative approaches such as ranking biotech stocks on size distribution may be of some utility.[26] Investors will also need to quantify patient populations to aid in valuation.

OTHER INVESTMENT CONSIDERATIONS

The biotech sector often has some of the most volatile share price performance of any sector of the market. For example, in 2007, the annual share price performance of the major biotech index ranged from +400 percent to –98 percent.[27] These results are not uncommon; intuitively, if there is a single factor, like the outcome of a clinical trial, that can make or break a company, this will cause the share price to react violently. Binary events or catalysts tend to make shares of smaller companies more volatile than those of larger companies because these events tend to be more important for the less diversified companies.

Catalysts are not limited to clinical events. Any change in the franchise that may have a material impact can be the cause of a big share move. Companies may have predetermined milestones to show that they are making business or clinical progress; these can include filings with the FDA, clinical trial enrollment goals, or moving a drug to the next stage of development. A payment in cash or some other remuneration, which can help offset costs and can change the financial complexion of the often smaller company, is often associated with achieving these milestones. A priority for investors is to ensure that the catalyst is in fact material; since it is recognized that investors use events like alliances as proxies for science quality, companies can overstate the importance of such an event. If an alliance is just a signal without material consequences for either party, it is unlikely to be successful.[28]

Moving a compound from early to middle stage (Phase I to Phase II, for example) may not be a sign of progress; rather, it may indicate that the company is so reliant on that compound for future growth and access to capital that it may ultimately fail. Investors can understand the motivation for continuing a failing project, although it does indicate poor corporate governance and may lead to negative outcomes anyway.[29] Investing in biotech requires an understanding that there can be wild price swings, if only because these companies tend to have higher betas (a measure of market movement) than the market, which implies that they will react with larger moves in general.

Biotechnology companies, even smaller ones, disseminate significant levels of information with which the analyst must contend. Like companies in other R&D-intensive industries, biotechnology companies tend to have more analyst coverage and hold more conference calls than companies in non-R&D-intensive industries.[30] This R&D intensity also allows insiders to have a far greater asymmetry of knowledge than is found in other industries—they are better positioned to judge the merits of intangibles like ideas and clinical progress than outsiders are.[31] The insider disclosure policy also influences the level of discourse. Researchers, both company-related and non-company-related, are likely to add to the information flow by publishing or presenting data at clinical conferences. It is incumbent on the analyst to be aware that there will be substantial data available that may move a stock, but that some of these data may be biased or incorrect. It is important to develop sources by which to judge the merit of new information as it becomes incorporated into the stock price.

Biotech as an industry is also subject to the occasional fad, and this can lead to outsized share price responses. It can be difficult to distinguish a fad from a genuine scientific breakthrough, but investors should be aware that fads do occur occasionally in the sector, recognize that the resulting performance is not sustainable, and sell their stocks when the valuation outpaces the return potential of the franchise.

CLINICAL TRIALS

Because smaller companies have so much riding on a few compounds, investors' emphasis is naturally placed on the clinical programs. As for the smaller pharmaceutical companies, contract research organizations (CROs) have improved smaller companies' ability to manage complex clinical trials. However, the existence of CROs does not guarantee that these programs will be carried out in a way that produces an approvable drug, even if the drug appears to have some type of therapeutic activity. Statistical significance in a trial does not ensure a successful product. Poor study design can waste valuable resources and lead to a negative outcome.[32] A poor clinical program reduces the attractiveness of a smaller biotech firm to both alliance partners and acquirers, making the program that much more important as a value-creating factor. A number of considerations go into deciding on the design of a clinical trial, including the endpoints (what change the drug is intended to create), how the endpoints are to be measured, when the endpoints will be measured, the number of patients in the trial, what types of patients will be included in the trial, how quickly patients will be able to be enrolled in a trial, and whether all trial participants will be measured or just those that complete the trial.

Selecting where the trial will be conducted is also important, as sites with more experience with a disease and in conducting research are more likely to be effective than less experienced sites.[33] Statistical analysis of data is also critical, as determining whether the outcome of a trial is statistically significant (whether the compound alters the disease course in a way that would not happen by random chance—i.e., whether or not it works) is generally what determines a company's ability to get a drug on the market. Unfortunately, this is one of the more complicated areas of investment analysis, and it involves a higher level of scrutiny. The disease and the potential outcome of the trial are likely to drive the statistical analysis; elements such as whether the population is normally distributed and how large the clinical impact will be play a role in deciding which analysis techniques to use. Trial design factors such as whether the trials will take all comers or whether there are exclusion criteria will affect the final results. In general, a larger trial population (number of patients enrolled) with a large therapeutic change that is easily measured in conditions that closely mirror real-world situations is preferred.

In certain situations, enrolling patients who have not been exposed to medicine for a given condition ("treatment naive") is difficult because many patients have had access to prior, often sophisticated treatments. Prior treatment often confounds results, as it makes it difficult to distinguish the effects of the experimental treatment from those of the previous treatment. Biotech companies have sought to conduct trials outside the United States to overcome this problem. However, because of other countries' own organic demand for medicines, it is not always easy to ensure that trial protocols (the process mandated by the trial design for consistency) are conducted with consistent rigor.

There are methods for quantifying the cost of trials and sample sizes based upon predetermined parameters,[34] but given the relative lack of success of most clinical trials, if either previous work, sample size, or clinical effect indicates that the results will be too close to call, investors without specialized knowledge in statistics or trial design should err on the side of caution. The clinical trial must take place in the context of safety: a drug could be proven efficacious, but if the side effect profile is poor or is not outweighed by the clinical benefits, the drug's regulatory and/or market success will be diminished.

REFORM

Biotech investors may view reform plans warily; this is a function of uncertainty and previous experience. Biotech stocks underperformed even pharmaceutical stocks' dismal performance during the Clinton health-care debate in the early 1990s.[35] The costliness of biotechnology drugs is likely to be a target of any health-care reform plan. The increasing number of biologic agents and the utilization of biotech drugs will only add to the already great cost pressures on the health-care system. The substantial price tags will keep access to these often life-enhancing or lifesaving products out of reach for many unless they are well insured.

A reform plan has relatively few options for dealing with the price of treatments, and they are similar to those for pharmaceuticals. Outright price caps, cost-effectiveness thresholds, and patient assistance programs are alternatives that a reform plan could utilize, but all of these could have unintended consequences, such as a reduction in innovative capacity. Unlike with pharmaceuticals, however, there is no well-developed generic pathway for biologics at present. The biotech industry is relatively young, so many of its products are still under patent protection. When Waxman-Hatch was passed, biotech as an industry was in its infancy, and the authors did not foresee the types of changes that would emerge two decades later. Bioequivalence does not necessarily exist in biotechnology the way it does in pharmaceuticals, as chemical composition can vary.

Manufacturing and delivery also pose challenges in determining bioequivalence; since the mechanisms of action of a drug are not always well elucidated, modest changes in its formulation or delivery can have substantial impacts on its efficacy and safety.[36] Given the expense and complexity of manufacturing (using live cells to produce the compounds), it is even unclear that a bioequivalent drug will be much less expensive.

It seems almost inevitable that a generic pathway will eventually be developed and that companies will enter the generic biologic field, with negative consequences for biotechnology innovator companies; however, it remains to be seen whether the magnitude of the detriment will be the same as it is for pharmaceutical companies.

As with pharmaceutical companies, a reform plan may not be a complete negative for shareholders. An expansion of access to care may increase volume,[37] and a reform plan could change the rules regarding partnering with universities or enhance the U.S. SBIR program, which could foster innovation. The government also spends a substantial amount of money on innovation through the National Institutes of Health (NIH). A reform package could make interaction between the NIH and the biotech industry more open, also possibly spurring innovation. Investors should be aware that an announcement of reform might have a negative impact on their biotech holdings, but that the devil will be in the details of the plan with regard to the impact on the sector.

A reform program may permit easier thresholds for label expansion (moving a compound from second line to first line) or lower the threshold for combination therapy (a common practice in biotech). A regulatory body may also allow greater use of surrogate markers (indications of disease progression that are not directly related to primary symptoms) or biomarkers (direct indications of diseases). There is no clear guidance on these mechanisms, so this could be clarified as part of a reform package, potentially making it easier for drugs to get approval.

In biotech, company-specific factors will ultimately drive returns, and there are other opportunities for the biotech sector that do not involve reform. Pharmacogenomics could have a profound impact on the future of drug discovery. Genome-wide association studies, among other techniques, may accelerate the drug discovery process and may lead to more opportunities.[38] The Internet may allow genetic information to be disseminated more widely and potentially allow for open-source R&D. Should R&D become more available, it could accelerate the research process,[39] although intellectual property concerns will remain an issue. Developing markets represent another opportunity for biotech companies, because as these economies' wealth increases, they will seek out biotechnological medical advances. Emerging markets are likely to be able to develop the infrastructure required to deliver such therapies as their economies improve. The market for certain types of biologic antivirals, for example, may be larger in certain emerging markets than in the North American market, so this could be a significant growth driver going forward.

THE FDA

The Food and Drug Administration is the U.S. agency that is responsible for protecting the public health by ensuring the safety and efficacy of food and medical products. The health-care portion of the agency is most relevant to health-care investors. In its capacity as watchdog of safety and arbiter of efficacy, the FDA is involved in most health-care products' life cycles in one way or another. The FDA is also helping to speed innovations that make medicines safer and more affordable and making sure that information about products is disseminated to the public in a timely manner.

The approval process is where most investors get confounded by the agency, given its sometimes confusing timelines, multiple acronyms, and varying subagencies. The FDA has specific sections for drugs, biologics, and medical devices, among others, and even different therapeutic sections (oncology and cardiovascular, for example), and these sections can have different philosophical approaches. In general, the approval process for a therapeutic agent goes through a series of discrete steps (see Figure 11-1). The law that dictates the process is the Prescription Drug User Fee Act (PDUFA) of 1993. This law was put into place to try to accelerate the approval process, and it involves product makers paying fees to the agency to encourage a speedy approval process. A standard review takes 10 months, and a priority review takes 6 months, although these are guidelines and approvals can be either faster or slower. A fast-track designation allows the company to schedule meetings and submit its applications in sections rather than submitting an entire application all at once. Fast track is independent of priority review and involves determining whether the product addresses an unmet medical need.

The process starts with an initial filing, referred to as an IND (Investigational New Drug application). This application proposes the clinical course of action to the FDA in order to gain permission to conduct clinical trials. Upon FDA approval, the company can go ahead with the clinical trials, and it does so through the various phases of the process. During this time, the company is likely to be interacting with the agency to keep it abreast of developments and receive guidance about the most efficient way to get to the next steps. Interacting with the agency successfully is a key competitive advantage, as some companies do this better than others.

F I G U R E   11-1

The FDA review process

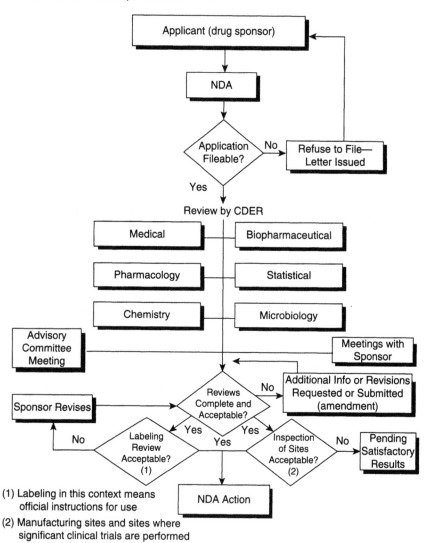

(1) Labeling in this context means
   official instructions for use

(2) Manufacturing sites and sites where
   significant clinical trials are performed

Source: FDA Web site.

Once the trials are completed, the company submits a New Drug Application (NDA) to the agency; the agency then has 180 days to accept the filing. There are different types of applications depending on the type of product: BLA (biologics license application) for biotech and PMA (premarket approval) for medical devices. Over the course of the approval process, the FDA may hold an advisory panel meeting. The function of such a panel is to have experts from outside the agency review the clinical issues. The panel then makes recommendations to the agency, which usually (but not always) follows the panel's recommendation; it can approve the compound; deem the compound approvable subject to additional requirements, such as more data or safety experience; or deem the product not approved.

If the compound is approved, the company then negotiates with the agency about the content of the label (the instructions for usage in the market). The broader the label, the more flexibility the company has in marketing the product, and the greater the possibility for a high level of sales. Once a product is approved, the company may be required to conduct a postapproval study, which is designed to detect issues after the product is on the market. If this study or some other form of agency surveillance detects product performance issues such as safety issues, the agency can require label changes or, in extreme cases, recall the product from the market. Having FDA approval gives companies a leg up in sales outside the United States, as other countries take their cues from the United States, as well as offering some protection against litigation risk should the product fail.

The company has some recourse if the agency deems a drug not approved or approvable. The recourse depends a great deal on the reasons for the lack of full approval. If the reason is safety-related, then it is incumbent on the company to run additional safety trials to document the way in which the agency misinterpreted the data. The same holds true for efficacy; if the company feels that the agency is in error with regard to the clinical value proposition, it needs to produce more data to convince the agency that this is an important drug. In the case of a drug that is deemed approvable, the agency is likely to dictate what additional data are needed. If the agency requests data that are impossible to get for clinical reasons, or if the acquisition of such data is prohibitively expensive, then the agency has functionally not approved the drug. The company can appeal to the legislature or to advocacy groups, but in the past this has yielded little in the way of positive outcomes. The agency does have a mechanism called a special protocol assessment (SPA), which is something of a memorandum of understanding that if a drug produces a certain outcome in a certain way, it will be approved. Although this document is not necessarily a guarantee of success, it does reduce the amount of miscommunication between company and agency—although a company should be in communication with the agency throughout the process anyway.

GENENTECH

In mid-2003, Genentech shares were mostly treading water after a relatively lackluster first quarter earnings report. Then in May of that year, the company presented the results of a trial for Avastin (a biologic) for colon cancer, which showed that the drug prolonged life. The results came as a surprise, because the drug had failed in a prior trial to treat breast cancer. Given the surprise, and the fact that colon cancer was not a successfully treated disease, Genentech's shares rocketed about 45 percent that day, on their way to over 100 percent gain for the year. Over the intervening years, the shares gained an additional 300 percent, on the strength of the usage of Avastin for other cancers besides colon, as well as progress Genentech made on its pipeline. In 2008, Roche announced its intention to purchase the shares of Genentech. The lessons learned for investors were that if a company can succeed in improving the outcomes of diseases with limited treatment options, the odds favor a positive response in the shares. Genentech had prior successes with other oncology drugs like Herceptin, which suggested they knew a great deal about the therapeutic area. Also, the drug did have some in-licensed technology (monoclonal antibodies), which had achieved positive clinical outcomes in other areas. These two factors, while not always conclusive, could have tilted analysis of the shares to the positive, given they are associated with success. In an era of health-care reform, the outcome might have been the same, although the magnitude of the share price jump may have been less. Avastin, though effective, is a very expensive drug costing in the tens of thousands of dollars for a single patient. Price controls or cost-effectiveness limitations under a reform plan may have put pressure on the company's ability to charge for and receive the price it ultimately did. Moreover, off-label usage, which spurred early growth of sales, may also be capped if such activities are restricted due to lack of evidence or cost considerations. Nevertheless, this was a breakthrough in cancer treatment and shareholders would have been rewarded.

NOTES

1. For a further discussion of the timelines in the development of biotechnology, see http://en.wikipedia.org/wiki/Timeline_of_biotechnology.
2. Also see "Biotechnology Industry Facts" for more discussion on the foundation of the biotech industry, available at http://bio.org/speeches/pubs/er/statistics.asp.
3. Rejin J. Guo, Baruch Lev, and Nan Zhou, "The Valuation of Biotech IPOs," December 2004; available at SSRN, http://ssrn.com/abstract=660281.
4. Joseph A. DiMasi and Henry B. Grabowski, "The Cost of Biopharmaceuticals R&D: Is Biotech Different?" *Managerial and Decision Economics* 28, no. 4–5 (2007): 469–479.
5. Christopher Adams and Van V. Brantner, "New Drug Development: Estimating Entry from Human Clinical Trials," FTC Bureau of Economics Working Paper No. 262, July 7, 2003; available at SSRN, http://ssrn.com/abstract=428040, or DOI, 10.2139/ssrn.428040.
6. "Fact Sheet Describing Recombinant DNA and Elements Utilizing Recombinant DNA Such as Plasmids and Viral Vectors, and the Application of Recombinant DNA Techniques in Molecular Biology," compiled and/or written by Amy B. Vento and David R. Gillum, Office of Environmental Health and Safety, University of New Hampshire, June 3, 2002, http://web.archive.org/web/20070322222148/http://www.unh.edu/ehs/BS/Recombinant-DNA.pdf.
7. Arlene Weintraub and Michael Arndt, "An Ache at Amgen? It Can't Make Enough of Its Hit Drug. And Rivals Are Pouring In," *BusinessWeek*, Dec. 9, 2002.
8. Aaron Smith, "Big Pharma Blurring the Lines with Big Biotech," CNNMoney.com, May 29, 2007, http://money.cnn.com/2007/05/25/news/companies/biotech/index.htm.
9. Lisa M. Jarvis, "Losing Their Religion: Biotechs Take a More 'Agnostic Approach' to Drug Discovery by Expanding into Small Molecules," *Chemical & Engineering News* 84, no. 44 (2006): 14–20.
10. Patricia M. Danzon, Sean Nicholson, and Nuno Sousa Pereira, "Productivity in Pharmaceutical Biotechnology R&D: The Role of Experience and Alliances," NBER Working Paper no. W9615, April 2003; available at SSRN, http://ssrn.com/abstract=394723.
11. DiMasi and Grabowski, "The Cost of Biopharmaceuticals R&D."
12. Sean Nicholson, Patricia M. Danzon, and Jeffrey McCullough, "Biotech-Pharmaceutical Alliances as a Signal of Asset and Firm Quality," NBER Working Paper no. W90007, June 2002; available at SSRN, http://ssrn.com/abstract=316786.

13. Guo, Lev, and Zhou, "The Valuation of Biotech IPOs."
14. Alexander Tsai and Josh Lerner, "Do Equity Financing Cycles Matter? Evidence from Biotechnology Alliances," June 1999; available at SSRN, http://ssrn.com/abstract=169789, or DOI, 10.2139/ssrn.169789.
15. Nicholson, Danzon, and McCullough, "Biotech-Pharmaceutical Alliances."
16. Ashish Arora, William B. Vogt, and Jiwoong Yoon, "Does In-house R&D Increase Bargaining Power? Evidence from the Pharmaceutical Industry," 2004; available at SSRN, http://ssrn.com/abstract=670304.
17. Danzon, Nicholson, and Pereira, "Productivity in Pharmaceutical Biotechnology R&D."
18. Michael R. Darby and Lynne G. Zucker, "Going Public When You Can in Biotechnology," NBER Working Paper no. W8954, May 2002; available at http://www.nber.org.papers/w8954.
19. Ibid.
20. Bronwyn H. Hall, Adam Jaffee, and Manuel Trajtenberg, "Market Value and Patent Citations," *RAND Journal of Economics* 36, no. 1 (2005): 16–38.
21. Mark Hirschey and Vernon J. Richardson, "Are Scientific Indicators of Patent Quality Useful to Investors?" *Journal of Empirical Finance* 11, no. 1 (2004): 91–107.
22. John R. M. Hand, "The Market Valuation of Biotechnology Firms and Biotechnology R&D," December 2001, http://papers.ssrn.com/sol3/papers.cfm?abstract_id=294471.
23. Ibid.
24. Tsai and Lerner, "Do Equity Financing Cycles Matter?"
25. Joseph H. Golec and John A. Vernon, "Financial Risk in the Biotechnology Industry," NBER Working Paper no. W13604; available at http://www.nber.org/papers/W13604.
26. Samuel C. Kou and Steven G. Kou, "Modeling Growth Stocks via Size Distribution," November 2001; available at SSRN, http://ssrn.com/abstract=300243, or DOI, 10.2139/ssrn.300243.
27. Bloomberg statistics.
28. Danzon, Nicholson, and Pereira, "Productivity in Pharmaceutical Biotechnology R&D."
29. Ilan Guedj and David Scharfstein, "Organizational Scope and Investment: Evidence from the Drug Development Strategies and Performance of Biopharmaceutical Firms," NBER Working Paper no. 10933, November 2004; available at http://www.nber.org/papers/w10933.
30. David Aboody and Baruch Lev, "Information Asymmetry, R&D and Insider Gains," *Journal of Finance* 55, no. 6 (2000).
31. Ibid.
32. Jessica Wapner, "Group Therapy, How Poorly Designed Trials for Cancer Drugs Are Hurting Patients, *Slate*, Jan. 10, 2008, http://www.slate.com/toolbar.aspx?action=print&id=218789.
33. Robert S. Huckman and Darren E. Zinner, "Does Focus Improve Operational Performance? Lessons from the Management of Clinical Trials," April 2005; available at SSRN, http://ssrn.com/abstract=715441.
34. Giampiero Favato and Roger Mills, "Valuation of Intangible Assets: Estimating Late-Stage Development Cost of Pharmaceutical R&D," August 2007; available at SSRN, http://ssrn.com/abstract=1012639.
35. Golec and Vernon, "Financial Risk in the Biotechnology Industry."
36. Andrew Pollack, "Trouble with Anemia Drug Is Reduced, but Issues Remain," *New York Times*, Sept. 30, 2004.

37. Margaret Blume-Kohout and Neeraj Sood, "The Impact of Medicare Part D on Pharmaceutical R&D," NBER Working Paper no. W13857, March 2008; available at SSRN, http://ssrn.com/abstract=1106583Golec.

38. Stephen F. Kingsmore, Ingrid E. Lindquist, Joann Mudge, Damian D. Gessler, and William D. Beavis, "Genome-wide Association Studies: Progress and Potential for Drug Discovery and Development," *Nature Reviews Drug Discovery* 7, no. 2 (2008): 221–230.

39. Bernard Munos, "Can Open-Source R&D Reinvigorate Drug Research?" *Nature Reviews Drug Discovery* 5, no. 9 (2006), 723–729.

CHAPTER 12

Investment Opportunities in Health-Care Services

The Blue Cross plan, created in Dallas, Texas, in 1929 to ensure that teachers who had babies would be able to pay their hospital bills, is acknowledged to be among the first broadly based health insurance plans. Ostensibly, this prepaid plan was meant to ensure that teachers were not bankrupted by pregnancy, but it appears to have been intended more as a protection for area hospitals' financial health. The intent of health insurance, like that of other forms of insurance, is to protect the policyholder from loss resulting from an unforeseen event. Insurance companies profit if the amount paid out in claims is less than the amount taken in through insurance premiums. As with other forms of insurance, risks can be managed because the prevalence of certain events (illness) is quantifiable if the population is large enough. The demand for services comes from potential patients who want to be protected from serious financial (catastrophic) loss as a result of illness. The value proposition for managed care is that coordinated care, as opposed to fee-for-service (the model in which patients seek out care on their own) leads to better outcomes because of its focus on delivering optimal care and patient compliance as well as on cost control. This modern model extends those attributes beyond catastrophic events to all aspects of acute conditions, chronic disease, and wellness.

In the intervening years, numerous models of health-care insurance have been developed, including staff and network versions of health maintenance organizations (HMOs). For investors, the major change in the industry came with the passage of the Health Maintenance Organization Act of 1973, which provided grants to encourage the development of HMOs. This law succeeded in encouraging the growth of the industry. A further refinement occurred during the Reagan administration, when the laws were changed to encourage private funding of HMOs. These law changes eventually culminated in the initial public offering (IPO) of U.S. Health Care Systems. As in many other subsectors in health care, changes in the law led to significant value creation for investors. Investors should be attuned to changes in legislation that may lead to the development of entirely new sectors or segments of health care, although companies with solid underlying fundamentals are more likely to benefit from secular changes than weaker ones are.

Managed-care organizations are where the rubber hits the road in the delivery of health-care services. In the twenty-first century, the vast majority of insured Americans (over 80 percent) are enrolled in some type of managed-care plan, either an HMO or a PPO (preferred provider organization).[1] There are also significant numbers of people enrolled in a government-sponsored HMO, either Medicaid or Medicare. Given the size of the market, the opportunity for positive stock returns is significant. An entire publicly traded industry has grown up to allow investors to participate in the financing and delivery of health-care services. The sector now has a market cap of well over $100 billion.[2]

At the highest level, the managed-care sector's business model is straightforward: take in premium payments and pay out insurance claims—the more revenue there is coming in and the fewer costs going out, the better the profit picture. The practical reality is more complex in that a company must gather (enroll) members at a premium that will offset their unknown future medical expenditures. This task is made even more difficult by the fact that health-care costs have generally been rising, meaning that in order to be successful, insurers will have to forecast cost growth that has yet to emerge.

Managed-care companies have at their disposal the customary insurance techniques, such as risk pooling and actuarial analysis, that help them deal with matching revenue to costs. Risk pooling is the aggregation of a large number of people into a group, thus spreading the financial risk of a quantifiable number (presumably relatively small) of medical cost events over a large group of people and the premiums they pay. Actuarial science quantifies how many people in a population will have a given amount of medical events. It applies statistics, probability, and other mathematical techniques to a population to determine future cost growth. Having a solid actuarial system gives a company a significant competitive advantage, but even good actuaries can have difficulty forecasting at times, particularly at times of great change.[3]

There are numerous challenges in forecasting medical costs. The first of these is moral hazard, which posits that the more coverage a person has, the more health care that person will utilize. Health-care demand is also motivated by many other factors, including some of the same types of behavioral finance actions that motivate investors, such as anchoring and acquiescence.[4] Not all populations are created equal; some populations are inherently more expensive than others, as companies, industries, and geographies with younger, healthier people will be less expensive than those with older people who have a poorer health status (preexisting conditions, for example). Many other variables, including income, gender, and ethnic status, also play a role in health-care demand.[5] Technology development has also influenced the health insurance process. As treatments get more complex, costs inevitably rise. The treatment of disease can involve several different types of providers (physicians and hospitals, for example). Physicians can prescribe either redundant (because of defensive medicine concerns) or ineffective (because of lack of information) treatments, which can raise costs unnecessarily and result in poor outcomes. Physician practice patterns can be widely variable,[6] and this too can add to the forecasting challenge. Enrollees switch plans relatively frequently, which means that the composition of the insured book of business can change markedly over time.

Financial difficulty for companies can arise when a population suffers a sufficiently high level of medical events that the premiums from the patients without events cannot cover the costs. A health plan that attracts a sicker population is said to be suffering from adverse selection. There are many possible causes for adverse selection: a plan may offer services that are more attractive to patients with higher medical needs (low-cost chronic illness maintenance, for example), or there may be asymmetry of information (the patients may have preexisting conditions and not tell the insurance companies about them). A health plan with substantial adverse selection in its population is very likely to find itself in a loss position. The converse is true also; if health plans can attract a population with above-normal health status, they can earn substantial positive returns. This is sometimes referred to as "cream skimming." There are laws in place to ensure that companies cannot exclude sick patients and enroll only healthy patients.

There are two sides of the health-care cost equation that managed-care companies can influence in an attempt to control costs: they can reduce either the utilization (how often a service or product is used) or the cost of the service or product. Some advocates have always feared that managed-care companies would deny patients the care that they needed (the utilization side) in order to save money, but in fact it appears that they derive much of their cost savings from discounts from retail prices for providers and products.[7] Denial of care can lead to both public relations repercussions and possible legal repercussions.[8]

The health plans obtain these discounts by developing networks of medical providers and offering members of these networks access to substantial markets. The larger the market share that a plan has, the greater the discounts it is likely to be able to obtain because it is in a stronger bargaining position in contract negotiations. The converse is also true: provider groups that have a substantial market share may be able to use their own market power to push back during contract negotiations; there have been instances where this has led to conflict. Scale and contracting ability are significant competitive tools that can separate one plan from another.

Health plans have put numerous processes and plan designs into place in an attempt to limit resource utilization (to prevent market problems like supply-induced demand) to what they consider optimal. Such processes include preauthorization certification and requiring primary-care providers to make referrals to specialists. Plan design initiatives including higher copays, deductibles, and co-insurance that shift some of the cost of the service or product to the patient, on the premise that patients will allocate resources more efficiently when they are exposed to cost. Higher costs seem to reduce the moral hazard of unnecessary provision of medical care. There are limits to cost sharing, however, as increased copays can lead to a decrease in compliance with treatments like prescription drugs or follow-up visits, resulting in higher downstream costs like hospitalizations.[9] Case management and disease management are tools that plans can employ once a disease state is encountered. Those plans that can best control costs while making sure that resources are allocated effectively to ensure health will maintain a competitive advantage.

Managed-care organizations operate in a competitive and highly regulated industry. Each state has an insurance division that is responsible for monitoring the industry; these agencies require frequent filings and have a wide variety of capital requirements that the company must contend with. There is significant competition, not just from other for-profit publicly traded organizations, but from provider formations, third-party administrators, and not-for-profit companies. The major not-for-profit companies like the Blue Cross & Blue Shield plans (the Blues) and Kaiser Permanente, among others, preceded the for-profit companies in many places and have substantial market share; they represent perhaps the biggest competitive challenge to the publicly traded companies. The smaller for-profit companies are less of a threat because their scale, in terms of both enrollment and the ability to invest in infrastructure such as actuarial systems, puts them at a competitive disadvantage. The Blues, for their part, have been converting from nonprofit status to for-profit status over the past few years. The market impacts and the impacts on public health from these conversions are not completely clear—the conversions may make the companies more efficient, but they may alter traditional relationships with area providers.[10]

Among the most important competitive considerations for managed-care companies is pricing power. Not-for-profits have, by their charter, less incentive to maximize profit and therefore can be more responsive to pricing issues than for-profits can be.[11] Managed-care companies, whether they are for-profit or not-for-profit, must base their prices on their cost trends, though, because if they price below their anticipated cost trend, they will find themselves in the position of losing money, which is not a sustainable state of being in the long run. The cost trend is composed of five main elements: physician costs, hospital inpatient costs, pharmacy (drug) costs, outpatient costs, and diagnostic and radiology costs.

The trend for each one of these costs has its own dynamics; for example, drug costs can move as a result of new products and patent expirations, while diagnostic costs can move as a result of new modalities in radiology. Some companies outsource or "carve out" the management of certain cost categories, such as pharmacy or mental health costs, but that varies by organization, and it isn't clear that a fully integrated model is necessarily better than an outsourced one.

Price plays an important role in the success of a managed-care offering, since there are relatively few ways to differentiate insurance products for consumers other than customer satisfaction and broad networks. One way in which plans can differentiate themselves from their competition is through product design. There are three broadly defined types of products in the commercial market: large-group, small-group, and individual plans. A fourth related product called an administrative services only (ASO) contract is designed for companies that self-insure (the client company takes the medical underwriting risk upon itself). Under an ASO arrangement, the managed-care plan processes claims and perhaps lets the company access its network or use some other component part of the full plan. There is no underwriting risk with these plans, but the upside is also more limited.

Each of the product lines has its own set of market dynamics, to which a successful company must be attentive. Within each of the product lines, a managed-care company can overlay plan design features like network size and copay requirements that can make the plan more or less attractive. Even in the same geography, a plan may have more success with one subtype than with another as a result of multiple factors, including price, scale, and reputation. Companies that can understand a given submarket and design and price their plans optimally will create shareholder value.

There can be a seasonal component to cost trends in that there is often a bolus of patients getting sick in the fourth and first quarters (flu season and so on). The overall cost of delivering care is often referred to as the medical loss ratio (MLR) or the medical care ratio (MCR). Since margins for managed-care companies are generally modest, changes in the MLR can have an outsized impact on financial performance. Sometimes companies will price below trend for strategic reasons, such as using a loss-leader approach to enter a new geography or a new product line. Eventually, however, the company will have to revert to more profitable pricing, or the strategy will fail. If other competitors in a given market follow suit and price below trend, they too may face negative consequences.

Paying a medical claim is referred to as claims adjudication. This process involves companies ensuring that the service was billed for properly (that there was no fraud), then sending the payment out to the provider. Providers obviously want to be paid as quickly as possible, and technology has allowed for greater speed of payment. There is some time lag, and this cash float between premium receipt and claim payout can be used to generate investment income, which can be a driver of managed-care returns. Sometimes claims made in one period are not resolved until the following period. Prior period adjustment is the reconciliation of the prior estimate of costs with the actual costs. Though the prior period adjustment is unrelated to revenue, it will show the true cost trend and should be analyzed carefully.

GOVERNMENT PROGRAMS

Government has been playing an increasingly large role in the provision of health-care services, either through regulation or through direct payment. The shift has been much more pronounced in recent years, with programs like managed Medicare, managed Medicaid, and Medicare Part D (the drug benefit) all seeing substantial growth.[12] These programs have both added to the bottom lines of managed-care companies and given the government more influence in the managed-care market. The underlying philosophy of the movement toward a more private company–centric approach to health care is that private entities can deliver care more efficiently at lower costs and with higher quality as a result of competition. It is too early to tell whether this is the case, given the limited evidence.[13] Beneficiaries will often choose a government-sponsored plan rather than a private plan, suggesting a "crowding-out" effect.[14] Beyond competition from the government, the medical utilization of the populations choosing these product lines differs from traditional commercial usage, so there are increased actuarial challenges to accompany the crowding-out factor. It is incumbent upon analysts to balance the potentially significant opportunity against the risks of these product lines when evaluating a managed-care company's foray into government programs.

INVESTMENT CONSIDERATIONS

Investing in managed-care companies has some challenges. There is the need to understand the insurance cycle, which, although it has waned somewhat as a result of information technology, still affects capital flows and can lead to counterproductive behavior.[15] The economy also plays a role in that in a stronger economy, workers will demand more comprehensive benefits, while in a weaker economy, they may utilize fewer health-care services and there may be member attrition as a result of job losses. Political considerations need to be part of the investment process in managed care, given that the government is an important player in the industry.

As in other sectors, the valuation challenge is to determine the value of the assets, current earnings, and future growth. For the most part, the assets of a managed-care company, assuming that it uses a network model, are its information systems, contracts, and membership. The value of a member is going to vary depending on the demographics of that member (age, sex, gender, and geography) and what type of product the member buys (group size, ASO, or government program). Generally these values can be determined from recent acquisitions of similar books of business. Member acquisition costs—the difference between what it costs to acquire a member and what that member ultimately returns—need to be considered, as they will help in quantifying potential. Much of the U.S. population is insured, but about 15 percent of the population is still uninsured, so growth can come about through gaining new members from the pool of the uninsured, through market share shift, through external corporate development activities like acquisitions, or by offering new products to capture more of the health-care spending. Companies that have new products, are entering new geographies, or have scale in existing geographies should be given a premium over those companies without similar capabilities. The ability to retain membership; actuarial predictability; risk pooling, which can be influenced by membership composition; stop-loss reinsurance protection; and organizational cost structure are also issues that need to be considered when investing in managed care.

Given the importance of in-market pricing, this is an immediate concern with respect to earnings, although over time, pricing is likely to converge to some price that yields a return on capital.[16]

REFORM

Although the problems in the health-care system are evident—the uninsured, cost inflation, access, and quality—there are only a few policy options when it comes to reform. Managed-care plans are the most obvious area in which reform can have a direct impact on the health-care market. There will be debate, as there has been in the past, over whether a public, public/private, or purely private form of managed care is the right solution. If history is a guide, the most likely outcome will be a mix of public and private entities, which should allow for investment opportunities.

The likely primary targets of reform will be access and cost. Insuring the entire population is a worthwhile goal, and there are several proposals for doing this, such as subsidies for premiums;[17] pay-or-play approaches, where employees and employers are required to either have or provide health-care insurance or pay into a pool that provides it for the uninsured;[18] or outright expansion of government programs like Medicaid and Medicare. None of these proposals has been attempted on a national scale, and each of them is likely to be tried at the state level before it is expanded. Investors should monitor the state programs for evidence of what types of programs are showing hints of success in improving access or controlling costs. If a local plan is well run by an investable company, it may generate even greater positive returns if it is expanded to other markets. The individual market with its significant inefficiencies and fragmentation seems the most logical target for reform, though other segments could also see their share of reform under certain scenarios.

A reform plan could also employ managed-care plans to address other market failure issues, such as dealing with variations in care through bonuses for optimal care and information technology support, asymmetry of information through diffusion of best practices and outcomes results, and moral hazard by utilizing optimal benefit design. These steps could reduce health-care costs, but they may also have unintended consequences. As with access issues, investors should be attuned to a plan's success in altering any of these market failures, as such a program could be adopted broadly.

Reform is not without its risks for managed-care investments. The more power the government has over the health-care process, the less flexibility a managed-care company will have in determining its own destiny; this can limit growth and makes watching the machinations of the government a more important investment consideration. Government power in managed-care markets could also manifest itself in other ways, including mandates on profit levels (mandating a minimum medical loss ratio, for example), mandates on enrollment (which could reduce the actuarial ability to control risks), outright price controls, mandates on the adoption of medical technology, mandates on service levels, or increased regulation, all of which could raise costs. Any proposal that limits flexibility for managed care will lead to a discount to valuation as a result of uncertainty as well as the presence of unintended consequences and potentially a negative shareholder return.

FUTURE OPPORTUNITIES

Because the health-care system has significant problems, there are substantial opportunities to correct those problems and derive positive shareholder returns through these solutions. As the medical industry accumulates more information about what types of interventions work in which settings, there will be opportunities to apply this knowledge in a real-time fashion rather than through the passive, often informal diffusion of information that has made some medical progress slower than it would otherwise have been.

The most likely future opportunities in managed care will come from consumerism, which will put more of the power over medical decisions into the hands of the patients. The information revolution has allowed information about therapies and providers to be freely exchanged. Health plans can harness this information and make it more available to patients so that they can make more informed decisions about a course of treatment or among treatment options. Quality of care can then be quantified and understood in the same way as the quality of many other consumer services—online retailers, for example. Making health-care report cards available may induce behavior change.[19]

Greater information may lead to behavior change on the part of patients if it makes them aware of methods that will enable them to lead healthier lives. Consumerism has the potential to alter patient/provider relationships and reduce information asymmetries, a cause of market failure. Information tools like electronic medical records could also serve to reduce variations of care and medical errors if they were programmed to alert providers to optimal care.

Decision support technology could alert both patients and providers to what constitutes optimal care as long as optimal care has been defined and as long as the motivation is really optimal care and not just optimal cost. Information can lead to a positive feedback loop; if patients and physicians can alert the managed-care companies to which therapies are optimal, a database can be developed, and quality can be improved over time through algorithm development using data analysis tools. Managed-care companies can channel consumerism and information technology and can manage care and drive shareholder returns more effectively.

Adaptive or value-based health plans are plans that are customized to an individual or a disease state, acknowledging that patients are heterogeneous and that different situations require different plan designs in order to lead to optimal clinical and financial outcomes. For example, it may be that in order to obtain an optimal clinical outcome, strict compliance with a therapeutic regimen is required. If achieving compliance with this regimen requires either very low or no copays for prescriptions or very high levels of intervention (coaching, advocacy) on the part of a provider or a health plan, the patient can be placed in a plan that provides these services. Some day, value-based plans may even be able to incorporate genetic information about an individual patient that comes from the burgeoning field of pharmacogenomics. The implementation of these plans will require an information-intensive approach to overcome asymmetries and price elasticity,[20] but ultimately technology should enable this as long as the information is available.

Adapting a plan to a person's genetic makeup may lead to optimal care; however, privacy concerns will be inevitable, and an ideal solution to this dilemma has yet to be proposed. Providers would than garner additional compensation for optimal care through a pay-for-performance reimbursement scheme. This could be an especially powerful approach for dealing with chronic diseases, which drive a substantial amount of the overall health system spending.

Value-based plans could make a medical home (a centralized location for patient information which is considered a hallmark of optimal care) actionable thereby which could improve medical quality and continuity of care. The risk that must be dealt with is that a value-based plan, if it is successful, may lead to selection bias (adverse selection) because high-cost patients will seek out optimal care. Additionally, since patients shift plans with some frequency, plans run the risk of improving outcomes for another plan. Companies that can master the development of value-based plans will have a competitive advantage.

The future may also hold changes in the way health insurance companies contract with providers. The existence of multiple plans and contracts exacerbates already complex situations by increasing the workload and paperwork component of the delivery of care and can lead to inefficiencies. In the future, there may be simpler contracts or even common contracts, where a provider has the same contract with all insurance companies or a single fee schedule. Given the myriad plan designs, this may be somewhat difficult to implement, but information technology may allow it to move toward reality, as reducing complexity in health care seems inevitable, although the timing is uncertain. A simpler claims adjudication process and appeals process in terms of coding and information exchange will go a long way toward reducing billing problems, which seem to arise for consumers with alarming frequency. A reduction in claims and billing issues will also go a long way toward improving the public's perception of health plans. Common contracts may reduce managed-care flexibility, which could limit discounts, but if the companies could reduce complexity, it is possible that they might be able to offset the discount risk with cost reductions.

Developed and emerging international markets offer another future opportunity for health plans. While systems in other countries tend to be more government-run, they still face issues similar to those in the United States, notably demographic shifts, medical cost inflation, and a need to deal with chronic diseases effectively. Although there are also cultural differences, health-care management practices honed in the United States may be useful to other nations that will have a much larger population with health insurance in the future as their economies grow. Although it is likely to require an expansion of skill sets and some experimentation, managed-care companies that can demonstrate success in countries outside the United States could access a future avenue of growth.

NON-HEALTH-PLAN MANAGED CARE

Pharmaceutical benefit managers (PBMs) are not health plans in the traditional sense, but they do engage in the management of health care. There are relatively few investment opportunities in this sector, but there have been more in the past, and there may be more in the future. PBMs and other non-health-plan management companies specialize in a particular area, which may allow them greater operating efficiencies. Some health plans outsource or carve out ancillary businesses that they feel can be executed better externally. The business challenges are similar to those of traditional health plans, as PBMs need to take in premiums and pay out for drugs. The level of financial risk is much lower, as PBMs often operate on an administrative basis and retain some of the savings that they generate for the client. PBMs drive savings by moving patients to less expensive therapeutic options, such as generic pharmaceuticals, or less expensive methods of distribution, such as mail order. They can also save costs by negotiating greater discounts from manufacturers, getting upside by retaining some of the discounts. Success in driving more generic utilization, either through shifting share from brands or through the emergence of new generic drugs, will also lead to upside for these companies. Shifting patients from traditional pharmacy distribution of drugs to mail-order delivery of drugs is yet another way for PBMs to capture upside. PBMs do face some of the same competitive challenges as health plans, as differentiation can be difficult beyond price.

Outcomes, compliance, ability to deal with complex disease and medicinal challenges, and customer satisfaction ratings may one day become more common metrics used to differentiate PBM products. PBMs have to compete with a retail channel that seems like it will grow in importance as consumerism becomes more common in health care. PBMs are also competing with some of their insurance company customers because as they move up the value chain and manage more of the health-care spending, they will come into conflict with some of their customers that are also trying to manage more of the health-care dollar. For companies and other large populations, such as unions, that self-insure, PBMs may offer value, but they need to deliver improved outcomes and transparency.

Beyond PBMs there are a wide variety of publicly traded health-care service companies, but as a group they tend to be difficult to characterize broadly because there are usually a small number of companies in each subsector, and they are often small-market capitalization companies, which can at times limit investment opportunities. These companies can range from drug distribution companies to contract research organizations, lab-testing companies, long-term care facilities, and even waste management. With these companies the same analytic techniques will apply as with the other sectors, with the goal of determining whether earnings and other company characteristics support the valuation. The overarching factor in forecasting a demand curve and ascertaining the long-term potential of the enterprise is to observe whether the company truly addresses value to the system either by decreasing costs, improving access, improving quality, or in some cases accelerating the innovation process. A major risk factor in the ancillary service sector is that government reimbursement often makes up a substantial portion of revenue, so the companies may be subject to volatile results based upon government changes. If the criteria are met, then the shares are potentially safe to be purchased. For the ancillary service business whose customers are other health-care businesses, investors need to watch the business conditions of the customers. A customer base in trouble may not necessarily be a negative thing if it means more outsourcing of services, but changes impacting business customers need to be considered in an investment in this sector.

HOSPITALS

Hospital inpatient spending is a significant proportion of health-care spending in the United States—30 percent.[21] As with the PBMs, there are relatively few equity investment options for directly participating in the industry. In an era of reform, the investment options could expand as lower levels of bad debt and charity care resulting from a reduced level of the uninsured may lead to higher returns for hospitals and make them more attractive as investments. There are some considerations that investors must be attuned to when looking at the facility sector. Hospital pricing is confusing, with different pricing levels often being determined by payer or patient type.[22] Hospital pricing may be addressable by reform efforts, and those hospitals with more efficient operations are likely to benefit. Geography also plays a role in hospital operations, in that an area with a growing population that is also well insured is likely to drive better financial results than an area that is seeing population outflows or in which the population is not well insured.

The competitive environment is also an investment factor, as more competition will naturally have an impact on financial returns. Because of the high level of capital costs, competition in inpatient facilities does not come online rapidly. The nature of the competition also matters because, as with health plans, for-profit hospitals face competition from nonprofits. For-profit hospitals can have lower costs than nonprofits,[23] which can influence competitive dynamics. The hospital industry also has significant levels of both consolidation[24] and closures,[25] and both factors need to be considered as a future possibility in any given region. Physician ownership of facilities has been and is likely to remain a hotly debated issue in the future because of the perceived or real conflicts of interest involved. In some locations, hospitals have established programs to share profits from optimal care, measured in terms of either cost or quality, with physicians. Sometimes referred to as gain sharing, this arrangement has been viewed with skepticism, as although on the surface it appears to align incentives, it may expose patients to negative outcomes if cost is the deciding factor in treatment decisions.

The hospital of the future is likely to have to contend with two important factors: quality metrics and a movement toward outpatient procedures. Determinants of quality are becoming more commonplace in the health-care industry, and hospitals are no exception. Although there may be an element of studying for the test (improving the metrics that are to be measured), ultimately multiple quality metrics will be measured and the results presented to the public at large. It will be costly for those facilities with lower quality scores to improve them,[26] but in order to compete in the future, hospitals will have to deliver solid quality metrics on both a relative and an absolute basis.

The movement toward outpatient care and shorter inpatient stays in hospitals is an outgrowth of improving medical technology. Minimally invasive surgery, among other developments, has led to decreases in the amount of time a patient stays in a hospital. While this is a welcome development for patients, hospitals will need to accommodate changes in treatment modalities and sites of care and deal with public health infrastructure problems like long waiting times in emergency departments if they are to drive future returns. Other potential hospital reforms include minimum staffing level requirements, greater accountability for outcomes, and stricter tax rules for nonprofits.

PHYSICIANS

Physician expense accounts for a substantial portion of health-care spending in the United States.[27] As with hospitals, there are limited investment opportunities to participate directly in physician services. There have been investable models in the past, such as physician practice management companies, and there may be in the future if physicians participate in the trend toward the corporatization of medicine or if reform makes physicians otherwise investable. Physicians cannot be avoided when discussing investment in health care because they control so much of the spending and because issues that affect physicians are likely to spill over into areas of the market that are investable. Among the key issues for physicians is incentives, which motivate behavior. Financial incentives for physicians is a topic that tends to be discussed in hushed tones because there is a perception of a completely altruistic doctor, although the subject has been well researched and physicians are known to be motivated by financial incentives.[28]

Given the substantial variations in care, there would seem to be room for optimization of medical practice. However, there is little consensus about what works in actual practice, and too much pressure on practice patterns can lead to charges that plans wish physicians to practice cookbook medicine or that optimal care is a red herring way to use cost rather than quality as a measure of what is optimal. The dynamics under which physicians operate are similar to those faced by other providers: geography plays a role in the cost and reimbursement structure, as do competition and referral patterns and whether the practice is a specialist or a primary-care group. Physician group size is also an investment consideration. Physicians are likely to be faced with having quality and cost metrics made available to current and future patients, and this opens up the question of measurement bias. Physicians remain a potent lobbying force, so it is unlikely that a reform plan will be overly detrimental to them; however, cost reduction efforts may lead to some revenue cuts. Medical societies are an important driver of physicians' behavior, and in the future they could be engaged as either self-regulating organizations (similar to some Wall Street entities) or arbiters of clinically optimal care.

The physician fee schedule that is dictated by Medicare is often a topic of debate in Congress, as continued increases in this schedule will ultimately put pressure on the Medicare budget. Medicare rates tend to be lower than commercial rates, so there is something of a cost shift involved in making Medicare rates acceptable. Medicare physician rates may be a flash point in any reform plan. As with other areas of reform, there may be offsets for price pressure, such as malpractice shields, reduction in administrative overhead, bonus payments for optimal quality steps, tax incentives for pro bono charity work, incentives to pick an underserved specialty or geography, convenience enhancers, and payment for time spent with patients (primary care) rather than by procedure volume. The same dynamics that apply to physicians also apply to nurses and other providers.

UNITEDHEALTH GROUP

Between 2000 and 2005, UnitedHealth shares returned 600 percent (including stock splits). It became the largest managed-care company by market capitalization. The success was driven by many factors. The company was early to invest in technology and systems, which allowed it to capture significant market share at the local level. The company was also early to realize at the corporate level that reducing variations in care was a good way to control costs as well as being an important differentiating marketing point. The company also increased its scale through a series of acquisitions. From an analytic perspective, the lessons are that a company that focuses on reducing variations through technology and market scale can create shareholder value. How managed-care companies fare in a reformed health-care environment will rest on the nature of reforms. If they are called upon to administer health benefits under a universal program or there is a move toward a more individual-driven system, the upside could be substantial. If the government takes health-care benefits upon itself or otherwise limits profitability, the results could be devastating. Reforms that improve our understanding of cost effectiveness or quality could be a boon to managed-care companies, as it could help managed-care companies direct patients to optimal care.

NOTES

1. Kaiser Family Foundation and Health Research and Educational Trust, "Employer Benefits 2006 Annual Survey," http://www.kff.org/insurance/7527/upload/7527.pdf.
2. Bloomberg statistics.
3. Colin Barr, "WellPoint Warning Hammers HMOs," http://dailybriefing.blogs.fortune.cnn.com/2008/03/10/wellpoint-warning-hammers-hmos/.
4. Jayanta Bhattacharya and Adam Isen, "On Inferring Demand for Health Care in the Presence of Anchoring, Acquiescence, and Selection Biases NBER Working Paper no. W13865, March 2008, http://www.nber.org/papers/w13865.
5. Jorge Munoz Perez and Tapen Sinha, "Determinants of Group Health Insurance Demand," November 2006; available at SSRN, http://ssrn.com/abstract=947345.
6. John E. Wennberg, "Perspective: Practice Variations and Health Care Reform: Connecting the Dots, *Health Affairs* Web Exclusive, Oct. 7, 2004, http://content.healthaffairs.org/cgi/content/full/hlthaff.var.140/DC2.
7. Avi Dor, Siran M. Koroukian-Hajinazarian, and Michael Grossman, "Managed Care Discounting: Evidence from the MarketScan Database," NBER Working Paper no. W10437, April 2004; available at SSRN, http://ssrn.com/abstract=532996.
8. John A. Humbach, "Criminal Prosecution for HMO Treatment Denial," *Health Matrix: Journal of Law-Medicine* 11, no. 1 (2001); available at SSRN, http://ssrn.com/abstract=273434, or DOI, 10.2139/ssrn.273434.
9. Avi Dor and William E. Encinosa, "Does Cost Sharing Affect Compliance? The Case of Prescription Drugs," NBER Working Paper no. W10738, September 2004; available at SSRN, http://ssrn.com/abstract=590724.
10. Mark A. Hall and Chris Conover, "For-Profit Conversion of Blue Cross Plans: Public Benefit or Public Harm?" *Annual Review of Public Health* 27 (April 2006).
11. R. Lawrence Van Horn and Gerard J. Wedig, "Competition, Price and Organizational Form: A Test of Price Convergence in the HMO Market," Organizational Economics of Health Care Conference, October 2003; available at SSRN, http://ssrn.com/abstract=468400, or DOI, 10.2139/ssrn.468400.
12. Michael Chernew, Phillip DeCicca, and Robert J. Town, "Managed Care and Medical Expenditures of Medicare Beneficiaries," NBER Working Paper no. W13747, January 2008, http://www.nber.org.papers/w13747.
13. Mark Duggan, "Does Contracting Out Increase the Efficiency of Government Programs? Evidence from Medicaid HMOs," NBER Working Paper no. W9091, August 2002, http://www.nber.org/papers/w9091.

14. Jeffrey R. Brown, Norma B. Coe, and Amy Finkelstein, "Medicaid Crowd-Out of Private Long-Term Care Insurance Demand: Evidence from the Health and Retirement Survey," NBER Working Paper no. 12536, September 2006, http://www.nber.org/papers/w12536.

15. Sean M. Fitzpatrick, "Fear Is the Key: A Behavioral Guide to Underwriting Cycles," *Connecticut Insurance Law Journal* 10, no. 2 (2004): 255–275.

16. Van Horn and Wedig, "Competition, Price and Organizational Form."

17. Jonathan Gruber and Ebonya L. Washington, "Subsidies to Employee Health Insurance Premiums and the Health Insurance Market," NBER Working Paper no. W9567, March 2003, http://nber.org/ papers w9567.

18. Richard V. Burkhauser and Kosali I. Simon, "Who Gets What from Employer Pay or Play Mandates?" NBER Working Paper no. W13578, November 2007, http://www.nber.org.papers/w13578.

19. Leemore S. Dafny and David Dranove, "Do Report Cards Tell Consumers Anything They Don't Already Know? The Case of Medicare HMOs," NBER Working Paper no. W11420, June 2005, http://www.nber.org/papers/w11420.

20. Mark V. Pauly and Fredric E. Blavin, "Value Based Cost Sharing Meets the Theory of Moral Hazard: Medical Effectiveness in Insurance Benefits Design," NBER Working Paper no. W13044, April 2007, http://www.nber.org/papers/w13044.

21. National Center for Health Statistics, *Health, United States, 2006 with Chartbook on Trends in the Health of Americans* (Hyattsville, Md.: National Center for Health Statistics Press, 2006).

22. Uwe E. Reinhardt, "The Pricing of U.S. Hospital Services: Chaos behind a Veil of Secrecy," *Health Affairs* 25, no. 1 (2006).

23. Daniel P. Kessler and Mark B. McClellan, "The Effects of Hospital Ownership on Medical Productivity, NBER Working Paper no. W8537, October 2001, http://www.nber.org/papers/w8537.

24. Jean M. Abraham, Martin S. Gaynor, and William B. Vogt, "Entry and Competition in Local Hospital Markets," NBER Working Paper no. W11649, September 2005, http://www.nber.org/papers/w11649.

25. Thomas C. Buchmueller, Mireille Jacobson, and Cheryl Wold, "How Far to the Hospital? The Effect of Hospital Closures on Access to Care," NBER Working Paper no. W10700, August 2004, http://www.nber.org/papers/w10700.

26. John A. Romley and Dana Goldman, "How Costly Is Hospital Quality? A Revealed-Preference Approach," NBER Working Paper no. W13730, January 2008, http://www.nber.org/papers/w13730.

27. National Center for Health Statistics, *Health, United States, 2006.*

28. David J. Cooper and James B. Rebitzer, "Managed Care and Physician Incentives: The Effects of Competition on the Cost and Quality of Care," *Contributions to Economic Analysis & Policy* 5, no. 1 (2006): 1409.

CHAPTER 13

Investing in Medical Technology

For the most part, medical technology has avoided being the target of direct health-care reform efforts in the past. Medical technology is a heterogeneous industry that encompasses a broad swath of products, ranging from commodities to high technology, that are used in a wide array of settings. A reform program would have to be prohibitively complex in order to affect the entire sector. Medical technology will not be completely unscathed by reform, of course, as it is affected by health insurance, notably managed care,[1] and health insurance may well be affected by reform. Thus, health-care reform will have its effects on medical technology indirectly, but it will have effects nonetheless. It is surprising that reform plans have not focused more on dealing with medical technology, as new technology has accounted for much of the growth in health-care costs over the last few decades.[2] If a reform plan is serious about controlling costs, it may take a more direct approach to dealing with medical technology, and that would most likely lead to discounted multiples on the shares of companies in the industry.

Medical technology reform initiatives can be as wide-ranging as outright price controls, comparative studies for efficacy, or alterations in the approval process. Health-care investors should be attuned to changes in reimbursement or regulatory paradigms, as they could have an outsized impact on the return potential for shares in the industry. Medical technology has benefits for a reform initiative. It can be a labor saver in terms of reducing the staff required, either by eliminating administrative work through electronic record keeping (health-care IT), or by requiring smaller staffs to perform a procedure or examination while producing similar outcomes. Medical technology can be used to reduce the length of hospital stays, which can lower costs given the expense associated with treatment in that setting. Medical technology, if it is applied correctly, could reduce future long-term comorbidity, thereby also reducing costs, improving outcomes, and increasing a patient's ability to be productive. Companies that can show the benefits of their technology for controlling costs, improving quality, or expanding access to medical care will be able to overcome the most onerous provisions in a reform plan and will be able to deliver increasing shareholder value.

BUSINESS MODELS

As befits such a diverse industry, there is a wide variety of business models that have been developed to distribute medical technology, and these are dependent on the nature of the particular products sold. Medical technology is a catchall term that includes both commodity and temporary products, like catheters, and permanent products, like cardiac stents. Another distinction among medical technology companies is whether the product is implantable, like a hip replacement, or is a larger piece of capital equipment, like a magnetic resonance imaging (MRI) machine. A third delineation is whether the product is used for direct patient intervention, like a catheter, or deals with the patient indirectly, like a genetic sequence analyzer. Distribution of medical technology products can entail selling in bulk, selling a product set that is dependent on an individual patient's need, bundling products together in a suite of products for the same or similar indications, selling the product combined with a service contract, or selling a product in a razor/razor blade model, where a piece of equipment is sold but disposable products are required for each procedure. Companies can mix and match these models to optimize revenue.

The sales infrastructure is determined in large part by the types of products that are being sold. Companies can choose to sell their products directly or to sell them through independent distributors. In the direct model, the sales force must identify the customer and the payer, although these are sometimes the same. For bulk commodity products, companies may reach out to larger institutions, group purchasing organizations (GPOs), or multiline distribution companies. For higher-value products like large pieces of capital equipment or expensive implantable devices like pacemakers, sales representatives may need greater technical knowledge and sell the products directly to hospitals or doctors; this may even include "scrubbing in" to advise physicians during procedures.

The sales cycle, process, and timelines will also be dictated by the type of product and the type of purchaser. While there are no absolute rules regarding sales time, generally speaking, the more expensive a product is, the longer it will take to sell that product. The more novel a product is, the longer it will likely take to see adoption in the provider community. Because there are a relatively small number of providers who perform particular procedures, medical technology companies require smaller sales forces than other subsectors of health care. Smaller sales forces generally have lower operating costs and better margins. Analysts need to consider both sales force efficacy and sales cycles as they develop revenue projections, as these can affect both near-term and longer-term projections and subsequent valuation metrics.

In addition to the sales infrastructure, analysts must also consider the adoption curve of new technology in its own right. Since medical technology is generally procedure-based and dependent on episodes of care rather than chronic usage, there will be wide variations in uptake depending on a number of factors. These factors include the incidence of disease, severity of disease, novelty of the product, cost of the product, type of physicians who administer the procedure (some specialties adopt faster than others), availability of substitutes, and penetration of existing technologies.

There is also a learning curve with procedures, and this learning curve can have an impact on the adoption of medical technologies.[3] The simpler a procedure is, the more quickly it is likely to be taken up. The more complex a procedure is, the slower its adoption may be. The availability of patients on whom to attempt the procedure may also affect the adoption curve. The referral pattern for a given procedure will also influence the learning curve for that procedure. Having a learning curve does offer companies some advantages, as the existence of the learning process will make demand for the product relatively sticky, since the time and expense of learning competing procedures or using competing products offer some barriers to physicians rapidly switching to substitutes.

A procedure that requires considerable experience to become proficient may be limited to high-volume procedure centers at first, diffusing to lower-volume centers only later. High-volume centers can have a competitive advantage, although this also encourages lower-volume centers to adopt new technology rather than risk losing patients to other centers. The adoption of technology by a site, especially a hospital, can be a complex decision process akin to the investment process for common stocks. Similar valuation approaches, like a real option approach[4] and internal rate of return calculations, come into play in the medical technology assessment process. Since the value of health-care procedures and the required aftercare can be substantial for facilities, there is an incentive to offer as wide a suite of procedures as possible. Given the value of patients, there is often a fight for these attractive customers among facilities, leading to an arms-race mentality among providers when it comes to implementing technology.[5] Such an arms race can lead to overcapacity and inefficiencies. Certificate of need (CON) programs, where a facility or operating company must prove to a regulatory body (usually governmental) that the new product or service is necessary in a given geographic area, have been developed in an attempt to moderate the potential inefficiencies and curb overusage and supply-induced demand. However, CONs do not operate in all places and success will likely vary depending on the level of restrictions. Resource allocation is one area that a reform plan may address that might affect the adoption of medical technology.

The medical technology business model (as it pertains specifically to devices) must also contemplate the Medicare reimbursement situation for a given product. Procedures are performed either in the hospital (inpatient) or on an outpatient basis. The site of service determines whether the procedure is paid for and often the rate at which it is paid. In general the government pays for medical devices by bundling them into global payments that include the device and other patient costs except physician payments. Diagnosis-related groups (DRG) is the system developed to classify and then reimburse hospitals for inpatients. The DRG attempts to pay the hospital for the resources used relative to the average inpatient case. A number of factors go into the calculation, including classification of disease, disease severity, and region in which the hospital is domiciled. It behooves the hospital to minimize the cost of the inpatient encounter as its margin is the difference between the payment and the cost. In the outpatient setting (either a hospital outpatient department or an independent ambulatory surgery center), medical devices are paid for under APC (ambulatory payment classification) codes. If the device is provided in a physician's office, it is paid under the Medicare physician fee schedule. From an investment perspective, analysts need to make sure that a code both exists and is of appropriate payment size that it can accommodate the price of the medical device. Commercial insurance usually benchmarks its payment rate either implicitly or explicitly of Medicare payment levels.

A reform process likely will have an impact on the adoption of medical technology, either directly, through price controls or direct negotiation with product makers (as with pharmaceuticals), or indirectly, by allowing surrogates who manage a reform plan's health benefits (e.g., HMOs) to set reimbursement rules that are either onerous or expansive, depending on some set of cost-effectiveness criteria. Included in reforms could also be a registry mechanism by which negative outcomes would be tracked as they are now done in other countries, or a more restrictive approval process. In the absence of reform, managed care has had an impact on the adoption of medical technology, particularly when it has greater penetration in a market.[6] If a reform plan grants insurance entities power over either price or market share, the impact on medical technology will be accentuated.

INNOVATION

As with the other therapeutic modalities, innovation is a key value-creating factor in medical technology. Increases in medical technology can both be profitable for the companies that innovate and provide a cost/benefit advantage for the entire system.[7] Innovation in this sector has generally been evolutionary, punctuated by the occasional revolution, such as stents for cardiovascular indications or intensity-modulated radiation therapy for oncology. In general, the evolutions have involved refining technique, either for consistency or for convenience, the types of materials used, and the size of the devices. The innovation cycle is affected by the regulatory process, which varies somewhat from that for pharmaceuticals and biotechnology. The FDA does have a premarket approval (PMA) process for what the FDA refers to as Class III devices (devices that support or sustain life); this is similar to the approval process for biotechnology and pharmaceutical products in that trials are required and the time frame is generally long.

In addition to this more traditional approval process, the FDA also has what is referred to as a 510(k) process for Class I and Class II devices—those involving less medical risk, like endoscopes. In this less rigorous approval process, the companies need only show that the product is substantially equivalent to something else that is already on the market (referred to as a predicate). Comparing a device with something else that is already on the market is substantially easier than showing efficacy against a placebo in a clinical trial. However, the returns are commensurate with the risk and effort, as PMA products have a higher value than 510(k) products because it is much harder for competitors to come to market with a similar device.

Medical technology and devices benefit from the same types of innovation that are occurring in other areas of technology, such as miniaturization, the acceleration of microprocessor speeds, innovation in software development, and greater understanding of materials sciences. Innovations in any of these areas will eventually find their way into medical technology, either by lowering the costs of the products, by making the clinical outcomes better, or by doing less collateral damage (making procedures faster or less invasive). Companies that can innovate can add shareholder value despite any conditions placed upon them by a difficult health-care reform plan.

INVESTMENT CONSIDERATIONS

One of the hallmarks of the medical device industry is the good visibility of its revenue relative to that of other industries. The incidence of disease and the procedures used do not vary dramatically over short periods of time unless a new type of surgery or a new product is developed. Especially good visibility is found with implantable products, which are predominantly used during cardiovascular and orthopedic procedures. Capital equipment sales can also be somewhat steady, but big-ticket items are affected by the availability of credit to institutions (as they are usually costly), along with certificate of need issues. Given the revenue contribution of these machines, a small number of cancellations or delays in purchase (because capital equipment has a much longer sales cycle) can have a dramatic impact on any given quarter's financial results.

Reimbursement visibility is an important investment consideration with medical technology investments. Procedures performed on patients over 65 (a substantial number) are subject to payments determined by Medicare. These payments are adjusted annually. Often they are adjusted upward; however, there have been occasions when the rates have been lowered or have not been raised sufficiently to allow for growth. These pricing changes occur at regular known intervals, and there is also a comment period for those companies that feel that the adjustments are unfair. Investors need to remember that changes in Medicare rates can also resonate throughout the commercial insurance sector and influence pricing. In addition, profit margins can be affected by raw material costs and production efficiency. Companies that can develop effective raw material sourcing and manufacturing processes (for example, sterilization) have a competitive advantage.

Because many technologies are quite similar, intellectual property is an important component of any medical technology investment thesis. There are numerous occasions where one company sues another for infringement, with the aim of either extracting a royalty arrangement or getting an injunction preventing a product from being put on the market. These patent cases can be long-time-frame events, and it appears that the courts are reluctant to prevent a product from being on the market.

Medical technology investing does not take place in a vacuum. There are often other approaches that are used earlier in the treatment course, either in combination with or instead of a procedure. As other modalities for treatment of a disease improve (pharmaceutical or lifestyle, for example), this reduces the benefit of a procedure-based approach. As evidence about the relative efficacy and cost/benefit of a procedure becomes more precise and available, more attention will be paid to using nonprocedure treatments, given the overall cost. For example, the cost/benefit advantage of percutaneous coronary interventions (PCI) over drug therapy is not always clear in all settings.[8] Investors should be aware of developments in other modalities in order to ascertain competition risk.

Because medical technology tends to be more an evolutionary than a revolutionary industry, as companies roll out new features, there is cannibalization risk—the risk that new products will steal share from old products, lowering the growth of the older product as buyers put off purchases until the next product comes out. The offset is that prices for new medical technology tend to be higher than those for older technology, leading to better margins. In an era of reform, more stringent requirements may be placed upon the addition of new features in order to garner improved reimbursement. Having a continuous stream of new products is a competitive advantage, as it allows for better pricing as well as new opportunities for growth. A new product cycle can offer companies an additional leg of growth as long as it does not also harm the existing franchise.

The smaller-market-capitalization medical technology companies have investment similarities to smaller-cap biotechnology and pharmaceutical companies. Smaller-cap medical technology companies tend to have a narrow set of product offerings, a limited pipeline, and often a need for capital. Consolidation is part of the business strategy both for small companies as an exit strategy and for larger companies as a way to develop new revenue growth. Novelty and growth of product sets, access to capital, intellectual property, pipeline, and sales ability are all factors that influence the valuation and attractiveness of a given acquisition. For companies that sell products in markets outside the United States, foreign exchange rates can play an important role in financial outcomes, as prices are usually lower outside the United States, and therefore a weaker U.S. dollar can provide a boost for margins.

For investors, the regulatory risk for medical technology is somewhat lower than that for other sectors, given the availability of a less strict approval process. There is another type of risk to which investors must be attuned, however. Medical technology has operator risk, which the other sectors do not have. Because the skill of the provider can vary, the outcome of medical technology usage can vary in cost and quality. There is the risk that when a product is taken out of a clinical trial environment and placed in a "real-world" environment, the performance of the product may decline, although a shorter learning curve can ameliorate this phenomenon. Investors should be aware that operator differences can affect the performance of the product and the subsequent financial results of the manufacturer. The possibility of recalls exists, although this is more of a risk with implantable devices, as having a device in a body tends to be a long-term proposition. Explants can be costly from a financial point of view as well as being harmful to a company's reputation.

Analyzing companies that produce non-patient-facing medical technology, such as life science tools, requires a modification of the approach used for other medical technology. These companies can be analyzed like other capital equipment companies, often with razor/razor blade strategies. The predominant difference between non-patient-centered technologies and traditional medical technology is the sales channels and call points: biopharmaceutical and industrial companies, laboratories, and academia. Therefore, it is important for analysts to track corporate capital expenditure trends, government spending on the sciences, and overall global economic activity, which will drive the demand for such equipment. These products tend to be less sensitive to changes in reimbursement and therefore should also be more resistant, though not necessarily immune, from health-care reform. Enabling technologies like genetic analysis could lead to great strides in the development of other therapeutic agents, and as these technologies prove themselves as "money makers," their adoption is likely to grow. Life science tools often share common traits with other medical technology, like using a razor/razor blade model selling capital equipment along with disposables so similar forecasting methodologies can be employed to analyze performance.

The valuation approach to medical technology will be driven by product offerings, the shape of the adoption curve, where in the adoption process a given product is, competitive factors (both other technologies and other modalities), sales force effectiveness, pipeline, and reimbursement (all else being equal, higher reimbursement is superior). In an era of health-care reform, companies that manufacture products that can reduce costs, improve outcomes, or expand access will receive a premium valuation relative to those that do not. The product or product portfolio will also determine valuations as higher-value products, given their margins, will merit a higher valuation, possibly offset somewhat by differences in visibility. Smaller companies tend to be more amenable to growth valuation approaches, while larger companies tend to be more amenable to traditional cash flow–based techniques or multiple-based techniques like price to sales or price to earnings.

FUTURE POTENTIAL

Changes in medical technology could have a profound impact on the way disease is detected and treated in the future. New imaging and diagnostic modalities, both genetic and radiologic, may allow diseases to be detected and treated before they reach the point where they either are incurable or produce significant complications. Late detection lowers the quality of potential clinical outcomes and increases the downstream costs.

Therapeutically, treatments will become less invasive, as it is apparent that the less a treatment affects the nondiseased parts of the body, the more successful it will be. As technology improves, intervention will become far more targeted. Such inventions as robotically assisted surgery and miniaturization, including down to the molecular size (nanotechnology), will continue to increase in sophistication and will lead to improved clinical outcomes through shorter recovery times (leading to reduced lengths of stay in hospitals) and reduced costs, both of which will be of tremendous importance to a health-care system that is undergoing reform.

Medical technology may also expand beyond the currently available parts of the body into areas that were previously unreachable. Anatomies like the brain and other major organs like the liver may see medical technology interventions resulting from changes in materials sciences or miniaturization. As information technology improves, so will the ability of implanted devices to monitor biological status continuously and report it in real time. Subtle changes in biological functions can be precursors to full-blown disease later on, and if they can be analyzed and interpreted, this could lead to early interventions. Pairing diagnostics with medical devices will be a part of future technological shifts. There will be greater pairing of drugs or biologics and devices as technology advances to the point where a device can determine when and how much of a drug should be released given a set of biological processes. The products will also become more portable as technology allows devices, both capital equipment and the procedure suites, to become smaller. Making devices more portable could allow greater access to procedures and reduced costs by having these procedures done in less expensive environments, such as the home.

Emerging markets will play an important role in the development of medical technology. These new locations can be a less expensive place to source components for technology, assuming that they are able to comply with safety standards. They can also serve as a less expensive place to develop new technology, as many countries are attempting to create their own medical technology infrastructure. The health-care demands in emerging markets may differ somewhat from those in developed markets, which may shift the types of innovation required of medical technology companies. Emerging markets will offer an additional growth component for medical technology as their economies grow; however, this growth is likely to be constrained at least initially by a lack of qualified personnel to perform the procedures. In order to be successful in these markets, medical technology will have to be rugged enough not to require an extensive support service, simple enough to encompass most potential users, and efficient enough to accommodate a large number of patients with a small number of machines.

INTUITIVE SURGICAL

In 2003, Intuitive Surgical shares were trading near their all-time low. The company had been embroiled in an intellectual property litigation with a company called Computer Motion. The IP was related to the companies' respective approaches to robotic-assisted surgery. The premise was that if robotic technology could automate at least some of a surgical procedure and make the procedure less invasive, variations in care would be reduced. Naturally, surgeons were initially skeptical, assuming that an unproven machine could not replicate their skill, so adoption was slow. Then in mid-2003, Intuitive reached a breakthrough and acquired Computer Motion. Once the financial burden and management distraction of a protracted legal case were removed, Intuitive was able to conduct significant market development efforts. Included in the development effort was the company's search for clinicians to conduct follow-on clinical trials for the Da Vinci robotic device. Intuitive Surgical was highly successful with its efforts. Annual revenue rose from below $100 million in 2003 to over $800 million in 2007. Its market share of all prostatectomies (versus traditional open surgery) has risen to above 50 percent. The share price increased over 8,000 percent between 2003 and 2007. The company has succeeded in great part due to the fact that robotic-assisted surgery has similar outcomes to traditional surgery but, because it is minimally invasive, it reduces the levels of traditional side effects such as impotence and incontinence, as well as reducing blood loss during surgery and length of stay in the hospital. After prostatectomy, the company gained market share in gynecological indications like hysterectomy and it is attempting to move into other areas like cardiac surgery.

Given equal or better clinical outcomes, most patients and physicians would choose the less-invasive procedure. Physicians would especially endorse it if they were paid a similar amount as for traditional surgery, though there will be many physicians who do not believe the outcomes are superior to their own. Market forces being what they are, the reluctant physicians may not have a choice if patients in a new consumerist model choose a robotic-assisted procedure. A robotic-assisted procedure that lowers comorbidities could save the system costs longer-term by reducing aftercare. The analytic lessons are that adoption of a revolutionary product can take time to develop, but once it hits an inflection point, hypergrowth is possible. In addition, improving outcomes, whether they are improved efficacy, fewer side effects, or reduced costs (preferably all three), can lead to a significant shareholder return. The more data a company can produce to validate its benefit to patients or the system, the more comfortable an analyst can be with his decision. In an era of reform, cost-effective hurdles will be high and products will need to show robust results in these measures. If a procedure can resonate with consumers, empowered by reform, this is another avenue of potential for growth.

NOTES

1. Núria Mas and Janice Seinfeld, "Is Managed Care Restraining the Adoption of Technology by Hospitals?" IESE Business School Working Paper, 2004; available at SSRN, http://ssrn.com/abstract=997984.

2. David M. Cutler, "The Lifetime Costs and Benefits of Medical Technology," NBER Working Paper no. W13478, October 2007; available at SSRN, http://ssrn.com/abstract=1020904.

3. Vivian Ho, "Learning and the Evolution of Medical Technologies: The Diffusion of Coronary Angioplasty," June 2000; available at SSRN, http://ssrn.com/abstract=240494, or DOI, 10.2139/ssrn.240494.

4. Rosella Levaggi and Michele Moretto, "Investment in Hospital Care Technology under Different Purchasing Rules: A Real Option Approach," FEEM Working Paper no. 75.04, May 2004; available at SSRN, http://ssrn.com/abstract=536002.

5. Farasat Bokhari, "Managed Care and the Adoption of Hospital Technology: The Case of Cardiac Catheterization," October 2000; available at SSRN, http://ssrn.com/abstract=284348, or DOI, 10.2139/ssrn.284348.

6. Mas and Seinfeld, "Is Managed Care Restraining the Adoption of Technology by Hospitals?"

7. David M. Cutler and Mark McClellan, "Is Technological Change in Medicine Worth It?" *Health Affairs* 20, no. 5 (2001): 11–29.

8. William E. Boden et al., "Optimal Medical Therapy with or without PCI for Stable Coronary Diseases," *New England Journal of Medicine* 356, no. 15 (2007).

CHAPTER 14

Conclusion

The capital markets have not been renowned for being a vehicle for social change. This is a shame. The market has an amazing ability to distinguish success from failure, and given its power, it could drive changes in health care. Though cataloging the numerous ways in which the health-care system fails and calls out for reform is easy, it is clear that there are no simple or cheap answers. The history of reform suggests that there will be broad but incremental changes in the way health care is delivered in the United States. These changes can have consequences far beyond their original intent and may lead to outsized investment gains for those who can interpret the longer-term effects successfully. If health-care reform goes beyond just incremental changes and strays into a revolution, the change will be volatile, but a prepared investor can profit from a revolution. Investors can also participate in positive social change by helping to harness market forces and create a virtuous feedback loop so that companies that create value for the health-care system and their shareholders are rewarded. Even if the status quo prevails, investing in health care can be a profitable exercise, as the industry has tremendous growth characteristics and the possibility of revolutionary change from within.

There are a number of factors that make reform, if not inevitable, at least highly likely. Demographic changes, technological advances, accelerating costs, and globalization are coming together to make transforming the health-care system a virtual necessity. Change will be a natural outgrowth of the increased information resulting from the advent of new media. Right now there is no health-care system in the United States per se; rather, there is an interconnected set of programs that provide health care. This is an unsustainable state of affairs. Most Americans believe that health care is a basic right, so on philosophical and social justice grounds, a reform program that leads to universal coverage is desirable.

Reform can take many shapes, and the program that is ultimately adopted can encompass a wide range of strategies. It could be narrow, focusing on major issues like the uninsured and health-care costs, or it could be broader, looking at quality and process issues in addition to cost and access. The government will have a significant role in reforming health care, either through an outright reform plan or through less aggressive measures. There will be many proposals, as there have been in the past, and there may be confusion during the process. Vested interests that prefer the status quo will stand in the way of health-care reform. It will take the will of the American public to force meaningful and long-term solutions to the health-care conundrum. A better health-care system will not just be better for citizens, but also be better for the national economy as the world becomes more competitive. A reform plan's ability to surmount the hurdles erected by its opponents will be driven by the momentum created by economic and social changes, both globally and internally.

As the environment for health care changes, the business models of market participants will have to adapt or the companies will become obsolete. The lines between corporations, government, and academics will continue to blur as stakeholders attempt to determine the optimal way to deploy capital to improve the health-care system and medicine. Even without the impetus of reform, health care is changing. Shifts in the way health care is delivered, increased information about diseases, alterations in the health-care labor force, and technological advances will all exert their own influence on the way the health-care system is shaped going forward.

Industrial transformation will lead to a tremendous opportunity to profit. For investors, knowing where to look and how to look there will help them ferret out investing ideas. Investing in health care is different from investing in other industries, and investors should bear this in mind when they attempt to analyze the sector. Health care is not impenetrable, however, and with a little work the analytic challenges become less complex. The same is true of understanding health-care reform. A study of where health-care reform is leading society can allow investors to foresee where the ultimate opportunity lies. Good public health is profitable, so those companies that make the system better will enrich their shareholders, and those that disadvantage the system will cause their shareholders losses.

The goal of stock picking is to value stocks appropriately, and when there is a decoupling between the price of a company's shares and the value of the company, to take advantage of that mispricing. Knowledge of changes in the health-care landscape allows investors to anticipate future stock movements before other market participants do, leading to outsized returns. Health reform of some type is inevitable, and developing an investment strategy before it occurs is one way to develop an edge over other market participants who lack this foresight. Health care is different from other industries because of its complex regulatory and payment systems, and because of economic considerations that require investors to understand nuance in order to be successful. At the company level, any company that improves the system should have ample opportunity to transform this into significant returns to shareholders. The problems in the health-care market are so large that there is ample opportunity for solutions—many of the problems do not appear to be insurmountable. Like other industries, health care also requires a management team and a competitive advantage to transfer the opportunity to shareholders, so analysis of these factors is also important to health-care investors.

The success of reform will ultimately be judged by whether all people can receive optimal care—basic, emergency, and elective— at a cost that does not lead to financial hardship for them or for society. There is still so much to be discovered in health care that it is possible that innovation will provide us with wonder therapies that will eliminate much of the burden of disease on society, but that is in the future, and although it is likely, the timing is uncertain. So we must work with the facts as we know them, and that means that the system will change and investors will profit. If investors profit from this book, they should be cautioned to spend their earnings wisely and take it easy on the cheeseburgers lest they become part of the problem rather than part of the solution.

INDEX

ABOUT THE AUTHOR

Les Funtleyder serves as health-care strategist for Miller Tabak + Co. He previously managed the health-care portfolio of the Minneapolis-based hedge fund Provident Advisors. Funtleyder makes frequent appearances on CNBC, Bloomberg, and National Public Radio.

CPSIA information can be obtained
at www.ICGtesting.com
Printed in the USA
LVHW041302021218
597325LV00002B/35/P